UNIVERSITY OF NORTH CAROLINA
STUDIES IN THE ROMANCE LANGUAGES AND LITERATURES
Number 91

TRADITIONALISM IN THE WORKS OF
FRANCISCO DE QUEVEDO Y VILLEGAS

TRADITIONALISM IN THE WORKS OF FRANCISCO DE QUEVEDO Y VILLEGAS

BY

DORIS L. BAUM

CHAPEL HILL
THE UNIVERSITY OF NORTH CAROLINA PRESS

DEPÓSITO LEGAL: V. 2.951 - 1970

ARTES GRÁFICAS SOLER, S. A. - JÁVEA, 28 - VALENCIA (8) - 1970

I would like to take this opportunity to express my sincere appreciation to Professor Fernando de Toro-Garland whose valuable advice contributed immeasurably to the successful completion of this study.

I also wish to acknowledge a generous grant from the University of North Carolina at Wilmington and the Kenan Fund which has helped make this publication possible.

* * *

In memory of my father.

D. L. B.

TABLE OF CONTENTS

	Page
INTRODUCTION	11
CHAPTER ONE: THE FORMATION OF QUEVEDO'S TRADITIONALISTIC ATTITUDE	15
The Years of Initiation (1580-1600)	15
An Increase of Intellectual Stimuli (1600-1609)	19
Practical Political Experience (1609-1621)	25
CHAPTER TWO: POLITICAL TRADITIONALISM	32
The Evolution of the Spanish Monarchy	32
The Monarchy under Felipe III	39
The *Política de Dios*	41
The Theme of Privanza	61
Quevedo and the Conde-Duque de Olivares	67
CHAPTER THREE: RELIGIOUS TRADITIONALISM	77
Spanish Catholicism	77
Quevedo's Religiosity	79
His Idea of Heresy and his Attitude toward the Jews	86
Quevedo and Seneca	89
His Attitude toward Erasmus of Rotterdam	98
The Defense of Santiago's Patronage of Spain	100
Quevedo and the Spanish Society of his Time	106
CHAPTER FOUR: LITERARY AND CULTURAL TRADITIONS DEFENDED	115
The Literary Critic	115
His Attack against Góngora	123
The Editor	131
His Defense of Spanish Culture	137
CHAPTER FIVE: TRADITIONALISTIC ASPECTS OF QUEVEDO'S STYLE	146

	Page
The Choice of Themes and Genres	146
Versification in Quevedo's Poetry	162
"Gongorismos" in Quevedo's Poetry	170
The Problem of "Conceptismo" in Quevedo's Style	175
CHAPTER SIX: THE LEGACY OF QUEVEDO'S TRADITIONALISM	182
Quevedo: Forerunner of Traditionalism in Post-Renaissance Spanish Literature	182
Eighteenth Century Traditionalism in Spain	186
Quevedian Traditionalism in the Nineteenth and Twentieth Centuries	189
CONCLUSION	199
BIBLIOGRAPHY	203

INTRODUCTION

The works of Francisco de Quevedo y Villegas, one of the most prolific authors of Spain's Golden Age, have been the inspiration for numerous studies by literary critics and historians who have brought to light the multiple facets of Quevedo's style and subject matter. Thanks to these investigations, the modern reader can appreciate the value of Quevedo not only as a satirist, for which he is most famous, but also as a political theorist, an historian, a theologian, a literary critic, a dramatist and a lyric poet.

Because Quevedo was a man of such diverse expression both as a writer and as a public figure of his time, there have been conflicting interpretations as to what inspired and motivated his works, particularly in regard to his satire. Was he angered, disillusioned, resentful, or was he laughingly sympathetic toward the foibles and idiosyncrasies of his fellow Spaniards? Why did Quevedo return so frequently to the satiric genre? Is there a connection between the spirit of these works and his more serious essays and poems? The answers to these questions require an analysis of other areas of his work in order to uncover clues to his true feelings and reactions toward his milieu.

With this realization in mind, I have approached the present study from a broad perspective including in it as many aspects as possible of Quevedo's life and work. My intention was to seek out and to substantiate the most pervasive and persistent creative motivation of Quevedo's writings, one which would not only help to consolidate the spirit of his work, but would also clarify aspects of his personality and ambition. As a result of this investigation, I have found that such a unifying motivation does exist in Quevedo's work and is the most constant and essential quality of his writing; it is what is herein recognized as a spirit of traditionalism.

The following pages endeavor to illustrate the thesis that Quevedo was, above all, a traditionalist, a firm and sincere advocate of the traditions of Spanish life. It is my belief that the goal of the majority of his works was to defend and preserve those traditions which he feared to be in jeopardy of extinction because of the neglectful attitude of the rulers, the educated classes and the common folk of seventeenth century Spain.

Before beginning this study, it is imperative to describe what is meant by the word "traditionalism" within the context of the time in which Quevedo lived. "Traditionalism" has no static definition except in its most rudimentary sense (i.e., the support of "traditions"), for as ages pass and men and their ideas change, the bases upon which traditions are formed and perpetuated also change. As Menéndez Pidal has said:

> Tradición es... la transmisión de conocimientos y prácticas con interés social o colectivo (idioma, arte, relatos, doctrinas, ritos, costumbres) hecha en todo o en gran parte oralmente, de viejos a jóvenes, de generación en generación. La materia tradicional, en cualquiera de sus manifestaciones, no es absolutamente fija; cambia, evoluciona con el tiempo.[1]

Therefore, what we think of today as "traditionalism" in Spain is not precisely the same as what it was in 1600.

First, it is essential to disregard all allusions to the traditionalism associated with the nineteenth century when Spain was torn internally by political rivalry and civil strife. The concept of traditionalism in the early seventeenth century cannot be confined to one area such as politics, nor should it be linked with political labels such as "reactionary" or "conservative." It would also be incorrect to assume that being a traditionalist necessarily presupposes an aversion to progress and evolution. Again I cite Menéndez Pidal:

> Un pueblo puede ser muy tradicionalista y muy evolutivo a la vez; el pueblo inglés, por ejemplo. En lo mismo que se conserve del pasado puede infiltrarse honda novedad y ade-

---

[1] R. Menéndez Pidal, *Poesía juglaresca y orígenes de las literaturas románticas*, 6th ed. Madrid: Instituto de Estudios Políticos, 1957, p. 364.

lanto, mientras lo que se innove puede entrañar retroceso y descenso. El culpable de las faltas retrógradas del pueblo español no es absolutamente el tradicionalismo; más bien a él se debe lo mejor que España ha producido, los frutos tardíos de su cultura, que luego diremos. La tradicionalidad en sí misma es una fuerza positiva, única manera de vivir una vida de personalidad fuerte. Lo negativo es el misoneísmo, la repulsión de todo lo nuevo, y eso sí, en ciertas épocas, ha obrado sobre el pueblo español como rémora en en connivencia con la vulgar apatía. [2]

The traditionalism to which I refer in the following pages concerning Quevedo's work is characterized by a devotion to the basic foundations of Spanish society and culture as they were understood in the Golden Age of Spain's existence. It is concerned with the preservation of certain ideals of physical and spiritual conduct not only in the realm of government, but also in religious, social and literary contexts. Most of the traditions which were a part of seventeenth century Spain had been cultivated for centuries before that time, but others were adopted later under the Catholic Kings and their immediate successors.

Finally, it must be realized that traditionalism, like any other form of intellectual expression, is ultimately defined in terms of the individual: "....la tradición es cambiante y evolutiva porque siempre en todo caso se halla sujeta a las variaciones que cualquier individuo trasmisor logre introducir, según su personal modo de comprender o interpretar el pensamiento común que recibe de la colectividad o según su propósito de oponerse a lo que la comunidad acepta." [3] Quevedo was influenced in his thinking by his environment; however, he, as an individual, was unique in his method of self-expression. For this reason, it will be seen that the importance he ascribes to maintaining the force of Spanish traditions is determined by more than merely a devotion to the past or a desire for historical continuity; it is based primarily upon his personal interpretation of the relevancy of ancient traditions to the solution of contemporary problems. As I discuss each aspect of Quevedo's

---

[2] R. Menéndez Pidal, *Los españoles en la historia* in *España y su historia,* Vol. I. Madrid: Ediciones Minotauro, 1967, p. 27.

[3] R. Menéndez Pidal, *Poesía juglaresca...,* p. 365.

traditionalism, this factor which distinguishes his writing from that of other seventeenth century authors will be noted.

The spirit of traditionalism in Quevedo's works cannot be linked with any group movement or "school" in his own time. Indeed, the unprecedented value of Quevedo's literary production is founded upon the singularity of his traditionalistic spirit in relation to the attitude of his contemporaries. Like a solitary voice in a desert of complacency, Quevedo's militant traditionalism represents an unparalleled effort to sustain the essential ideals of Hispanic culture amid the apathy which invaded national life at every level during the early seventeenth century. Other writers joined him in combatting one or another of the aspects of literary, social or political deterioration, but none of his colleagues took the same comprehensive stand against all forms of national decay as did Quevedo, nor did any of them support traditions with the same persistence and tenacity.

In order to clarify the sources of Quevedo's traditionalistic attitude, I have begun my study with an analysis of the first forty years of his life when this attitude developed and matured under a variety of influences. Specific areas of traditionalism in his work are examined in separate chapters, and a final section is devoted to my interpretation of Quevedo as a forerunner of the modern current of Hispanic traditionalism in literature. I have purposely enlarged the scope of my study to encompass this view of Quevedo's legacy to subsequent generations as I feel that it will contribute to a reevaluation of Quevedo's significance, not only within the Golden Age, but also within the larger boundaries of all modern Spanish literature.

November, 1968

CHAPTER ONE

THE FORMATION OF QUEVEDO'S TRADITIONALISTIC ATTITUDE

THE YEARS OF INITIATION (1580-1600)

Francisco Gómez de Quevedo y Villegas was born in Madrid on September 17, 1580, at a time when Spain basked in the glory of being the most powerful nation in Europe. The reigning Monarch, Felipe II, had perpetuated and reinforced the belief of his father, Carlos I, that Spain's holy mission was to unite the world under the banner of Catholicism. Spurred on by this messianic spirit, Spain sought and attained dominion over vast territories in the Old and New Worlds.

During his reign, Felipe II became known as "the prudent king." Following the example of his father, he maintained a strong hold over the reins of government, and he alone had the final word in all decisions of policy and administration. His earnest desire was to seek peace within Europe and to consolidate the varied segments of the Spanish kingdom under his rule.

Spanish society at this time was rigidly stratified. At the top of the hierarchical structure were the high clergy and the nobility, followed by the bourgeoisie, the ordinary townsfolk, the literati, the soldiers, and finally, the peasants. Social mobility was slight. However, the Monarch and the nobles were accustomed to patronizing writers and artists who might otherwise be unable to support themselves by their profession.[1] With the aid of this enlightened

---

[1] One might recall here the success of Lope de Vega under the patrona-

attitude, Spain experienced a Renaissance of the arts which has never since been equalled in her history.

Despite the structural contrasts of society, almost all Spaniards of this period shared two beliefs: first, that their religion was the only valid hope for the salvation of mankind, and second, that their nation and ruler had been chosen by divine providence to impart this message to the rest of the world:

> Estos dos caracteres —el nacional y el religioso— que definen la esencia de la expansión española por el mundo no son realmente otra cosa que la manifestación necesaria del alma española, de la hispanidad, cuya sustancia espiritual acaba de madurar durante el reinado de los Reyes Católicos, después de casi ocho siglos de germinación en la Península. La nación española sabe ahora ya que su definición, su sustancia ideal, la misión que Dios le ha conferido en la economía del mundo es nada menos que la defensa de la fe cristiana. [2]

This was the Spain into which Quevedo was born. Unlike many other artists of his era, he had the advantage of a noble heritage. At the time of his birth, both of his parents were performing important services in the Court of Felipe II. His father, Pedro Gómez de Quevedo, had previously distinguished himself in the Court of Carlos I and was later appointed secretary to Felipe II's fourth wife, Ana de Austria. María de Santibáñez, Quevedo's mother, held the coveted post of lady-in-waiting to the Queen. Although young Francisco was brought up in the Court, both sides of his family came originally from the Valley of Toranzo in the northern province of Santander, often referred to as "la Montaña." This Cantabrian region has been a stronghold of traditionalism throughout Spanish history. As early as 718, the Moorish invaders discovered that the rugged northerners would not tolerate subjugation, and as the Moors retreated to the south, the seeds of the modern Spanish State were sown in the north. [3] Quevedo's ancestry

---

ge of the Duke of Sessa, as opposed to the poverty and hardship of Cervantes who had no patron.

[2] Manuel García Morente, *Idea de la hispanidad*. Madrid: Espasa-Calpe, S.A., 1961, pp. 194-195.

[3] See William Atkinson, *A History of Spain and Portugal*. London: The Whitefriars Press, Ltd., 1960, p. 62.

was worthy of great pride. It was considered to be among the most illustrious of that region of Spain, and Quevedo was conscious of his duty to honor this noble Castilian heritage in his own words and deeds. [4]

Although family background was an important influence in the formation of his character, two other factors of his adolescent experience must be taken into account. Quevedo lost both parents before he reached adulthood, and consequently, he was left to find his own way in life at an early age. [5] Also, the fact that he grew up in the sophisticated milieu of the Court and not in the serene mountain atmosphere of his ancestors is significant. In Madrid, with the nobility of Spain surrounding him, Quevedo became aware of the intricacies of the courtly society of his generation at an age when most children might still be enjoying the illusions of childhood innocence. These two factors hastened a more mature and realistic approach to life in a young man who would soon become his society's foremost critic.

Shortly after his father's death in 1586, Quevedo's mother sent him to the Colegio Imperial de Madrid, a famous school run by the Jesuits and patronized by the children of the nobility. Quevedo studied there for four years; and for the rest of his life he retained the influence of this early Jesuit education, primarily in his respect for the ethical virtues of asceticism, so engrained in the Jesuit Order

---

[4] It is now known that among Quevedo's papers found after his death was a manuscript called *El linaje de Villegas* in which he traced his ancestry back to the thirteenth century. See S. Serrano Poncela, "Quevedo, hombre político" in *Formas de vida hispánica*. Madrid: Editorial Gredos, 1963, p. 73. Quevedo's awareness of his illustrious background is also evident in these words of a penniless "hidalgo" from *La vida del Buscón*: "Veme aquí vuesa merced un hidalgo hecho y derecho, de casa y solar montañés, que si como sustento la nobleza, me sustentara, no hubiera más que pedir." *Obras completas*, ed. Felicidad Buendía, Vol. I. Madrid: Aguilar, 1964, p. 319. Hereafter cited as *Obras* I (1964).

[5] Some of Quevedo's biographers, including Fernández-Guerra, have suggested that Quevedo's mother's court activities kept her too busy to give her son the affection he deserved, thus partially engendering the bitterness and cynicism of his later life. However, Luis Astrana Marín rejects this theory as purely hypothetical and without basis. See Quevedo, *Obras completas*, ed L. Astrana Marín, Vol. II. Madrid: Aguilar, 1952, p. 155 (Note). Hereafter cited as *Obras* II (1952).

by its founder, Ignatius Loyola.[6] There was none of the usual schoolboy reticence in young Francisco. As his first biographer, Pablo Antonio de Tarsia, described it, "... exhortarle al curso literario era espolear caballo, que a toda rienda corría."[7]

In 1596, he commenced another four years of study at the renowned University of Alcalá de Henares. According to Tarsia, Quevedo was a precocious student: "... fué dotado del ingenio tan dilatado, que, no pudiendo contenerse entre los límites naturales, sobresalía con admiración de sus maestros."[8] His intellectual prowess was fully demonstrated during his years at Alcalá where he pursued a degree in Theology. Because of his insatiable desire for knowledge, Quevedo acquired a well-rounded humanistic education; not only did he master Latin, Greek, French, Italian, Hebrew and Arabic, but he also dedicated his attention to philosophy, law, astrology, mathematics and medicine.[9]

Contrary to what might be expected of a young man of such astounding mental capacity, Quevedo also sought the adventures and intrigues of ordinary town life. While at Alcalá, he kept company with people from both extremes of the social spectrum, but he particularly enjoyed sharing the rowdy picaresque life of which he would later write with familiarity in *La vida del Buscón* (1626): "A despecho de su ejecutoria y de sus hábitos, alternó con buscones y tahures, rufianes y cotorreras, llegando a saber de germanía tanto como de lenguas clásicas."[10]

Quevedo was a sturdy youth. However, he was afflicted from birth by myopia and a club foot. These physical defects were the object of constant ridicule by fellow students, and yet they became

---

[6] Many years later, Quevedo wrote to the Jesuit Father, Juan de Pineda, upon the occasion of certain polemics: "Sola una pesadumbre me ha hecho vuestra paternidad, y es obligarme a responder a un religioso de la Compañía de Jesús, cuya reverencia y respeto creció conmigo desde los primeros años; a quien debo, desde la gramática, los estudios, y pudiera deber mucha virtud y grandes progresos, si a sus diligencias no se hubiera opuesto mi incapacidad y distraimentos." *Obras* I (1964), 382.

[7] *Vida de Don Francisco de Quevedo y Villegas* (1658-1662) in *Obras* II (1952), 856-857.

[8] Ibid., p. 856.

[9] Ibid., p. 858.

[10] Gabriel Maura y Gamazo, *Conferencias sobre Quevedo*. Madrid: Editorial "Saturnino Calleja," 1946, p. 23.

a source of inner strength to Quevedo, as he learned to buffet his contemporaries with his sharp wit and verbal counterattacks.

From an intellectual point of view, Quevedo's stay at the University of Alcalá was an important formative period in his life. It was during these years that he acquired a solid background of knowledge which was later to win him the admiration of many of his learned countrymen such as Lope de Vega and Cervantes, and of foreigners as well.

An Increase of Intellectual Stimuli (1600-1609)

Following the successful completion of his work at Alcalá in 1600, Quevedo decided to return to the Court, temporarily located in Valladolid where the new King, Felipe III, and his "privado," [11] the Duke of Lerma, had assumed residence. Quevedo went to Valladolid because he sought the professional and social stimuli of court activities. And yet, as a native of Madrid, he mourned the effects of this change which left his city destitute:

> . . . .
> Eres lástima del mundo,
> desengaño de grandezas,
> cadáver sin alma, frío,
> sombra fugitiva y negra,
> aviso de presunciones,
> amenaza de soberbias,
> desconfianza de humanos,
> eco de tus mismas quejas.
> Si algo pudieren mis versos,
> puedes estar, Madrid, cierta,
> que has de vivir en mis plumas,
> ya que en las del tiempo mueras. [12]

What greeted Quevedo in Valladolid must have been a source of acute disappointment. In the short space of two years since the

---

[11] The terms "privado" and "valido" are used in Spanish to refer to the favorite minister of the king. The corresponding words "privanza" and "valimento" signify the state of being a favorite minister. Since I shall employ these terms frequently in my study, I shall hereafter omit the quotation marks.

[12] "De Valladolid la rica," *Obras*, II (1964), 347.

death of Felipe II in 1598, the atmosphere of the Court had been altered considerably. The most noticeable change was in the nature of the King. In contrast to Felipe II who had been a capable and strongwilled monarch, Felipe III was weak and malleable. Soon after becoming king, he called upon the Duke of Lerma to assume the majority of his own responsibilities while he turned his attention to religious and social pursuits. To fill his abundant leisure hours, the King requested all manner of entertainment, and thus Valladolid became the seat of idle wealth and ostentation. The noble families who were once content to live in the surrounding provinces hastened to the Court where the King encouraged their participation in his recreation. As Von Ranke has observed:

> ¡Cuán distinta era esta corte de la de Felipe II! Un favorito investido de Poder real. Una gran familia noble, a la cabeza de los negocios: el acceso al Rey abierto a los Grandes... En esta emulación de magnificencia volvieron a incorporarse a la Corte. En ella encontramos cabezas de familia que no menos que con veinte carrozas, y acompañados de un tropel de nobles, hacían sus visitas. Las damas eran acompañadas por sus palafraneros a caballo, y de todos los nobles de su Casa. Por esta unión de la Corte y de los Grandes, se formó una extraña mezcla de ceremonial y lujo.... [13]

The profligacy of the nobility in Valladolid was offset by the proverty of the lower classes and by the growing imbroglio of an immoral and money-hungry bureaucracy. Quevedo, who as a boy was familiar with the Court of Felipe II, must have been shocked by the changes wrought in so brief an interlude. In another poem about Valladolid written when the Court left there in 1606, he said:

> . . . .
> La primera vez que la vi,
> te tuve en las apariencias
> por arrabal del infierno,
> y en todo muy su parienta.
> Mas ya sé, por tu linaje,
> que te apellidas cazuela,

---

[13] Leopold Von Ranke, *La monarquía española de los siglos XVI y XVII*, trans. Manuel Pedroso. México: Editorial Leyenda, S. A., 1946, p. 84.

THE FORMATION OF QUEVEDO'S TRADITIONALISTIC ATTITUDE 21

> que, en vez de guisados, hace
> desaguisados sin cuenta.
> No hay sino sufrir agora,
> y ser en esta tormenta
> nuevo Jonás en el mar
> a quien trague la ballena.
> Podrá ser que te vomite
> más presto que todos piensan,
> y que te celebren viva
> los que te llorarán muerta. [14]

It was at this time that Quevedo began to write short works of satire directed against the society of the Court. His natural inclination toward this literary genre was further stimulated by his studies and by various personal contacts he made during this period. While in Valladolid, Quevedo continued his theological studies, later receiving his minor clerical orders. His knowledge of religion and ethics must have been influential in heightening his concern for the degenerate society surrounding him. At the same time, he initiated correspondence with the distinguished Belgian humanist, Justus Lipsius. Through Lipsius, Quevedo came to appreciate more fully the works of Seneca, the classical Cordoban philosopher who exalted the virtues of abstinence and moral fortitude. [15] Quevedo also spent many hours working with the Spanish historian, Padre Juan de Mariana, who heartily condemned the social customs of the day. A further formative influence must be found in Quevedo's reading of classical Latin satirists such as Juvenal, Martial, Horace and, particularly, the third century satirist Lucian of Samosata. [16] Lucian, like Quevedo, had lived in an epoch of impending decadence, and he despised the hypocrisy he saw around him. His biting satires of social customs reinforced Quevedo's own inclination to employ this method of protest against the society of the Court of Felipe III.

---

[14] "No fuera tanto tu mal," *Obras* II (1964), 288.

[15] In Chapter III, I discuss this influence in depth.

[16] See Margarita Morreale, "Luciano y Quevedo: La humanidad condenada," *Revista de Literatura*, Tomo VIII, núm. 16, oct-dic. de 1955, pp. 213-227; and B. Sánchez Alonso, "Los satíricos latinos y la sátira de Quevedo," *Revista de Filología Española*, Tomo XI, Cuadernos 1 and 2, 1924, pp. 33-62, and 113-153.

In the period of 1600 to 1608, Quevedo wrote the following satiric works: *Capitulaciones matrimoniales* (c. 1600), *Premáticas y aranceles generales* (c. 1600), *Epístolas del Caballero de la Tenaza* (1600-1606), *El sueño del juicio final* (1606-1607?), *El alguacil endemoniado* (1607) and *El sueño del infierno,* later entitled *Las zahurdas de Plutón* (1608). He also wrote several poems in the same vein, including the celebrated letrilla, "Poderoso caballero es don Dinero." The satire of some of these early works has been termed "burlesque" as it appears on the surface to be a jovial mockery of social figures and customs. The amusing caricatures contained in his sketches were well received by the public which enjoyed laughing at its own idiosyncrasies. However, beneath Quevedo's wit and humor lay a deadly serious criticism of the corruption that had been allowed to permeate Spain.

Although the greater part of his writings during this period were short satiric and poetic works, Quevedo also produced two essays in prose of a non-satiric nature. In 1606, he wrote *Discurso de las privanzas,* a brief treatise which he dedicated to Felipe III; and in 1609, he started writing *España defendida y los tiempos de ahora,* an essay which he never completed. These two works, which shall be discussed at length in the following chapters, are significant because they show that Quevedo was concerned with tradition from the earliest days of his literary career. In both of these works, he expresses his fear that Spain is weakening and losing faith in ancient customs. These words from *España defendida* are indicative of his concern:

> Prolijo fuera y vanaglorioso en querer contar por menudo todas las cosas que nos sucedieron a los españoles gloriosamente en los días que han pasado, sin callar que ha habido hijo suyo que llora estos tiempos y el verla viuda en parte del antiguo vigor, y osa decir que la confianza de haberle tenido introduce descuido de conservarle.
>
> Han empezado a contentarse los hombres de España con heredar de sus padres virtud, sin procurar tenerla para que la hereden sus hijos. [17]

---

[17] *España defendida y los tiempos de ahora, Obras* I (1964), 524.

This preoccupation, unclouded by satire or burlesque, was then and continued to be the motivation behind the majority of Quevedo's work.

Since Quevedo was not inclined toward writing autobiographically and since there is a scarcity of his letters and documents during this period of his life, not much is know about his experiences between 1606 and 1609. In effect, this problem can be extended to encompass his entire life. Until recent studies by objective and critical authors, Quevedo's biographers have included as much fantasy as reality in their works. Beginning with Pablo Antonio de Tarsia who wrote a biography of Quevedo twenty years after his death, many other biographers have written of duels, scandals, amorous exploits and other adventures which were mostly fictitious in substance.[18] This is not to suggest that Quevedo was celibate or that he led an uneventful existence. He was adept in the handling of arms and in courting women, but his prowesses took on legendary proportions as he became a famous literary figure of his time. Throughout history such exaggeration of the qualities of villains or heroes has been common. The public does not bother to romanticize the life of a man who does not lend himself to such dramatization. Certainly Quevedo had proven himself to be a colorful court figure, and the public read his unpublished manuscripts (particularly the *Sueños*) that circulated through Madrid arousing their curiosity as to the nature of a man who would dare to mock so blatantly the customs of their society. Within these circumstances, it is not surprising that rumors became accepted as truths.

Because of this romantization, it is generally ignored that Quevedo suffered more than his share of discomfort during his lifetime. He was never able to live in the manner customary to his noble birth because the majority of his inheritance was left to him in the form of notes for debts owed to his family by residents of La Torre de Juan Abad, near Madrid. Beginning in 1609 and for many years thereafter, Quevedo was constantly involved in unsuccessful

---

[18] The two modern critics most influential in pointing out these myths are Luis Astrana Marín and James O. Crosby. See, for example, Astrana Marín's notes to Tarsia's biography of Quevedo in *Obras* II (1952), 851-896; see also Crosby, "Quevedo and the Court of Philip III: Neglected Satirical letters and New Biographical Data," *PMLA*, Vol. LXXI, 1956, pp. 1117-1126.

law suits in an effort to recover this money. In a poem which he once wrote about La Torre, his remorse is clear:

> . . . .
> Aquí cobro enfermedades,
> que no rentas ni tributos;
> y mando todos mis miembros
> y aun destos no mando algunos.
> De Madrid salí, y de juicio,
> y sin dinero, y sin gusto,
> vuelvo triste y enlutado
> como misa de difuntos. [19]

Though we know that he was found of female attention, Quevedo married only when he reached the age of fifty-two. After three months, he and his wife parted ways, as he found her to be a disagreeable companion, and thus, most of Quevedo's life was spent in solitude without the love of family or offspring. Moreover, on three separate occasions he was either exiled or imprisoned, apparently for political reasons, the last and worst of these being from 1639 to 1643 in the convent of San Marcos de León. Many critics have attributed Quevedo's caustic temperament to these experiences. However, they exaggerate this side of his character while overlooking the more emotional and tender aspects of his nature which are revealed in lesser-known prose and poetry. Examples of this may be found in his love poems to "Lisi," a name he used to shield the identity of Luisa de la Cerda, a noblewoman of the house of Medinaceli whom Quevedo loved in secret for many years. [20] Among the many sonnets he wrote which were inspired by Lisi is this famous verse:

> Cerrar podrá mis ojos la postrera
> sombra que me llevare el blanco día;
> y podrá desatar esta alma mía
> hora a su afán ansioso lisonjera;
>
> mas no de esotra parte en la ribera
> dejará la memoria en donde ardía;
> nadar sabe mi llama la agua fría,
> y perder el respeto a ley severa;

---

[19] "De ese famoso lugar," *Obras* II (1964), 303.
[20] See *Obras* II (1964), 116-139.

> alma a quien todo un Dios prisión ha sido,
> venas que humor a tanto fuego han dado,
> médulas que han gloriosamente ardido,
>
> su cuerpo dejarán, no su cuidado;
> serán ceniza, mas tendrá sentido;
> polvo serán, mas polvo enamorado. [21]

We do injustice to Quevedo if we forget this emotionally sensitive aspect of his nature. The pugnacity and asperity with which he attacked other situations was, perhaps, the result of an unusually keen sensitivity to the world around him.

PRACTICAL POLITICAL EXPERIENCE (1609-1621)

In 1609, Quevedo met Don Pedro Téllez Girón, Duke of Osuna, and thus began a new phase of his life. Quevedo saw in Osuna the possibility of a future patron and protector, and consequently he dedicated several works to the Duke in order to woo his favor. This opportunistic approach was characteristic of the epoch, and is explained by an artist's need to be aggressive if he wished to improve his economic status and gain valuable experience.

Having just returned to the Court from a highly successful military campaign in Flanders, the Duke was trying to make amends for his youthful misconduct by gaining the favor of the King and the powerful Duke of Lerma. As S. Serrano Poncela points out in an acute analysis of Osuna and Quevedo's long relationship, the Duke was an anachronism in seventeenth century Spain:

> Se ofrece la historia de la vida y hazañas de don Pedro Téllez Girón, duque de Osuna, como algo teratológico subrayado por la escasa estatura de los tiempos y los hombres entre quienes le tocó vivir. Fue un ejemplar humano tardío y desambientado del Renacimiento, hecho de la madera de los grandes capitanes y aventureros que en el siglo anterior se habían dado en España con varia suerte... A su vez, la necedad y el espíritu gallináceo del monarca le cerraron el paso a toda empresa grande. Osuna significó para España

---

[21] *Obras* II (1964), 123.

la última posibilidad de conquistar el poderío naval del Mediterráneo, aunque nadie lo entendió así. [22]

A lover of adventure, the Duke was the type of man who would have become a famous military leader under Carlos I, but whom Felipe III saw only as an indiscreet upstart. When in 1611 the King granted him the Viceroyalty of Sicily, it was substantially because of the Duke's battle record in Flanders and because of the marriage contrived by Osuna between his son and the granddaughter of the Duke of Lerma.

Mistrust on the part of his superiors did not bode an auspicious future for the Duke of Osuna, yet he set out for Sicily from where he promptly invited Quevedo to join him as his court poet. This relationship was advantageous to both men, as the Duke acquired a distinguished protegé and Quevedo received an opportunity to observe a foreign environment while under the protection of a most desirable patron. In addition, as Serrano Poncela suggests, Quevedo probably saw the chance to exercise his influence in political matters, recognizing in himself the potential of being an enlightened minister to Osuna. [23] Whatever the motive, Quevedo left his residence in La Torre and arrived in Sicily in 1613.

The Viceroy soon found that Quevedo was not only a respected writer, but also an astute diplomat and political adviser; before long he began entrusting Quevedo with diplomatic missions as his personal representative and confidant. Osuna, a straight-forward man of action, lacked the essential diplomatic qualities of finesse and savoir faire, and he thus availed himself of Quevedo's dexterity in these qualities. In many aspects, the two personalities complemented each other, and their relationship soon became one of mutual admiration and friendship.

Under these favorable circumstances, Quevedo began his brief career in politics. One of his first assignments from the Duke was to organize a clandestine transferral of the city of Nice to Spanish control. For a time, it seemed as though the scheme would work,

---

[22] S. Serrano Poncela, "Quevedo, hombre político," in *Formas de vida hispánica*. Madrid: Editorial Gredos, 1963, p. 66.
[23] Ibid., p. 69.

THE FORMATION OF QUEVEDO'S TRADITIONALISTIC ATTITUDE 27

but then it was discovered, and Quevedo had to flee Nice and acknowledge failure.

In 1615, Quevedo was chosen by the Sicilian Parliament to present in person to the King of Spain the triennial tribute of that Viceroyalty. During the eight months that he remained in Madrid, he carried on a lively and informal correspondence with the Duke of Osuna. In addition to his official functions, Quevedo performed some private business for the Duke:

> He had entered Madrid as a diplomatic envoy, and to the money he had brought for the King [300,000 ducats] there were soon added another thirty thousand ducats from Osuna. This was to be used in maintaining the good will of various important courtiers by lavish gifts, a practice so common at the Court that no Viceroy could hold his post unless he indulged in what was tantamount to bribery.[24]

As James Crosby has proved, Quevedo's influence had no bearing upon Osuna's appointment as Viceroy of Naples, a coveted position which was granted to him by Felipe III before Quevedo's appearance in Madrid.[25] In any event, this mission afforded Quevedo the opportunity to observe court intrigues and functions from an insider's viewpoint, an experience which must have impressed upon him the urgent need for political reform.

Once back in Italy, Quevedo became more indispensable than ever to Osuna. The Duke possessed power equivalent to that of a monarch in his territory of Naples, and Quevedo, an unofficial secretary, performed all the duties of a privado. According to Neapolitan reports of the time, Quevedo held private audiences, received all official inquiries, managed the Viceroyalty's finances, and even accompanied the Duke on his amorous escapades.[26] Whether to gain his favor or simply to laud his genius, the local literati showered him with flatteries.[27]

---

[24] J. O. Crosby, "Quevedo and the Court of Philip III: Neglected Satirical Letters and New Biographical Data," p. 1122.
[25] Ibid., p. 1125.
[26] See Serrano Poncela, pp. 75-76.
[27] Among these, Jerónimo Rivera referred to Quevedo as "Novello Icaro audace," and Juan Perelio added exuberantly, "Quevedo e un sole, ed sua pena un raggio." Cited by Serrano Poncela, p. 76.

Osuna became a powerful viceroy, practicing what Serrano Poncela calls "un paternalismo feudal que se correspondía con la fibra autoritaria y soberbia de su carácter." [28] He tended to administer justice in an arbitrary and extra-legal fashion which gained him as many enemies as allies. This aggressive approach was Osuna's by nature. Quevedo may not have agreed with everything he did, but he must have welcomed the Duke's authoritative command as a refreshing contrast to the indifference and weakness of Felipe III.

Quevedo wrote very little while he was involved in the affairs of Italy with the Duke of Osuna. One of the works he did commence in the summer of 1617 was the first part of the *Política de Dios y gobierno de Cristo*. [29] This work, which I shall treat fully in the second chapter, can be considered the most complete expression of Quevedo's political credo, as it sets forth the outlines of a system of government based upon the Scriptures. One wonders what moved Quevedo to write his *Política* at a time when he was very busy with little opportunity to relax over pen and paper. The answer, perhaps, lies in his constant involvement in political matters and his growing awareness of and preoccupation with the deteriorating state of government in Spain. Through his own practical experiences, Quevedo had formulated his theories of the ideal political situation: one in which morality and justice functioned in harmony.

From the first days of his arrival in Italy, Osuna had conceived the audacious notion that he could gradually establish Spanish supremacy over Mediterranean naval power by reorganizing Spain's

---

[28] Ibid., p. 77.

[29] James O. Crosby expresses the opinion that Quevedo did not begin the *Política* until 1619 because he was too busy working for the Duke in Italy to have written it in 1617. He says that Quevedo's statement in the 1626 first edition's dedication that he had written it "diez años ha" is just a vague reference, not necessarily a specific designation of the year he wrote the first part. See Crosby, *The Sources of the Text of Quevedo's "Política de Dios."* New York: The Modern Language Association of America, 1959, p. 1 (Note). However, it must be pointed out that Quevedo refers again in the first edition of 1626 to the same time span: "Yo escribí sin ambición; diez años callé con modestia;" *Obras* I (1964), 531 ("A los doctores sin luz"). Because of this, I hesitate to follow Prof. Crosby's opinion.

The second part of the *Política* was written in 1635 and published posthumously in 1655.

relations with the principal Italian governments in Savoy, Venice and Rome.[30] His objective in 1617 was to destroy Venice's commercial and naval hegemony in the Adriatic and Mediterranean Seas by secretly inciting a rebellion from within Venice while offering outside support from Spanish ships. Knowing the state of public finances and Felipe III's pusillanimous nature, Osuna hoped to win his consent to this plan by assuring the King of anonymity in the conspiracy itself.

In early 1617, Quevedo made a trip to see the Pope and the Spanish Monarch in an effort to enlist their support in this project. He met with no success in Rome, but apparently returned to Naples in 1618 with the unofficial authorization of Felipe III to proceed with the undertaking. This was a great diplomatic coup for Quevedo, and it can be considered the high point of his political career.

To add to his triumph, he was named a Knight of the Order of Santiago, an appointment which he had actively sought with the Duke's help.[31] Apart from the honor of being made a Knight, the appointment also brought with it special political and social privileges of inestimable value. Since its members were selected on the basis of merit and not birthright, the Order of Santiago was comprised of the most respected figures of Spanish society, among them, Calderón de la Barca, Guillén de Castro, Diego Saavedra Fajardo and Diego Silva Velázquez.

Exactly what part Quevedo played in the actual implementation of the Venice conspiracy has been obscured by the passage of time. Neither he nor Osuna ever admitted under inquiry or in writing that there had been a plan to overthrow the Venetian government, and consequently there are conflicting accounts as to just what did or did not occur. We do know that Quevedo later felt compelled to defend the Duke on numerous occasions and that he wrote several works to this effect, including the fragmentary *Mundo caduco y desvaríos de la edad* (1621), *Lince de Italia u zahorí español* (1628) and *La república de Venecia llega al Parnaso*. In each of these

---

[30] See Serrano Poncela, p. 79.
[31] One of the four military Orders of Knighthood in Spain initiated during the Reconquest, the Order of Santiago was conferred only by royal decree.

is found a scathing condemnation of the Venetians and of the Duke of Savoy who was Osuna's most powerful adversary in Italy.

Osuna's Venetian conspiracy, like the one in Nice, ended in failure. The crafty Venetians decided to appeal directly to Felipe III, trying to convince him that the Duke was as much a threat to Spain as he was to Venice. In 1619, Quevedo left Naples to return to Madrid, and a year later the Duke was relieved of his Viceroyalty. Osuna's frequent visits with Quevedo upon his return to the Court aroused suspicion, and Quevedo was exiled to his residence in La Torre de Juan Abad. When Felipe IV became king in 1621, Osuna was also confined to prison where he died a few years later.

The Venetian affair had backfired and caused the eventual downfall of the Duke. Quevedo, as his righthand man, was forced to accept Osuna's defeat as his own. Despite the many times he attempted to vindicate them both in his later writings, Quevedo could not overcome the disillusionment he felt upon realizing that all his earlier hopes for political success had been frustrated in so short a time. He had admired Osuna for his energy, aggressiveness and valor, traditional traits in Spanish heroes and conquerors. The following sonnet eulogizing the Duke illustrates the esteem Quevedo felt for his former patron:

> Faltar pudo su patria al grande Osuna,
> pero no a su defensa sus hazañas;
> diéronle muerte y cárcel las Españas,
> de quien él hizo esclava la fortuna.
>
> Lloraron sus invidias una a una
> con las propias naciones las extrañas;
> su tumba son de Flandes las campañas,
> y su epitafio la sangrienta luna.
>
> En sus exequias encendió al Vesubio
> Parténope, y Trinacria, al Mongibelo;
> el llanto militar creció en diluvio.
>
> Dióle el mejor lugar Marte en su cielo;
> la Mosa, el Thin, el Tajo y el Danubio
> murmuran con dolor su desconsuelo. [32]

---

[32] *Obras* II (1964), 18.

Quevedo thought that these qualities, with the aid of his own counsel, could make the Duke a great leader, but historical circumstances had proved him wrong. Quevedo was discouraged and embittered, but he did not renounce his ideas, nor did his failure prevent him from trying to recreate a similar relationship with the Conde-Duque de Olivares and the Duke of Medinaceli in later years.

Perhaps this period of six years in Italy can best be understood in terms of a sobering influence in Quevedo's life. His personal experiences in the political arena had brought deceptions, but they had not defeated his desire to see Spain's decline halted. If anything, he had been impressed by the reality of this decline and by the necessity of his fighting against it.

These first forty-one years in Quevedo's life constitute the period during which his traditionalistic attitude was gradually taking shape. By the time he settled once again in Spain in 1621, he had reached the stage of maturity both as a man of action and as a writer. As I shall describe in the following chapters, Quevedo spent the remaining twenty-four years of his life defending the values which he had formulated as a younger man.

CHAPTER TWO

POLITICAL TRADITIONALISM

THE EVOLUTION OF THE SPANISH MONARCHY *

The monarchical tradition in Spain originated during the Visigothic invasion of the fifth century A. D. Although the Visigoths initially occupied territory in Spain by virtue of a pact or "foedus" with the Roman Empire, this agreement was broken in the latter part of the fifth century when the Empire ceased to be a viable political force in the Iberian Peninsula. [1] At that time, the Visigoths were ruled by an elected monarch:

> Cuando los Visigodos se asientan en las Galias y después en España, son, pues, un pueblo organizado políticamente como una comunidad nacional de guerreros y sus familias, constituida sobre una base militar y para la determinación y cumplimiento del derecho; su órgano es la asamblea popular... de todos los hombres libres con capacidad para empuñar las armas; en ella se dicta el derecho, se administra justicia, en la que se refiere a las cuestiones que afectan a toda la comunidad (traición, deserción, etc.); se elige al jefe de la comunidad o Rey, expresándose la voluntad del pueblo mediante el ruido de las armas, que revela el asentimiento de la asamblea a las decisiones propuestas. [2]

---

* I purposely begin this chapter with an historical analysis of Spain's political traditions so that the background of Quevedo's political traditionalism may be clear to the reader.

[1] Luis García de Valdeavellano, *Historia de España de los orígenes a la baja Edad Media*. Madrid: Revista de Occidente, S. A., 1952, p. 254.

[2] Ibid., p. 253.

The political dominion of the Visigoths was soon established in Spain. However, alongside the new political force, there continued to exist a cultural and spiritual tradition which had been established by the Roman Empire: "... la tradición imperial universalista, encarnada en el nombre de Roma y recogida por la Iglesia cristiana, se mantenía viva en el pensamiento de las clases cultas de las antiguas provincias sometidas a los 'bárbaros' y en la persistencia del Imperio de Oriente, que intentará con Justiniano la reconstrucción política del 'Orbis romanus'." [3] In the sixth century, the Visigothic King Leovigildo tried to unite his kingdom by imposing the heretical beliefs of Arianism upon the orthodox Hispano-Roman peoples under his rule. His efforts were futile since Roman orthodox Christians far outnumbered Arians. [4] With the same hope for spiritual as well as political unity, his successor, Recaredo, adopted the Hispano-Roman faith, and at the Third Council of Toledo in 587, the Visigothic people declared their adoption of the faith of Rome. Thus began the close alliance between the Catholic Church and the state in Spain:

> La unidad de las conciencias se había logrado con la conversión al Catolicismo; la Iglesia católica fue en adelante un elemento de gran importancia en el Estado visigodo, y los hispano-romanos lograron no sólo una victoria espiritual, sino también política. [5]

The Visigothic monarchy came to an end in 711 when King Rodrigo was defeated by the Moorish invaders. The Arabs succeeded in establishing political dominion over most of the Peninsula with the exception of the Asturian region in the north. There, in 718, a new monarch was named by the people: "... la rebeldía de los astures provocó el nacimiento de un nuevo Reino cristiano que, firme en su resistencia contra el Islam, no tardó en buscar su razón de existir, el modelo de sus instituciones y la fuerza de su ideal expansivo en la vieja tradición unitaria del Estado hispano-godo." [6] Although the Visigothic system of an elected monarch was continued

---

[3] Ibid., pp. 259-260.
[4] Ibid., p. 277.
[5] Ibid., p. 281.
[6] Ibid., p. 507.

in the Asturias-Leonese Kingdom, this practice became a mere formality as the prestige of royal ancestry acquired a decisive influence and the monarchy became essentially hereditary.[7] As the Reconquest gathered momentum and more territory was recaptured from the Moors, the kingdoms of Castilla, Aragón and Navarra were created and inspired by the same spirit as that of Asturias-León: "Las monarquías que se forman en los territorios de la Reconquista, aunque escindidos y separados entre sí, mantienen la conciencia de ser continuación de la monarquía visigoda, sólo accidentalmente destruida por las armas del invasor."[8] Each of these kingdoms was motivated by the same desire to defend the Christian faith, and this spirit of service to Christianity, according to Menéndez Pidal, was the basis of future national unity: "... la vieja concepción de la reconquista, como misión histórica de España, se robustece, desde el siglo XII, afirmando que el sojuzgamiento de los infieles es empresa exclusiva de los españoles en beneficio de toda la Cristiandad."[9] This unity was finally accomplished under the reign of Fernando and Isabel in the late fifteenth century.

Numerous medieval texts such as the *Siete Partidas* of Alfonso X and the *Poema de Mío Cid* confirm the tradition of monarchical authority which has been honored in Spain since the Visigothic era. The preservation of the kings' power in the medieval realms of Spain was due largely to the limited penetration of feudalism in the Peninsula:

> Las circunstancias históricas especiales derivadas de la invasión musulmana, de la guerra de reconquista y de la forma de realizar la colonización de los territorios nuevamente incorporados al dominio cristiano, no sólo impidieron el completo desarrollo en la mayor parte de España de un Feudalismo organizado, sino que contribuyeron también a la formación de una Sociedad y de unas clases sociales constituidas sobre bases bastante diferentes de las que habían llegado a servir de apoyo en toda Europa al nuevo sistema social y político.[10]

---

[7] Ibid., p. 567.

[8] José María Font Rius, *Instituciones medievales españolas*. Madrid: Consejo Superior de Investigaciones Científicas, 1949, pp. 19-20.

[9] R. Menéndez Pidal, *Cristiandad e Islam* in *España y su historia*, Vol. I. Madrid: Ediciones Minotauro, 1957, p. 379.

[10] García de Valdeavellano, p. 540.

The Spanish states maintained their public character and did not succumb to the private vassal-lord relationship to the same degree as in other European countries during the Middle Ages.[11] Therefore, the monarchs never lost their authority, nor did the people relinquish their rights as public citizens.

This does not imply, however, that a monarch possessed absolute power over the state. In accordance with Hispano-Visigothic tradition, a king was not above the power of the law:

> Según la doctrina eclesiástica, el poder real viene de Dios y se ha de emplear en regir rectamente al pueblo o, en caso contrario, se pierden el nombre y la condición de Rey, como advirtió San Isidoro al incorporar a sus "Etimologías" el viejo proverbio "Serás Rey si obras rectamente", y que Horacio había recogido en el primer libro de sus "Epístolas" y que San Isidoro completó al añadir "si no obras rectamente no lo serás."[12]

The king's power, being based upon Christian principles of human dignity and generosity, was limited in that he was expected to respect his subjects' individual rights as human beings and as his equals in the eyes of God. His duty was to administer the kingdom in the manner best suited to the benefit of the people. This concept was expressed in the *Siete Partidas* wherein the king is described as "vicario de Dios en el imperio para fazer justicia en lo temporal."[13] The following metaphor from the same thirteenth century document is also indicative of the desired relationship between a king and his subjects: "el es alma e cabeza e ellos miembros."[14] Just as the body only functions appropriately under just and reasonable commands from the mind and heart, so equally does a kingdom flourish under a judicious monarch.

In spite of the fact that this tradition was kept alive in the spirit of the people during the Middle Ages, the Spanish realms endured the rule of several ineffective monarchs. Immediately preceding the Catholic Kings was Enrique IV (1454-1474). The degeneracy and

---

[11] Font Rius, pp. 28-29.
[12] García de Valdeavellano, p. 301.
[13] *Las Siete Partidas del Sabio Rey Don Alonso*, ed. Gregorio López, Vol. I. Madrid: 1611, Segunda Partida, Título I, Ley I.
[14] Segunda Partida, Título I, Ley V.

corruption of his Court was harshly criticized in two anonymous works, *Coplas del Provincial* and *Coplas de Mingo Revulgo*. Shortly thereafter, however, Spain embarked upon a period of great exploits and accomplishments under the joint rule of King Fernando of Aragón and Queen Isabel of Castilla. Their successful rule, under which Spain became a united kingdom, was the result of a scrupulous concern for authoritative leadership and a militant spirit of defense of the Christian faith against the infidels. Fernando, whose attention was directed primarily to Spain's international politics, has been praised by many writers, i.e., Castiglione, Machiavelli, Saavedra Fajardo and Gracián. His policy has been described succinctly by Gómez de Mercado:

> Por todos los medios procuró Don Fernando la paz entre los príncipes cristianos, la bendición del Pontífice, la unidad de Europa, ...buscando la defensa de la fe, de la cultura de Occidente, frente a la amenaza que se presentaba violenta y casi invencible de los turcos.[15]

Isabel, who administered the internal policies, was endowed with what Menéndez Pidal has termed "el espíritu selectivo," the unusual ability to single out the most capable public servants to perform duties of importance to the Church and the state: "Gracias a la amplitud, austeridad y perseverancia en el esfuerzo selectivo, lograron los Reyes Católicos volver las tornas y trocar el curso descendente que la invidencia había dado al país durante los reinados anteriores."[16] These qualities necessary for effective leadership and national unity were the constant preoccupation of the Catholic Kings.

Anticipating his imminent death, Fernando wrote a Last Will and Testament in 1516 in which he included advice to his grandson and successor, Carlos I.[17] It was his hope that Carlos, who was educated in Brussels and unfamiliar with Spanish life and idiom, would leave his foreign counselors behind and come to Spain with

---

[15] Gómez de Mercado, *Dogmas nacionales del Rey Católico*. Madrid: Ediciones Cultura Hispánica, 1953, p. 208.

[16] Menéndez Pidal, *Los españoles en la historia* in *España en su historia*, Vol. I, p. 51.

[17] See Gómez de Mercado, Apéndice III, pp. 416-427.

the purpose of continuing the policies of his predecessors. The young King, a strong contender for the Holy Roman throne to which he was elected in 1519, was slow to follow his grandfather's advice. However, by 1528, Carlos I had formulated the concept of "el imperio cristiano."[18] Inspired by the tradition of a united Christian Empire which had originated in Spain in the Middle Ages and was revived by Fernando and Isabel, Carlos I, in collaboration with his advisers, el doctor Mota, Alfonso de Valdés and Antonio de Guevara, expounded his idea of Christian peace and unity led by Spain:

> Carlos V [his title as Emperor] se ha hispanizado ya y quiere hispanizar a Europa. Digo hispanizar porque él quiere trasfundir en Europa el sentido de un pueblo cruzado que España mantenía abnegadamente desde hacía ocho siglos, y que acaba de coronar hacía pocos años por la guerra de Granada, mientras Europa había olvidado el ideal de cruzada hacía siglos, después de un fracaso total. Ese abnegado sentimiento de cruzada contra infieles y herejes es el que inspiró el alto quijotismo de la política de Carlos...[19]

Carlos I, who as a youth was indecisive and inhibited, became a forceful and authoritative leader as he matured. Throughout his reign of forty years, Carlos maintained strict control over the government: "... la unidad del todo descansaba en la persona del Monarca. Es cierto que los poderes de éste aparecían limitados por las distintas constituciones de sus territorios, por la política de sus vecinos y por la complicación de los negocios; pero siempre hasta los últimos años, le vemos decidir por su propio criterio y ejercer su potestad suprema con independencia de toda influencia extraña."[20]

When Carlos I abdicated the throne of Spain in 1556, he left the title of Holy Roman Emperor to his brother, Fernando, while his son, Felipe, became the next King of Spain. His decision to divide these authorities was influenced by the realization that the Protestant Reform movement in Germany had made his ecumenical

---
[18] Menéndez Pidal, *Idea imperial de Carlos V*. Madrid: Espasa-Calpe, S. A., 1955, p. 18.
[19] Ibid., p. 28.
[20] Leopold Von Ranke, *La monarquía española de los siglos XVI y XVII*, trans. Manuel Pedroso. México: Editorial Leyenda, S. A., 1946, p. 44.

ideal impossible.[21] Since the Pope refused to recognize the new Emperor, that title lost its power and universal significance. Nevertheless, as Menéndez Pidal points out, the concept of a united Christian Empire mainained its traditional force in Spain:

> ...la idea de la *universitas christiana* que mantuvo Carlos V, de tan hispana que era, continuó siendo la base de la política, la literatura y la vida toda peninsular; a ella sacrificó España su propio adelanto en el siglo de las luces, queriendo mantener, en lo posible, la vieja unidad que se desmoronaba por todas partes.[22]

From his father, Felipe II inherited the noble aspiration to defend the traditions of Catholicism against the infidels and the Protestants. His zeal in this endeavor was even more pronounced than that of Carlos I; his religiosity has been described by Von Ranke as

> ...una especie de religión fundada en el convencimiento de que él ha nacido para mantener este culto externo, que él es columna de la Iglesia, y que él así cumple una misión buena. Con esto consigue que la mayoría de los españoles, imbuidos de análogos sentimientos, ...no sólo le amen sino que le veneren, y le adoren, y que consideren sus órdenes como sagradas, que nadie puede quebrantar sin ofender a Dios.[23]

Another admirable characteristic of Felipe II was his prodigious capacity for administrative work:

> Todos los asuntos de su vasto Imperio convergían en su mesa. Todos los acuerdos de alguna importancia, propuestos por sus consejeros, se le presentaban con el margen del papel en blanco, y doblado, para que él anotara las correcciones o las modificaciones que creyera convenientes. Los memoriales, las cartas a él dirigidas, las consultas de sus ministros y los informes secretos, todo venía a parar a sus manos. Su trabajo, y su placer, consistía en leerlos, reflexionar sobre su contenido y dar respuesta a todos.[24]

---

[21] See Menéndez Pidal, *Idea imperial de Carlos V*, p. 31.
[22] Ibid., p. 32.
[23] Von Ranke, p. 26.
[24] Ibid., p. 23.

However, unlike his predecessors, he was not adept at selecting the appropriate men to fulfill important tasks and lead his military exploits. This, according to Menéndez Pidal, was the primary failing of Felipe II and one of the major causes of national disillusionment and decline. [25]

The Monarchy under Felipe III

Shortly before his death in 1598, it is said that Felipe II lamented the fact that God, having graced him with a great kingdom to rule, did not grant him an heir worthy of inheriting it. [26] The King foresaw the inefficacy and laxitude which would characterize the reign of his son, Felipe III.

The new King did not inherit any of the traits or abilities which had distinguished his ancestors; he was not interested in the affairs of state, nor was he inspired by the prospect of religious wars in Europe. [27] He was extremely pious, but his main concern was his own salvation. Because of his weak character, he was easily dominated by the strong personality of his favorite companion, Francisco Gómez de Sandoval y Rojas, later Duke of Lerma:

> Al subir al Trono Felipe III, no hubo ya duda sobre el futuro. El primer acto del Rey fue recibir juramento de Lerma, su primera orden, una orden sin igual, fue que la firma de Lerma valiera tanto como la propia firma del Rey; los primeros favores fueron concedios a Lerma. Al aniversario de la muerte del Rey se vio que Lerma lo era todo en el nuevo orden de cosas. [28]

Having gained such unprecedented control over the King and the government, Lerma became a jealous guardian of his position:

> En vano daba el Rey sus audiencias, en vano acomodado en la mesa esperaba a los peticionarios. Que todo lo que

---

[25] See Menéndez Pidal, *Los españoles en la historia* in *España y su historia*, Vol. I, pp. 54-55.
[26] Von Ranke, p. 30.
[27] Ibid., p. 31.
[28] Ibid., pp. 79-80.

trataban era sólo ser oídos del Ministro omnipotente, quien les hacía esperar largos meses antes de recibirlos. Lerma se convirtió en el punto central de un Reino, que administraba en su propio interés. [29]

One of many travelers in Spain at this time, the Venetian Ambassador, Simon Contarini, did not fail to notice this relationship between Felipe III and his privado. From an account of his journey in 1605 comes the following observation:

El estado de las cosas de España no es bueno, porque deseando los pueblos mejorarse del Gobierno de Felipe II han alcanzado otro más desigual y confuso y de menos despacho, y lo que con más extremo sienten, es conocer que no tienen Rey, y del poder del Duque hablan diferentemente, unos que le tienen hechizado; otros que el natural es servil, cada uno como le parece... [30]

When the Duke of Lerma finally lost the King's favor in 1618, his son, the Duke of Uceda, assumed the duties and privileges of being the favorite minister; Felipe III was incapable of governing on his own: "Era un hombre de un natural demasiado bueno, demasiado débil, demasiado piadoso para su cargo." [31]

During the reign of Felipe III, Spain continued to be the supreme territorial power in Europe. Her dominion over the New World, the Low Countries, Italy and her support of the Empire in Germany required the maintenance of military forces on land and at sea. These foreign commitments necessitated large sums of money and man power which could thus not be used on the Peninsula. Local industry and agriculture which had flourished in the sixteenth century suffered a severe set-back in the early seventeenth century due to the effects of depopulation. The wealth which Spain acquired in the Indies was either channeled into the costs of war, spent outside Spain on imported industrial products or remained in the

---

[29] Ibid., p. 81.
[30] *Relación que hizo a la República de Venecia Simón Contarini, al fin de el año 1605, de la Embajada que había hecho en España*, cited by José García Mercadal, *España vista por los extranjeros*, Vol. III. Madrid: Biblioteca Nueva, 1917, p. 51.
[31] Von Ranke, p. 90.

pockets of the nobles and clergy who were exempt from taxation. The extravagance and corruption of the Court under Lerma's authority was notorious, and lavish banquets were frequently given for the King and foreign visitors:

> En el banquete dado por el duque de Lerma [in honor of the English Ambassador in 1605] las salas estaban colgadas con telas de oro y tapicerías de brocado, y los aparadores, que llegaban hasta el techo, veíanse llenos de piezas de plata, oro macizo y cristal de roca, guarnecidos con pedrería, y vidrios venecianos y catalanes, finos barros portugueses y frascos de plata y cantimploras con vinos y cerveza al uso de Inglaterra.[32]

The Court became the seat of an ostentatious and vain nobility and a mecca for the poor who lived like parasites in a day-to-day existence.

This, then, was the unhappy state of the monarchy under Felipe III. Without the guidance of a powerful and determined king, the Spanish nation began to lose the unifying moral and political spirit of the century before. When Felipe III died in 1621, the new King, Felipe IV, was confronted with the problems of a nation in decline.

The "Política de Dios"

During the twenty-three years of Felipe III's reign, Francisco de Quevedo had abundant opportunities to observe the King and his privados at close range. Not only did he frequent the Court and mingle with the court society as a nobleman in his own right, but he also interviewed the King and the Duke of Lerma as an unofficial representative of the Duke of Osuna, Viceroy of Sicily and, later, of Naples. Defending his ability to appraise and comment upon the affairs of government, Quevedo mentioned his qualifications at the conclusion of a short work written in 1621 analyzing a letter of Fernando el Católico:

---

[32] García Mercadal, p. 44.

...lo que he escrito lo he estudiado en el tumulto destos años, y en catorce viajes, que me han servido más de estudio que de peregrinación, siendo parte en los negocios que de su real servicio me encomendó su majestad, que está en el cielo, y con su Santidad y los potentados. [33]

From both perspectives, that of a citizen and a politician, Quevedo saw the corrupt state of the government and realized the danger to the nation if it were allowed to continue unchecked.

In the face of this realization, Quevedo began to write the *Política de Dios y gobierno de Cristo* in the summer of 1617. [34] Although Quevedo intended this work for Felipe III, he did not conclude the first part until 1621 at which time the King died. He therefore dedicated it to Felipe IV and the Conde-Duque de Olivares, his valido, and sent it to Olivares with the hope that it would be of benefit to the new government: "Dar a leer a vuecelencia este libro es la mejor diligencia que puede hacer el conocimiento de su integridad, para darse por entendido del cuidado con que asiste al Rey nuestro señor, en valimiento ni celoso ni interesado." [35]

The *Política de Dios* contains the nucleus of Quevedo's political philosophy. Its primary purpose was to present to the Monarch and to his privado a code of ethics based upon the Holy Scriptures which Quevedo believed to be the answer to a revival of the vigorous and just leadership which Spain had known in the past. The idea that princes should follow the teachings of the New Testament was not an original one in Spain; it had been broached by Padre Pedro de Rivadeneyra in his *Tratado de la religión y virtudes que debe tener el príncipe cristiano* (1595). [36] What is original in this work by Quevedo is his tone of urgency and his will to impress his point

---

[33] "Carta del Rey don Fernando el Católico al primer Virrey de Nápoles," *Obras* I (1964), 707.

[34] When the first part of the *Política* was printed in 1626, some 12,000 copies were made in that year alone, an unprecedented demonstration of popularity not equalled by any other contemporary work, including Cervantes' *Quijote*. This popularity is evidence of Quevedo's respected position in Spanish society. See J. O. Crosby, *The Sources of the Text of Quevedo's Política de Dios*. New York: The Modern Language Association of America, 1959, p. 5 and p. 48.

[35] "Al Conde-Duque," *Política, Obras* I (1964), 530.

[36] See Monroe Z. Hafter, "Sobre la singularidad de la *Política de Dios*," *Nueva Revista de Filología Hispánica*, vol. XIII, 1959, p. 102.

upon the Monarch: "Exegeta y predicador a la vez, arrogante y modesto, Quevedo está siempre presente como el intermediario, como el portador de la verdad indispensable." [37] It was impossible for Quevedo to remain outside his work and to depersonalize it, as did so many other writers of political literature, because (1) he was thoroughly convinced that the example of Christ was the best model of conduct for a monarch, and (2) he felt that it was his patriotic duty to urge this upon Felipe IV so that he would not repeat the mistakes of his father. The fact that Quevedo added a second part to the *Política de Dios* some fifteen years later, in 1635, is evidence of his unfailing desire to impart his message. [38] Although Quevedo was primarily writing for the benefit of the Spanish Monarch, he also tried to emphasize the transcendence of his ideas: "Estos preceptos generales hablan en lenguaje de los mandamientos con todos los que los quebrantaron y no cumplieren, y miran con igual entereza a todos tiempos, y señalan las vidas, no los nombres." [39] When Quevedo wrote these words, he might well have been thinking of the French government, then in the hands of the minister, Cardinal Richelieu. [40]

In his dedication of the *Política* to Felipe IV, Quevedo's initial statement reveals the message of his work: "Tiene vuestra majestad de Dios tantos y tan grandes reinos, que sólo de su boca y acciones y de los que le imitaron puede tomar modo de gobernar con acierto y providencia." [41] The only true and perfect king was Christ, God's incarnation on earth whose mission among men was to set an example for all rulers to follow: "Cristo sólo supo ser rey; y así sólo lo sabrá ser quien le imitare." [42] In contrast to other political writers of his time who chose Fernando el Católico as their model ruler, [43] Quevedo looks only to Christ. This is not to say that he

---

[37] Ibid., p. 104.

[38] For the sake of organization and clarity, my discussion of the *Política* will be based upon both the first and second parts.

[39] Política (Pt. II, "A quien lee..."), Obras I (1964), 585.

[40] Quevedo's antipathy toward Richelieu was expressed in his *Carta a Luis XIII* (1635) and in a short satire entitled *Visita y anatomía de la cabeza del Cardenal Armando de Richelieu* (1635).

[41] *Política* (Pt. I), *Obras* I (1964), 528.

[42] *Política* (Pt. I), *Obras* I (1964), 538.

[43] See Baltasar Gracián, *El Político* or Saavedra Fajardo, *Introducción a la Política y Razón de Estado del Rey Católico Don Fernando*.

does not mention other Spanish kings, but he does so merely in the manner of a side-comment as in the following lines to Felipe IV: "Mucho tenéis que copiar en Carlos V, si os fatigaren guerras extranjeras, y ambición de victorias os llevare por el mundo con glorioso distraimiento." [44]

In a preface to the first part, Quevedo invokes a warning to any ruler who might contradict God's designs. His words expose the strength of his convictions and are almost startling in their frankness:

> A vuestro cuidado, no a vuestro albedrío, encomendó las gentes Dios nuestro señor y en los estados, reinos y monarquías os dió trabajo y afán honroso, no vanidad ni descanso, si el que os encomendó los pueblos os ha de tomar cuenta dellos si os hacéis dueños con resabios de lobos...
> Y con nombre de tiranía irá vuestra memoria disfamando por las edades vuestros huesos y en las historias serviréis de ejemplo escandaloso. [45]

The most important tradition which Quevedo defines in the *Política* and the one which actually comprises the "raison d'être" of his work is that of the maintenance of monarchical authority. This authority is invested in a king by God and it carries with it the responsibility to reign over men in His image, following His will and commandments: "Señor, la vida del oficio real se mide con la obediencia a los mandatos de Dios y con su imitación." [46] The concept of monarchical sovereignty cannot be equated with absolutism, for the king has been entrusted by God with the duty of working for the well-being of his people. I have shown previously how this reasoning has been a tradition in Spain since the sixth century, and Quevedo reaffirms it in this manner:

> La primera virtud de un rey es la obediencia. Ella, como sabidora de lo que vale la templanza y moderación, dispone con suavidad el mandar en el sumo poder. No es la obediencia mortificación de los monarcas; que noblemente

---

[44] *Política* (Dedication), *Obras* I (1964), 529.
[45] *Política* (Pt. I, "Prefación"), *Obras* I (1964), 532.
[46] *Política* (Pt. II, Chapt. I), *Obras* I (1964), 590.

reconocen las grandas almas vasallaje a la razón, a la piedad y a las leyes. Quien a éstas obedece bien, manda; y quien manda sin haberlas obedecido, antes martiriza que gobierna. [47]

Quevedo's defense of this duty recalls a similar statement by Dante in the *Monarchy* (c. 1312):

> ...the Emperor... in accordance with philosophical teaching, is to lead mankind to temporal happiness. None would reach this harbour — or, at least, few would do so, and only with the greatest difficulty — unless the waves of alluring cupidity were assuaged and mankind were freed from them so as to rest in the tranquillity of peace; and this is the task to which that protector of the world must devote his energies who is called the Roman Prince. His office is to provide freedom and peace for men as they pass through the testing-time of this world. [48]

The task of maintaining authority within these limits will not be an easy one, says Quevedo, recalling the sorrows and rejection of Christ on earth: "Señor, si en palacio hacen burla de Cristo, Dios y hombre y verdadero Rey, bien pueden temer mayores excesos los reyes. ..." [49]

In order to be respected and to conserve his authority, a king must seek justice in all his decrees: "La justicia se muestra en la igualdad de los premios y los castigos, y en la distribución, que algunas veces se llama igualdad. Es una constante y perpetua voluntad de dar a cada uno lo que le toca." [50] Quevedo underlines the necessity of a ruler being flexible in his attitude toward the dispensation of justice: "Ser justo, ser recto, ser severo, otra cosa es; que inexorable es condición indigna de quien tiene cuidados de Dios, del padre de las gentes, del pastor de los pueblos." [51] In the *Partidas* of Alfonso X one reads a similar plea that a king be

---

[47] *Política* (Pt. II, Chapt. XVI), *Obras* I (1964), 640.

[48] Dante Alighieri, *Monarchy and Three Political Letters*, trans. Donald Nicholl. London: Weidenfeld and Nicolson, 1954, p. 93.

[49] *Política* (Pt. I, Chapt. I), *Obras* I (1964), 534.

[50] *Política* (Pt. I, Chapt. III), *Obras* I (1964), 539.

[51] *Política* (Pt. I, Chapt. III), *Obras* I (1964), 540.

merciful toward his subjects, "aviendo merced dellos, faziéndles merced, quando entendiere que lo han menester." [52]

A just king must always consider the needs of the people ahead of his own interests: "Buena voluntad es con la que el príncipe quiere más el público provecho, que el propio; más el bien del reino, que el suyo; más el trabajo de su oficio, que el deleite de sus deseos." [53] However, Quevedo does not mean to say that a monarch can justify nefarious deeds by explaining them as necessary for the good of the state. No "razón de Estado" is an excuse for evil:

> Los perversos políticos la han hecho [la razón de Estado] un dios sobre toda deidad, ley a todas superior. Esto cada día se les oye muchas veces. Quitan y roban los estados ajenos; mienten, niegan la palabra; rompen los sagrados y solemnes juramentos; siendo católicos, favorecen a herejes e infieles. Si se lo reprenden por ofensa al derecho divino y humano, responden que lo hacen por materia de Estado, teniéndola por absolución de toda vileza, tiranía y sacrilegio. [54]

When writing this in 1635, Quevedo could well have been thinking of the government of Richelieu. The powerful Cardinal had initiated territorial conquests and employed unscrupulous tactics during the Thirty Years' War (1618-1648), and Quevedo was particularly incensed by the recent plunder of Tillimon by French troops. [55] The French declaration of war against Spain in Flanders in 1635 was, in his opinion, motivated purely by greed and was an overt act of aggression against peace-loving Christians. Writing to Louis XIII, Quevedo denounced French tactics:

> Syre, si llamáis tener paz con nosotros, hacernos en Flandes una guerra desmentida, y en Alemania pública, y en Italia con un amparo mal rebozado fatigar la cristiandad, ¿por qué llamáis guerra nuestra justa defensa? Ocasionarla y no quererla, ni es justicia ni es valor. [56]

---

[52] Segunda partida, Título X, Ley II.
[53] *Política* (Pt. II, Chapt. XVI, *Obras* I (1964), 643.
[54] *Política* (Pt. II, Chapt. VI), *Obras* I (1964), 602.
[55] See "Carta a Luis XIII," *Obras* I (1964), 887-903.
[56] *Obras* I (1964), 895.

In his defense of monarchical virtue and his opposition to wars of territorial expansion purely motivated by the "razón de Estado," Quevedo's attitude is reminiscent of that of Antonio de Guevara, a counselor of Carlos I. In his work entitled *The Dial of Princes* (*El reloj de príncipes*), Guevara wrote:

> Do not think, Romans, to be the more victorious, for that ye assemble great armies, or that ye abound in treasures, neither for that you have greater gods in your aid, or that ye build greater temples, nor yet for that ye offer such great sacrifices. For I let you know, if ye do not know it, that no man is in more favor with the gods, than he which is at peace with virtue. [57]

Quevedo, in a manner traditional to the ideals of the Spanish monarchy, could not conceive of religious precepts separated from the attainment of national goals. He was a firm opponent of the tactics of Machiavelli, and he would never have agreed to these lines from *The Prince* (1513):

> It must be understood that a prince and particularly a new prince cannot practise all the virtues for which men are accounted good, for the necessity of preserving the state often compels him to take actions which are opposed to loyalty, charity, humanity, and religion. [58]

The *Política de Dios* is essentially a rejection of such thinking. Machiavelli's theories foreshadowed modern European politics, whereas Quevedo espoused the traditional concept of morality in governing nations.

Closely linked with the tradition of monarchical authority is the problem of the relationship between a king and his ministers. The burdens of his office require that a monarch accept the counsel and services of other capable men:

---

[57] Antonio de Guevara, *The Dial of Princes*, trans. Sir Thomas North. London: Philip Allan & Co., 1919, p. 110.

[58] Niccolò Machiavelli, *The Prince*, trans. and ed. Thomas G. Bergin. New York: Appleton-Century-Crofts, Inc., 1947, p. 51. In 1606, Quevedo wrote of Machiavelli: "No le impugno aquí más, porque pienso ocupar parte de mi vida en escribir contra todas sus obras..." *Discurso de las privanzas, Obras* II (1952), 1400.

> Señor, criados han de tener los reyes, unos más cerca de su persona que otros, y la voluntad no será en todos igual, y determinará con más afecto en algunos; y entre ellos podrá ser que uno sólo sea dueño de la voluntad del príncipe. [59]

This kind of relationship between a king and a privado is desirable as long as the power of the monarch remains supreme:

> A los reyes la majestad de Dios, cuando ordenó que naciesen reyes, dióles la administración y tutela de sus reinos: hízolos padres de sus vasallos, pastores: y todo esto les dió con darles el postrer arbitrio en todo lo que les consultaren y propusieren sus consejos y vasallos y reinos. Pues si eso diese un rey a otro hombre, ¿qué guardaría para sí? Nada; porque la corona y el cetro son trastos de la figura, embarazos y vanos. ¿No era renunciar el reino? Sí; no puede negarse, y es cortés manera de hablar. Era despreciar la mayor dádiva de Dios, y obrar contra su voluntad en perjuicio de tantas almas. [60]

There is no doubt that Quevedo was referring to Felipe III and the Duke of Lerma when he wrote this. As was noted, the King granted Lerma powers of authority equal to his own, and the Duke abused this power to the detriment of Spain. Again and again, Quevedo emphasizes the importance of a ruler being subservient to no one except God: "El corazón de los reyes no ha de estar en otra mano que en la de Dios. ... No sólo deben los reyes no andarse tras otro, ni dejarse llevar donde otro quisiere, sino que inviolablemente han de mirar que los que le siguieron a él puedan decir y digan: ves que lo hemos dejado y te hemos seguido." [61]

The twelve men who became Christ's disciples left their families and worldly ambitions behind and dedicated themselves entirely to their Master. Likewise, a good privado must forsake his own interests for those of the king and his people: "Señor, quien viniere a vuestra majestad, si no amare su real servicio y el bien de sus vasallos y la conservación de la fe y de la religión más que a sus padres, mujer y hijos ... no sea discípulo, no acompañe, no

---

[59] *Política* (Pt. I, Chapt. XVII), *Obras* I (1964), 569.
[60] *Política* (Pt. I, Chapt. XVII), *Obras* I (1964), 570.
[61] *Política* (Pt. I, Chapt. XX), *Obras* I (1964), 576-577.

asista."⁶² The Duke of Lerma had made sure that his relatives benefited by his exalted position; as Von Ranke says:

> Se preocupó en primer término en engrandecer a su familia. Nombró a su hermano Virrey de Valencia, a su cuñado Lemos, Virrey de Nápoles; de sus yernos, el uno fué General de las Galeras españolas, el otro Presidente del Consejo de Indias; su tío, Borja, fué Presidente del Consejo de Portugal... Los más importantes cargos del Reino se convirtieron en patrimonio familiar de su casa. ⁶³

Enumerating the ideal qualities of a minister, Quevedo says that he should always remain in the shadow of the king and seek only to aid, not to outshine his superior: "Ha de ser el ministro luz participada; no ha de tomar la que quiere, sino repartir la que le dan. Ha de ser medio iluminado, para que la majestad del Príncipe se proporcione con la capacidad del vasallo." ⁶⁴ His dedication to his work should be such that a privado feels no envy or vanity in the performance of his duties in relation to the king: "No es criado ni ministro del rey el que afecta la grandeza en tal manera, que no sólo es igual a su rey, antes superior; éste es envidioso de la corona, émulo del poder, tirano, criado a los pechos del favor, y alimentado y crecido por la soberbia del desconocimiento y la codicia." ⁶⁵ A monarch should suspect the loyalty of a valido who endeavors to distract him by offering him entertainment and encouraging him to be lazy: "Quien divierte al rey, le depone, no le sirve." ⁶⁶ In writing this, Quevedo was aware of the special attention which the Duke of Lerma had devoted to arranging all manner of entertainment for Felipe III. When he was not hunting, playing ball or dining at sumptuous banquets, the King was able to attend plays given by either of the two companies which were retained at the Court for his amusement. However, as Von Ranke points out, ⁶⁷ this atmosphere was beneficial if only for the reason that it stimulated the

---

⁶² *Política* (Pt. I, Chapt. XII), *Obras* I (1964), 558.
⁶³ Von Ranke, pp. 83-84.
⁶⁴ *Política* (Pt. II, Chapt. XI), *Obras* I (1964), 622-623.
⁶⁵ *Política* (Pt. I, Chapt. XVII), *Obras* I (1964), 568.
⁶⁶ *Política* (Pt. I, Chapt. IV), *Obras* I (1964), 541.
⁶⁷ See Von Ranke, p. 86.

literary and artistic talents of the time, not the least of which was that of Quevedo himself.

What Quevedo has made clear in the above list of necessary qualifications for a good privado is that a monarch must excercise his powers of discrimination and selection in obtaining the proper minister. Unlike other kings before him, Felipe III did not possess this ability to select the best men to perform the duties of minister. However, the problem in his case was deeper than that. Despite all the precautions a ruler may take in choosing a privado, he fails if he himself is not a strong, authoritative individual. Felipe III lacked this quality. Although he was an extremely religious man, he was not able to imitate Christ in the aspects which are most crucial to a successful king: "Aquel señor que, no queriendo imitar a Cristo, se deja gobernar por otro, no es señor, es guante; pues sólo se mueve cuando y donde quiere la mano que se lo calza." [68] A king who neglects to exert true leadership fails himself, his kingdom and God. This was the tragic paradox of the reign of Felipe III whose religiosity could not make up for his deficiencies as a ruler.

A king, by the nature of his office, is a public figure: "El rey es persona pública; su corona son las necesidades de su reino: el reinar no es entretenimiento, sino tarea; mal rey el que goza sus estados, y bueno el que los sirve." [69] In order for him to be a just ruler, he must be accessible to his subjects just as Christ was available to those who sought his help:

> Rey que se esconde a las quejas y que tiene porteros para los agraviados y no para quien lo agravia, ése retírase de su oficio y obligación, y cree que los ojos de Dios no entran en su retiramiento, y está de par en par a la perdición y al castigo del Señor, de quien no quiere aprender a ser rey. [70]

A king must hold audiences which do not allow favoritism of the rich over the poor, and he should guard against a privado who may wish to assume this duty or who may show preference toward the powerful over the weak. [71] By emphasizing this duty of a monarch,

---

[68] *Política* (Pt. II, Chapt. II), *Obras* I (1964), 593.
[69] *Política* (Pt. I, Chapt. XVI), *Obras* I (1964), 567.
[70] *Política* (Pt. I, Chapt. XVI), *Obras* I (1964), 567.
[71] *Política* (Pt. I, Chapt. XVI), *Obras* I (1964), 567.

Quevedo defends a traditional principle of the king being the final arbitrator of justice which has been respected in Spain since the Middle Ages. Describing the administration of justice in the twelfth and thirteenth centuries, Román Riaza and A. García Gallo say: "La administración de justicia fué considerada como atribución del Estado, según la concepción de la época, es decir, del rey, rechazándose la existencia de jurisdicciones de tipo privado." [72] This concept is historically substantiated in Spain's first known epic poem, *Poema de Mío Cid* (c. 1140). More than one half of the third and final "cantar" is devoted to the details of the Cid's plea for justice in an audience before the King, Alfonso VI. This practice continued through the reign of the Catholic Kings, after which time it fell into disuse;

> La intervención personal del monarca en la administración de justicia, a la manera como se había hecho en la Baja Edad Media, continuó bajo los Reyes Católicos, que, los lunes para oír peticiones y los viernes para escuchar las quejas de los presos, se sentaban en público, rodeados del *Consejo real*. Luego, los reyes se fueron desentendiendo de esta carga, de forma que el Consejo de Castilla vino a ejercer, en nombre de aquellos, sus funciones judiciales. [73]

During the reign of Felipe III, it was the Duke of Lerma who assumed the task of dispensing justice in place of the King, and Quevedo heartily condemns this in the *Política*:

> Dar audiencia los ministros es forzoso, y pueden cometer gran crimen y escandaloso en el modo de darla, por ser la acción de singular majestad en los reyes, y en España y Castilla particularmente, no hacer otra con los vasallos en que personalmente el rey ejercite la jurisdicción y soberanía; y si ésta se imita por el criado, es desautoridad; y si se igualase, sería atrevimiento; y si se excediese, lo que Dios no quiera, sería acción que aun ponerle nombre no se puede sin culpa. [74]

---

[72] Riaza and García Gallo, *Manual de Historia del Derecho Español*. Madrid: Librería General de Victoriano Suárez, 1935, p. 411.

[73] Ibid., p. 578.

[74] *Política* (Pt. I, Chapt. XVI), *Obras* I (1964), 567.

Just as a king must respect his duties to his subjects, so must these subjects render service to their ruler. The preservation of a monarchy, as with any society, depends upon the cooperation of all its individual parts to sustain the unity of the whole. In order for a king to maintain and protect his kingdom, he needs financial support. The custom of a king collecting tributes had been traditional in Spain since the Visigothic era and was inherited from the Roman system of exacting taxes: "... los reyes visigodos aceptaron en su provecho el sistema financiero de Roma, simplificándolo, por lo que sufrió alguna modificación." [75] Quevedo is adamant in his defense of this tradition:

> No puede haber rey ni reino... sin tributos. Concédenlos todos los derechos divino y natural, y civil y de las gentes. Todos los súbditos lo conocen y lo confiesan; y los más los rehusan cuando se los piden, y se quejan cuando los pagan a quien los deben. Quieren todos que el rey los gobierne, que pueda defenderlos y los defienda; y ninguno quiere que sea a costa de su obligación. Tal es la naturaleza del pueblo, que se ofende de que hagan los reyes lo que él quiere que hagan. [76]

Here Quevedo recognizes one of the chief problems of a monarch who, in trying to support his realm for the benefit of his people, is accused of injustice because of taxation. However, should he ask for tributes when there is no need for them, a monarch is guilty of greed: "Señor, Cristo cansado del camino pidió agua; pidió con necesidad: esto es lo primero que se ha de hacer. Lo segundo, pidió agua sentado sobre la fuente, que es pedir lo que hay, y donde lo hay sobrado. Lo tercero, pidió agua a quien venía a sacar agua, a quien traía con que dar y sacar lo que se le pidiese." [77] In requesting tributes, a king must imitate Christ who asked only of those who could afford to give. Writing this in the second part of the *Política*, Quevedo was conscious of Felipe IV's difficulties in collecting taxes levied upon the various provinces of Spain in order to pay for the costs of foreign wars. The local "cortes," or governing bodies of the six provinces, resented these demands for money as they con-

---

[75] Riaza and García Gallo, p. 143.
[76] *Política* (Pt. II, Chapt. VIII), *Obras* I (1964), 609.
[77] *Política* (Pt. II, Chapt. IX), *Obras* I (1964), 615.

sidered them excessive.[78] Felipe IV faced a severe economic crisis, and he was forced upon several occasions to devalue the currency which resulted in oppressive inflation. The Conde-Duque de Olivares had tried to curb spending and improve the economy, but his efforts were futile as this contemporary report shows:

> ...El conde de Olivares atiende sobre todo con mucho estudio a los asuntos de la Hacienda, la cual reducida como está al extremo, se procura con nuevas ideas y ahorro en los gastos dejarla en mejor estado y para ello hay junta permanente en casa del Conde que no piensa en otra cosa.
> ...los ingresos de España están muy disminuidos, tanto por la expulsión de los moriscos como por el poco número de hombres que quedan y la carga de tributos que soportan. El conde de Olivares había demostrado que quería empezar por la Casa Real reduciendo sus gastos a 36 mil escudos al mes; pero habiendo aumentado este año a 72.000 con los gastos extraordinarios que producirán el mantenimiento de ochenta galeones además del grandísimo gasto que se hace en Flandes, poco se podrá deducir de estos planes.[79]

In matters of taxation, Quevedo is particularly concerned with the importance of taxing those who can best afford to give and who are most in need of protection for their private interests.[80] He thus appears to be in favor of relinquishing the tradition of exempting the nobles and clergy from taxation in the interest of insuring a more important tradition, that of the unity and support of the populace:

> El Espíritu Santo dice "que la riqueza del rey está en la multitud del pueblo". No es pueblo muy poderoso, Señor, el que yace en rematada pobreza: es carga, es peligro, es amenaza; porque la multitud hambrienta ni sabe temer, ni

---

[78] See Martin Hume, *The Court of Philip IV: Spain in Decadence.* New York: Brentano's [1927], p. 618.

[79] "Dos enviados genoveses resumen la política exterior e interior de los primeros tiempos de Olivares," cited by Fernando Díaz-Plaja, *La historia de España en sus documentos: el siglo XVII,* Vol. III. Madrid: Instituto de Estudios Políticos, 1957, p. 116.

[80] See Pedro Pérez Clotet, *La Política de Dios de Quevedo.* Madrid: Editorial Reus, S. A., 1928, pp. 158-159. Pérez Clotet equates Quevedo's doctrine of tributes with the modern individualist school of economics founded by Thiers.

> tiene qué; y aquel que los quita cuanto adquirieron de oro
> y plata y hacienda, los deja la voz para el grito, los ojos
> para el llanto, el puñal y las armas. [81]

When a king loses his subjects' support, the unity of the state is threatened. This is the basic factor of any political association, and one which the astute Machiavelli, often the object of Quevedo's disdain, recognized with these words: "The best fortress a prince can have is simply in not being hated by his people, for if the people hate you your fortresses will not save you. . . ." [82] Quevedo would have disagreed with Machiavelli's means to achieve this end, but he would not have disputed the logic of the end in itself. He knew that the solid foundations of the monarchy in Spain had been built upon this premise, as the *Siete Partidas* expresses it: "El mayor poderío, y mas complido, que el emperador puede aver de fecho en su señorío, es quando el ama a su gente, e es amado della." [83]

This brings up the discussion of a problem which Quevedo touched upon in the *Política* but which he treated in greater detail in another political work, *Marco Bruto,* written in 1632. The topic in question is tyrannicide: can the murder of a king be justified if he has become a tyrant? [84] Quevedo's answer is unequivocal:

> Grave delito es dar muerte a cualquier hombre; mas darla
> al rey es maldad execrable, y traición nefanda no sólo
> poner en él manos, sino hablar de su persona con poca
> reverencia, o pensar de sus acciones con poco respeto. El
> rey bueno se ha de amar; el malo se ha de sufrir. Con-
> siente Dios el tirano, siendo quien le puede castigar y depo-
> ner, ¿y no le consentirá el vasallo, que debe obedecerle?
> No necesita el brazo de Dios de nuestros puñales para sus
> castigos, ni de nuestras manos para sus venganzas. [85]

---

[81] *Política* (Pt. II, Chapt. XII), *Obras* I (1964), 626.
[82] Machiavelli, p. 64.
[83] Segunda Partida, Título I, Ley III.
[84] The distinction between a tyrant who rules with the legitimate right to the throne and the one who has usurped the throne did not concern most seventeenth century writers because of their particular historical circumstances. See José-Antonio Maravall, *La Philosophie Politique Espagnole au XVIIe Siècle*. Paris: Librairie Philosophique J. Vrin, 1955, p. 314.
[85] *Marco Bruto, Obras* I (1964), 860.

During the sixteenth century, the majority of political theorists in Spain defended the right of the people to commit tyrannicide:

> Le XVI⁶ siècle, en effet, sauf de rares exceptions, avait présenté une défense chaleureuse et même exagérée du tyrannicide. Certes, quelques-uns, comme Vitoria, s'étaient permis de s'élever contre l'opinion générale et de dénier aux sujets le droit de mettre fin aux jours du tyran. Mais les auteurs catholiques espagnols et les réformés français s'étaient déclarés en faveur de cette faculté de la république contre le tyran. Soto, Suárez, Molina, Mariana, sur des tons différents, s'accordent pour accorder le droit de tuer le tyran. [86]

In his work, *Del rey y de la institución real,* Padre Juan de Mariana affirms the following:

> Es siempre sin embargo saludable que estén persuadidos los príncipes de que si oprimen la república, si se hacen intolerables por sus vicios y por sus delitos, están sujetos a ser asesinados, no sólo con derecho, sino hasta con aplauso y gloria de las generaciones venideras. [87]

The conflict in opinion between Quevedo and Padre Mariana is explained by their differing interpretations of the concept of sovereignty. Those who, like Mariana, defended tyrannicide based their opinion upon the belief that a tyrant, having overstepped the boundaries of his powers, is subject to judgment by his subjects:

> El poder, la soberanía, según ellos la ha puesto Dios en el pueblo que, mediante un pacto— que ahora ocupa el punto central de la doctrina—, la transmite al rey; éste no se convierte, sin embargo, en un simple mandatario. El Estado, la comunidad, tiene, por consiguiente, pleno poder contra el rey, a quien deberá fidelidad y obediencia mientras la dirija rectamente, pero a quien podrá deponer en cuanto, infringiendo el pacto, obre contra el Derecho divino y el humano, convirtiéndose en tirano. [88]

---

[86] Maravall, *La Philosophie...*, p. 319.
[87] Padre Juan de Mariana, *Del rey y de la institución real,* Cap. VI, in *Obras.* Madrid: Biblioteca de Autores Españoles, 1950, p. 483.
[88] Riaza and García Gallo, p. 509.

Other writers who held this opinion in the sixteenth century were: Alfonso Orosco in *Regalis institutio* (1565), Juan de Espinosa in *Cynacepanos o Diálogo en laude de las mujeres* (1580) and Diego Hurtado de Mendoza in *Diálogo entre Caronte y el Ánimo de Pedro Luis Farnesio, hijo del Papa Paulo III*. [89]

Quevedo is in agreement with these authors insofar as he upholds the Isidorian tradition, "Rex eris, si recte facies; si non facies, non eris." [90] When a king ceases to rule in accordance with the laws of God and nature, he has become a tyrant and no longer deserves to be called a king:

> ¿Qué llama Dios ser rey? ¿Qué llama no serlo? Cláusulas son éstas de ceño desapacible para los príncipes, de gran consuelo para los vasallos, de suma reputación para su justicia de inmensa mortificación para la hipocresía soberana de los hombres. Señor, la vida del oficio real se mide con la obediencia a los mandatos de Dios y con su imitación... Muchos entienden que reinan porque se ven con cetro, corona y púrpura (insignias de la majestad, y superficie delgada de aquel oficio); y siendo verdugos de sus imperios y provincias, los deja Dios el nombre y las ceremonias, para que conozcan las gentes que pidieron estas insignias para adorno de su calamidad y de su ruina. [91]

According to Quevedo, a tyrant no longer deserves the title of king, and he only conserves the outer trappings of his office. It does not follow, however, that the sovereignty of the king reverts to the people, permitting them to depose him. Quevedo feels that the misdeeds of a king can only be judged by God; the people must not take justice into their own hands: "El rey bueno se ha de amar; el malo se ha de sufrir." [92] In many cases, God permits a tyrant to reign as a punishment to the people: "A muchos, sin ser ya reyes, permite Dios el nombre y el puesto, porque sus maldades llenen el castigo de las gentes." [93]

Quevedo's opposition to tyrannicide is more thoroughly understood when the historical circumstances in which he lived are taken

---

[89] Pérez Clotet, p. 108.
[90] García de Valdeavellano, p. 301.
[91] *Política* (Pt. II, Chapt. I), *Obras* I (1964), 590.
[92] *Marco Bruto*, *Obras* I (1964), 860.
[93] *Política* (Pt. II, Chapt. I), *Obras* I (1964), 590-591.

into account. When writing the following words in the *Política,* he was undoubtedly implicating Felipe IV who had become more concerned with his own pleasures than with the administration of his kingdom as the years wore on:

> Hay tiranos de dos maneras: unos pródigos de la hacienda suya y de la república, por tomarse para sí no sólo el poder que les toca, sino el de las leyes divinas y humanas. Otros son miserables en dar caudal y dineros; y son pródigos en dar de sí y de su oficio; *y pasan a consentir que les tomen y quiten su propia dignidad, por no perder un instante de ocio y entretenimiento.* [94] (Emphasis added.)

This concept of tyranny by the lack of authority on the part of the monarch or the delegation of this authority to others became popular in the seventeenth century,[95] influenced by the examples of the Duke of Lerma, the Conde-Duque de Olivares and Cardinal Richelieu. In view of this, to endorse tyrannicide would be tantamount to supporting public opposition to the King at a time when Spain was desperately in need of political unity. Quevedo was not a believer in the ability of the people to govern themselves:

> Mal entendió Marco Bruto la materia de la tiranía, pues juzgó por tirano el que con la valentía y el séquito de sus virtudes y sus armas, asistidas de afortunados sucesos, en una república tomó para sí solo el dominio que la multitud de senadores posee en la confusión apasionada... Las leyes sacrosantas mejor se hallan servidas de uno que las ejecuta, que de muchos que las interpretan.[96]

Therefore, Quevedo and other opponents of tyrannicide in the seventeenth century, supported the tradition of supreme monarchical authority, even at the cost of tyranny, in order to preserve the unity of the kingdom:

> La raison décisive de l'inébranlable opposition des écrivains du XVIIᵉ siècle à toute reconnaissance du droit de résistance est basée sur la conscience historique et sur la claire

---

[94] *Política* (Pt. II, Chapt. IX), *Obras* I (1964), 617.
[95] See Maravall, *La Philosophie...,* pp. 315-316.
[96] *Marco Bruto, Obras* I (1964), 869.

notion des circonstances de l'époque que nous découvrons en eux. C'est la sécurité de l'Etat qu'ils veulent solidement établir, pour se defendre contre ces maux à nul autre pareils que sont les divisions et les révolutions... En matière d'idées politiques il ne suffit pas de procéder scientifiquement de déduction en déduction, selon les règles de la logique formelle, il faut aussi compter avec le temps dans lequel nous vivons, comme chaque fois qu'on se réfère a l'homme. [97]

The final chapters of the second part of the *Política de Dios* are devoted to the topic of war, its justifications, and how a king should conduct himself in time of war. Quevedo states that the first war was declared by God against the angels who fought with Lucifer to upset the peace of heaven. "¡Santa batalla!" exclaims Quevedo, and he continues, "Quien con herejes hace guerra a católicos, no sólo es demonio sino infierno." [98] This militaristic rejection of the infidels finds its traditional strength in the attitude of the Spanish realms of the Middle Ages during the Reconquest. Defining the reasons for a king's existence on earth by divine authority, the *Siete Partidas* explicitly states that a monarch (1) must be the defender of national unity "por toller desacuerdos entre las gentes e ayuntarlas en uno," (2) must be just, "facer fueros e leyes," and (3) must defend Christianity "para amparar la fe de nuestro Sr. Jesu Cristo, e quebrantar los enemigos della." [99]

Quevedo's logic in justifiying war is eminently simple: "Guerra que es instrumento de la venganza de Dios en sus enemigos, en su justicia, se justifica. Asistir a la cause de Dios es ser ministros suyos: ser medio de su providencia es calificación de la victoria." [100] War must not be waged as an end in itself or purely for the sake of aggression: "Buscar y cobrar la paz con la guerra, es de ángeles y serafines; buscar la guerra con la guerra, no; buscar la guerra con la paz, aún menos. Y estas dos cosas son la mayor ocupación y fatiga del mundo." [101]

---

[97] Maravall, *La Philosophie...*, p. 321.
[98] *Política* (Pt. II, Chapt. XXIII), *Obras* I (1964), 693.
[99] Segunda Partida, Título I, Ley I.
[100] *Política* (Pt. II, Chapt. XXII), *Obras* I (1964), 677.
[101] *Política* (Pt. II, Chapt. XXIII), *Obras* I (1964), 693.

As pointed out in preceding pages, Quevedo was opposed to war for the purpose of territorial expansion; however, he firmly believed in the virtue of defensive war when territories under Spanish Catholic rule were threatened by aggression on the part of heretics or those states inspired by Machiavellian tactics. This attitude is evident in *Lince de Italia u zahorí español*, a short work written by Quevedo in 1628 and addressed to Felipe IV. Here Quevedo demonstrates his familiarity with Spain's problems in Italy. His intent is to caution the King against the aggressive nature of the Duke of Savoy and of the Republic of Venice:

> La distinción de Italia me parece ésta y verdadera: en ella muchos son señores en el nombre, vuestra majestad lo es en la sustancia; el sumo Pontífice lo puede ser por sus estados y pretensiones; el duque de Saboya lo pretende ser por su orgullo; y el rey de Francia, por su poder y razones que finge; Venecia (que busca la paz con la boca, y la guerra con los dineros) siempre procurará la inquietud de los reinos de vuestra majestad, más en Italia que en otra parte, porque sólo con eso se contrapesa ella con Italia y con vuestra monarquía, y sabe que en otros países es menester encender la guerra y soportarla, y que en Italia ella se atiza sin fin. [102]

Since Spain was the most powerful of these interests in Italy, her position was the most vulnerable and the most delicate:

> Conjura contra sí todos los potentados (que se aúnan a ser contraste al grande peso de vuestro poderío en aquellas balanzas cuya igualdad los hace parecer libres) y con ellos los príncipes que siempre están desvelados por aquellas coronas. Ganar vuestra majestad más en Italia, juzgan sus potentados que les está mal; por eso la guerra que vuestra majestad en Italia hiciere, ya sea ofensiva o defensiva, les ha de ser sospechosa aun al propio que vuestra majestad defendiere: hoy se ve la experiencia de esto. Culpa es de la grandeza incomparable de vuestra majestad, que los desiguales la teman como todopoderosa, sin fiar nada de justicia. [103]

---

[102] *Lince de Italia u zahorí español, Obras* I (1964), 800.
[103] *Lince de Italia..., Obras* I (1964), 788.

In spite of this thankless position, says Quevedo, Felipe IV must protect his interests and find a way to halt these aggressors. The justification for this is the same as is found in the *Política*: "El asistir a la religión, Señor, es la verdad de los príncipes, y de todos lo primero."[104]

For Quevedo, religion and war must support and sustain each other; they cannot be separated without disastrous results:

> ¿Qué tiene que ver el púlpito con la materia de estado y guerra? Yo probaré que no tiene menos que ver, que el freno con el caballo, y la medicina con la enfermedad, y que la materia de estado, sin las riendas del Evangelio y de la religión, correrá desbocada; y la guerra, sin los remedios de la doctrina, será incurable dolencia y contagio rabioso.[105]

Neither the most common soldier nor the king will fear the outcome of a battle if their trust is in God: "Señor: sólo Dios da las victorias, y el pecado los vencimientos y las ruinas."[106] A soldier's courage is doubly reinforced if he sees his king fighting by his side: "Rey que pelea y trabaja delante de los suyos, oblígalos a ser valientes."[107] This tradition, inherited from the Middle Ages, was observed by Carlos I,[108] but his successors had preferred to remain in the Court and avoid appearances at the battle front.[109]

Quevedo's pride in the history of successful collaboration between the Catholic Church and the Spanish monarchy is frequently expressed in the *Política*: "La mayor monarquía que ha habido y hay, ¿no es la de España en lo temporal y en lo espiritual? ¿No es victoria toda ella de Santiago mártir, soldado de Cristo, capitán general nuestro? ... Él nos llamó en lo espiritual; nosotros en lo temporal le llamamos."[110]

---

[104] *Lince de Italia...*, *Obras* I (1964), 802.
[105] *Política* (Pt. II, Chapt. XXIII), *Obras* I (1964), 694.
[106] *Política* (Pt. II, Chapt. XXIII), *Obras* I (1964), 683.
[107] *Política* (Pt. I, Chapt. VI), *Obras* I (1964), 545.
[108] See Von Ranke, p. 14.
[109] Felipe IV wanted to go to the front in 1642, but Olivares kept him away. See Gregorio Marañón, *El Conde-Duque de Olivares: La pasión de mandar*, 4th ed. Madrid: Espasa-Calpe, S. A., 1959, p. 342.
[110] *Política* (Pt. II, Chapt. XXIII), *Obras* I (1964), 692-693.

Quevedo was not alone in the defense of this tradition. Writers throughout the sixteenth century had proclaimed the unity of Church and State; these famous lines by Hernando de Acuña, from a sonnet dedicated to Carlos I, have immortalized this sentiment:

> Ya se acerca, señor, o es ya llegada
> la edad gloriosa en que promete el cielo
> una grey y un pastor sólo en el suelo,
> por suerte a nuestros tiempos reservada. [111]
> ... ...

Quevedo was well aware that this tradition had become the source of Spain's unity and the inspiration for great deeds of glory. He also knew that the political atmosphere of his time threatened the destruction of this tradition. Out of his desire to prevent this evolved the *Política de Dios y gobierno de Cristo*. It is, as we have seen, a work motivated by a very realistic appraisal of contemporary events, yet it is also inspired by a strong sense of moral idealism. This Don Quijote-Sancho Panza duality of idealism and realism in Quevedo's character is, in itself, a tradition in Spain.

THE THEME OF PRIVANZA

The topics of government which are treated in the *Política de Dios* reappear in other works by Quevedo, offering proof of his constant concern for Spain's political situation. Such topics are rediscovered not only in his predominantly political writings, but also in his prose satire, poetry and drama. Having seen in the *Política* how Quevedo emphasizes the importance of the authority of a monarch and considering the failings of Felipe III and Felipe IV in this regard, it is not surprising that his most oft-repeated theme in the realm of politics is that of privanza:

> The themes of the relationship between monarch and favorite, which Quevedo treated in the First Part of the *Política de Dios,* was to become one of his predilections,

---

[111] Reprinted in *Floresta lírica española,* ed. José Blecua. Madrid: Editorial Gredos, 1957, p. 110.

and was to be set forth at length in such later works as the *Discurso de todos los diablos,* the *Vida de Marco Bruto,* and *La fortuna con seso y la hora de todos.* And although in the long Second Part of the *Política de Dios,* ...a variety of political topics are introduced, the theme of the favorite remains by far the most important. [112]

As early as 1606, Quevedo wrote a short essay entitled *Discurso de las privanzas* which he dedicated to Felipe III. [113] If the date attributed to this work is authentic, then the *Discurso* may be established as Quevedo's first attempt at serious political literature, and his choice of the theme of privanza becomes even more significant. When the *Discurso* was written, the Duke of Lerma had already established his influence over Felipe III, and it was undoubtedly this menacing situation that inspired Quevedo's work. [114] His intention in this essay is to outline the nature of privanza, the qualities necessary for becoming a worthy privado, and the status of a privado in relation to a monarch. In describing this relationship, Quevedo employs the popular metaphor of the moon and the sun:

> Así han de ser el privado y el rey; que como la Luna se esconde delante del Sol y tanto más luce con sus mismos rayos cuanto más se aparta de él, el privado ha de esconderse delante del príncipe, no ha de competir con él en luz. Ausente dél, ha de suplir como pudiere su falta. [115]

Quevedo's implication is that the Duke of Lerma's authority should not be allowed to eclipse that of the King. However, this was already an accomplished fact. Realizing this, he concludes his *Discurso* with these words of consolation: "Adviértase que, aunque fueron durables muchas privanzas malas, que no lo son ya: y que,

---

[112] J. O. Crosby, *The Sources of the Text of Quevedo's Política de Dios,* p.2.

[113] See Apéndice VI of *Obras* II (1952), 1385-1404. This date was suggested by the editor, Luis Astrana Marín; p. 1385 (Note).

[114] Upon concluding the *Discurso,* Quevedo offers words of praise for the King's privado. This was most likely a mere formality, and it does not detract from, but rather softly disguises, his critical intentions. See *Obras* II (1952), 1404.

[115] *Discurso de las privanzas, Obras* II (1952), 1388.

si algunas lo son, que aguardan tiempo en que no lo han de ser." [116]

The theme of privanza reappears a short time later in the *Sueños*, written between 1607 and 1622. The relentless satire of these short works does not exclude the topic at hand. In *El alguacil endemoniado*, a devil describes hell to the author who thereupon asks if there are any kings where he has come from. The devil answers: "... uno se condena por la crueldad ... otros se pierden por la codicia ... y otros se van al infierno por terceras personas y se condenan por poderes, fiándose de infames ministros." [117] In *El sueño de la muerte*, Quevedo tells of a conversation between himself and a deceased magician. The latter asks the author if there are still men on earth who vie for positions as privados. When Quevedo replies that there are such men, the magician says: "... quiero que te les digas a esas bestias que en albarda tienen la vanidad y ambición que los reyes y príncipes con azogue en todo , si le quieren apretar, se va; así sucede a los que quieren tomarse con los reyes más mano de lo que es razón." [118] These words reflect a new perspective on the author's part. He is no longer pleading for monarchical authority over privados; rather he is warning those who might aspire to privanza of the precarious fortunes of such a position. Writing this in 1622, Quevedo had reason to be optimistic, for Felipe IV had just assumed the throne and appeared to be a far stronger king than his father had been. Outwardly, Felipe IV's government was a forceful negation of the preceding twenty years: Felipe III's ministers were punished, committees were organized to effect social reforms, and war was renewed in Holland. [119] What most of the Spanish populace did not realize was that the Conde-Duque de Olivares had skillfully placed himself behind the scene, purposely making his uncle, Baltasar de Zúñiga, Felipe IV's first privado. [120] Olivares was already well entrenched as the King's favorite, but he wisely preferred to remain in the background for a few years so as not to provoke the mistrust of the people. Quevedo was aware of the Conde-Duque's influence over the King and his

---

[116] *Discurso de las privanzas, Obras* II (1952), 1403-1404.
[117] *Obras* I (1964), 137.
[118] *Obras* I (1964), 186.
[119] See Marañón, pp. 52-54.
[120] Ibid., p. 51.

role in the selection of Zúñiga, but he considered it more admirable than reprehensible:

> Tal elección aconsejó a su majestad la modestia del conde de Olivares, a quien bastó el ánimo a quitarse para otro lo que no ha podido caber entre padres y hijos. Y para ver cuánto talento sobraba al conde de Olivares, no es menester más de ver el conocimiento con que le dejó pasar; que quien sabe despreciar el poder es el benemérito; y el que le codicia, es el temerario; y en el uno es gloria lo que deja, y en el otro peligro lo que tiene. [121]

Quevedo was confident that Felipe IV would be a more authoritative leader:

> Sus manos nos prometen a Carlos V; en sus palabras se lee y se oye a su abuelo, y en su religión resucita su padre. Su entendimiento es el que ha dispuesto lo que habéis oído; su voluntad, la que no se deja adormecer de lisonjas, ni robar de diligencias, ni vencer de ruegos... Quiere ser obedecido, y no violentado. [122]

The theme of privanza is found in Quevedo's moral and satirical poems. One of his sonnets describes the precarious nature of valimiento (privanza), [123] and the same sentiment is expressed in a romance about Álvaro de Luna, the privado of Juan II, who met an unhappy end:

> ... ...
> Ve de Luzbel la privanza,
> que cayó por su soberbia;
> que aun los ángeles peligran
> en la privanza y alteza.
> Fuiste cohete en el mundo,
> subiste a las nubes mesmas,
> subiste resplandeciente,
> bajas, ya ceniza, a tierra. [124]
> ... ...

---

[121] *Grandes anales de quince días, Obras* I (1964), 735.
[122] *Grandes anales de quince días, Obras* I (1964), 761.
[123] See "Descansa, mal perdido, en alta cumbre," *Obras* II (1964), 30.
[124] "A los pies de la Fortuna," *Obras* II (1964), 358-359.

In 1627, Quevedo wrote a three-act play entitled *Como ha de ser el privado*. Although he invented different names for his characters, the play is an obvious portrayal of the relationship between Felipe IV and Olivares. Both the ruler and the valido are described as being virtuous and conscientious men; Quevedo's effort to flatter them is evident throughout. In one scene, the privado is praised by a member of the court in this way:

> Viste más común que yo;
> tiene tan escasa mesa,
> que si a indecente no pasa,
> a indigna de suya llega.
> A Dios da parte del día,
> y tan cabal la que resta
> a todos, que es un ministro
> que a lo demás avergüenza.
> ... ...
> Encuadernada es su vida;
> sus días, de una estampa mesma;
> su despacho, sin ejemplo;
> sin igual, su suficiencia;
> sin pasión, al que es indigno
> del premio acorta la rienda;
> y a el que es digno, con pasión
> los merecimientos premia. [125]

Although Quevedo's intent to flatter the Conde-Duque accounts for much of the praise-filled descriptions in the play, such flattery was not without foundation. The death of his only daughter in 1626 had brought about an accentuation in Olivares' religiosity and asceticism, and he became a model of piety and devotion in the Court. [126] This play has been described as "una defensa tan cínica de Olivares que produce una reacción de antipatía en el lector." [127] It is my opinion that Quevedo's motivation in writing it was opportunistic but not cynical. As I shall endeavor to prove in the next section of this chapter, Quevedo, despite certain reservations, admired the Conde-Duque and his frequent flattery of him was not totally lacking in sincerity.

---

[125] *Como ha de ser el privado* (Acto III), *Obras* II (1964), 358-359.
[126] See Marañón, pp. 176-177.
[127] Ibid., p. 126 (Note 6).

Again, in 1632, in his work, *Marco Bruto,* Quevedo discusses the problem of privanza. Not even Julius Caesar was astute enough to take precautions against evil ministers:

> No es sólo César el príncipe que ha muerto a manos de sus consejeros. A más han muerto malos consejos que sus enemigos. En esto son parecidas las leyes a la medicina. Matan los médicos y viven de matar, y la queja cae sobre la dolencia. Arruinan a un monarca los consejeros malos, y culpan a la fortuna; y los unos y los otros son homicidas pagados. [128]

In another work, *Virtud militante* (1634-1636), he discusses the sin of ingratitude and has this to say about the plight of a privado:

> Los privados de los reyes pasan sin saber qué es agradecimiento, porque aunque den a todos lo que piden, ninguno dice que recibió lo que merece. Si dan a todos, dicen todos que los igualan, y que con eso, los afrenta. Si da a pocos, dicen los mismos que lo hizo a más no poder... Los privados son mártires (digámoslo así) de la lealtad a sus reyes, del amor a sus patrias. Tal es la naturaleza suya, que el delito es la prosperidad. Y así como el hombre adolece porque es hombre, así el privado padece solamente porque lo es. [129]

Might Quevedo have been thinking of Olivares when he wrote this? Since 1623, the Conde-Duque had endured the fickle nature of the public who criticized him with impunity and only praised him in moments of military victory. [130]

The theme of privanza was a partial inspiration for one of Quevedo's last works, *La vida de San Pablo Apóstol,* written in 1643. The political import of this work is revealed in its last lines. After recounting the exemplary life of St. Paul, Quevedo says, "... ahora, a costa del clarín del Evangelio, Pablo, hablemos con los ministros de los emperadores y monarcas." [131] His hope is that the virtuous and steadfast qualities of St. Paul, as a minister of Christ, may serve as an inspiration to those who are ministers of temporal kings:

---

[128] *Obras* I (1964), 849. This is a typical example of the low esteem in which Quevedo held the doctors of his time.
[129] *Obras* I (1964), 1247.
[130] See Marañón, pp. 56-57.
[131] *Obras* I (1964), 1532.

Vosotros, que por permisión y providencia divina sois lados de los príncipes y gozáis de su más familiar asistencia, no quitéis los ojos de la cabeza de Pablo y de su garganta... Incesablemente os está aquel rostro yerto gritando a los que asistís a los reyes y cerráis sus lados en vuestra asistencia. Atajad las impías maquinaciones de los magos que los encantan, arruinad los tramoyeros que los divierten... Pasad en la caridad del alma más allá de la vida el amor a vuestros monarcas. [132]

From 1606 until two years before his death, Quevedo referred repeatedly to the problem of privanza. The seriousness of his preoccupation with this theme is understood when one sees how it penetrates not only his political writings, but also his works of satire, drama, poetry, philosophy and theology. To what may we attribute this insistent concern? It can only be explained by the critical situation in which the Spanish monarchy found itself throughout Quevedo's lifetime. He had returned to the Court as a young student in 1600 to discover that a privado had taken over the authority of the monarch. During his service to the Duke of Osuna in Italy, he became even more conscious of the corruptibility of a privado since he had the opportunity to deal directly with Lerma as a representative of Osuna at the Court. In 1621, Quevedo had reason to hope that the new monarch and his favorite would not repeat the errors of their immediate predecessors. He soon found out that Felipe IV was as impotent a ruler as his father and that the privado was one again the source of authority. The only course left open to Quevedo was that of trying to encourage virtue and justice in the privado, Olivares in this case. The manner in which he approached this task and the nature of the relationship between him and the Conde-Duque deserve amplification.

QUEVEDO AND THE CONDE-DUQUE DE OLIVARES

Gaspar de Guzmán, Conde-Duque de Olivares, was the valido of Felipe IV from 1622 until 1643. A detailed psychological study of this famous, often considered infamous, minister has been pub-

---

[132] *Obras* I (1964), 1532.

lished by Gregorio Marañón.[133] In this work, the author seeks to vindicate Olivares who has been misunderstood by many historians and has been cast into the same mold with money-hungry and self-centered privados like the Duke of Lerma. According to Marañón, the Conde-Duque was a dedicated statesman plagued by his misinterpretation of Spain's needs in the seventeenth century and motivated by "el afán de mando por el mando mismo":[134]

> Uno de los grandes defectos del Valido de Felipe IV fue, pues, el ser mucho más mandarín que gobernante; cuando lo que hubiera podido salvar a España —si aceptamos el hacer hipótesis sobre el pasado intangible— hubiera sido un hombre lleno de genial prudencia y de milagrosa habilidad para adaptar a las circunstancias nuevas la nueva Monarquía; que ya no podía ser la de Carlos V, en la que soñaba Guzmán, sino otra más humilde, menos imperial, fuerte por su fuero moral más que por el material poderío. Pero al Conde-Duque, a favor de los flujos de su humor alternativo, se le iba toda la energía en las apariencias del mando y descuidaba la realidad práctica de los problemas.[135]

The Conde-Duque deserves to be remembered as more than just another privado of the seventeenth century. He alone, of all the privados who rose to power under the last Hapsburg rulers in Spain, had a definite program of government.[136] Evidence of this is found in a document which Olivares wrote and presented to Felipe IV in 1625, the first lines of which are as follows:

> Señor: En obedecimiento de lo que V. M. se dignó mandarme, pongo con todo respeto y voluntad A L.R.P. de V.M. esos borrones; asegurando a Vuestra Majestad que son producidos de mi lealtad y dispuestos según lo poco que alcanza la experiencia de mis años. Repito, Señor, que son borrones; pero que pueden instruir mucho el gran entendimiento de V. M. Reconózcalos bien V. M., léalos muchas veces, sin permitir que otro alguno los examine y tome conocimiento de ellos, para que no se publiquen, que

---

[133] See Marañón, *El Conde-Duque de Olivares: La pasión de mandar.*
[134] Ibid., p. 101.
[135] Ibid., p. 102.
[136] Ibid., p. 305.

entonces más servirán de daño que de provecho; pero será al contrario, si V. M. los guarda para sí y usa de ellos en los tiempos, casos y con la prudencia con que adornó el Cielo a V. M. Entonces se verá claro su fruto y V. M. logrará los aplausos y gloria que le desea, Señor, su más leal vasallo y rendido criado.[137]

In this address, the Conde-Duque described what he considered the most urgent problem with which the King had to cope: the unification of the monarchy. In view of the vast territories under Felipe's rule, Olivares thought that the only solution to this problem was to eliminate disparity by establishing the laws and style of political procedure of Castille as the model to which the other realms should conform:

> Tenga V. M. por el negocio más importante de su Monarquía, el hacerse Rey de España; quiero decir, Señor, que no se contente V. M. con ser Rey de Portugal, de Aragón, de Valencia, Conde de Barcelona, sino que trabaje y piense con consejo mudado y secreto, por reducir estos reinos de que se compone España, al estilo y leyes de Castilla sin ninguna diferencia, que si V. M. lo alcanza, será el príncipe más poderoso del mundo.[138]

Olivares knew that this could not be accomplished overnight, but he believed that gradually it could become a reality.[139] The justification for such action was not only the necessary unity of the monarchy, but also the defense and propagation of Catholicism:

> ... que V. M. procure poner la mira en reducir sus reinos del estado más seguro, deseando este poder para el mayor bien y dilatación de la Religión Cristiana, conociendo que la división presente de leyes y fueros, enflaquece su poder y le estorba conseguir fin tan justo y glorioso, y tan al servicio de nuestro Señor.[140]

Part of the Conde-Duque's program of government was concerned with the economic problems of state. In 1621, he sent a

---

[137] Ibid., Apéndice XVIII, pp. 440-441.
[138] Ibid., p. 445.
[139] Idem.
[140] Idem.

document to the King advising him to curb government expenditures:

> Casi todos los Reyes y Príncipes de Europa son émulos de la grandeza de V. M. Es el principal apoyo y defensa de la Religión Católica; y por esto ha roto la guerra con los holandeses y con los demás enemigos de la Iglesia que los asisten; y la principal obligación de V. M. es defenderse y ofenderlos. El fundamento para todo, es la hacienda; la del patrimonio de V. M. está vendida o empeñada. Vive hoy V. M. de lo que contribuyen sus vasallos, desangrándose para esto con verdadero amor y fidelidad. [141]

In an effort to improve administration within the Spanish provinces, Olivares directed the formation of Juntas, or departments, to study specific problems and facilitate their solution. He also instructed that attention be given to the increase of local industry and commerce, and to obstruct social immorality and lavish spending, he issued various decrees to promote reforms. Certainly, all of these intentions were noble and well-founded. However, as Marañón points out, their beneficial effect was minuscule. [142] The plethora of Juntas only increased the bureaucratic entanglement of the affairs of state. The fomentation of commerce and industry was abandoned because of more urgent problems of war, and the attempt at social reform had little effect upon moral corruption. The failure of these programs can be attributed to the admirable but unattainable goal of the Conde-Duque's political philosophy:

> ...la política interior fue, en sus manos, un puro desastre... Desastrosa tenía que ser por el error inicial de la concepción centrífuga de nuestro poder; por querer hacer de España el centro de una política imperialista, concepto siempre discutible y en su tiempo ilusorio; en lugar de la nación peninsular, agrícola, comercial, industrial en lo posible y, sobre todo, civilizadora, como depositaria de una gran cultura y como madre y rectora de una lengua universal. [143]

---

[141] Marañón, Apéndice, XVII, p. 439.
[142] Ibid., pp. 319-326.
[143] Ibid., p. 319.

The initial contact between Olivares and Quevedo was made by Quevedo himself in 1621 when he dedicated his *Política de Dios* to the Conde-Duque and sent it to him from his exile in La Torre de Juan Abad. Undoubtedly, Quevedo sought Olivares' influence in procuring a release from his confinement, and yet his tributes to the privado did not cease when he achieved freedom in 1623. From that date until Olivares' fall from power in 1643, Quevedo wrote numerous pages in support and praise of the Conde-Duque. Some of these I have already mentioned; others are included in several letters to the privado and one to the Condesa de Olivares, a poem entitled "Epístola satírica y censoria contra las costumbres presentes de los castellanos" (1624), *El chitón de las tarabillas* (1630) and *La rebelión de Barcelona* (1640). During the same period, however, we have seen that Quevedo frequently elaborated upon the problems of privanza and that he sustained his opinions from the first part of the *Política* that a privado should always remain in the shadow of the king who holds supreme authority over the government. The optimism Quevedo expressed upon the advent of Felipe IV's reign is understood since the new King punished his father's former privados and appeared to be exerting the strong leadership which the author desired. What is not so easy to understand is Quevedo's enthusiasm and praise for the Conde-Duque long after the time when his power over Felipe IV was obvious in the Court. Was Quevedo not supporting exactly the type of privado he had condemned in his *Política* and which he was continuing to decry in other works?

Our opinion of Quevedo's integrity and sincerity is lowered if we admit this dualism in his writing. A partial explanation may be found in his understandable need for the financial protection which the Conde-Duque's favor afforded to him and to other artists.[144] In my opinion, however, this is not sufficient justification. His support of Olivares is better comprehended if the fact is accepted that Quevedo, then reaching his years of fullest maturity, realized the inevitability of Olivares' power and decided to compromise his principles in accordance with this realization. Felipe IV was, in many ways, every bit as ineffective a monarch as his father

---

[144] Ibid., pp. 144-146. This custom of seeking patrons from among the nobility was the normal practice of artists in the Golden Age.

had been, and a mature appraisal of his character would indicate the futility of protest against an inevitable state of affairs. Quevedo must have seen that a privado was necessary, for as Marañón points out, Felipe IV lacked the essential qualities for carrying out his office alone:

> Esta sucinta pintura del alma del Rey, flotando, inerte; como un trozo de madera en las olas, nos explica su conducta en la vida pública y exculpa a su Valido, el Conde-Duque, de la acusación más fuerte que sus contemporáneos le hicieron y transmitieron a los comentadores futuros: el de captar la voluntad del monarca. No la captó, porque no existía. Porque no existía, la sustituyó. Fue su privanza y dictadura, como todas las que ha conocido la Historia, un fenómeno de la biología pura. En la naturaleza todo tiende a remediarse, sustituyéndose los órganos y las actividades que flaquean, lo mismo en un ser vivo que en una organización social, por otros más fuertes. [145]

It is my opinion that Quevedo decided to support and defend Olivares because he understood this situation. But beyond this, it is possible that he was sincerely drawn to the Conde-Duque's defense because he saw in the privado's political philosophy many ideals similar to his own. In three basic areas, the unity of the monarchy, the defense of Catholicism and the criticism of social corruption, they were both seeking the same goals. Olivares was inspired by the same spirit of political traditionalism as Quevedo. Both of them wanted to strengthen the bonds of political and religious unity which had motivated the Spanish ideal of a Christian Empire. Neither one of them would renounce the conviction that this goal be pursued even at the cost of war. In addition to this, both men were austere in their moral habits, devoted to the Jesuit order and distrustful of the Spanish nobility in political matters. [146] I would even venture the opinion that Quevedo saw in Olivares the successful achievement of the power he himself would have liked to wield in the government, but which he knew he could never attain.

---

[145] Ibid., p. 237.
[146] Ibid., p. 91. Quevedo wrote in the *Política,* "La nobleza junta es peligrosísima, porque ni sabe mandar, ni obedecer." (Pt. II, Chapt. XXII), *Obras* I (1964), 681.

One other aspect of their relationship remains to be discussed. Late one evening in December of 1639, Quevedo was in the house of the Duke of Medinaceli, a friend and patron, when, without warning, two officials of the Court walked in, summarily arrested Quevedo and carried him off to the convent of San Marcos de León where he was imprisoned. There are no official documents or reports by his contemporaries which give any credible explanation for this imprisonment, and Quevedo repeatedly denied any knowledge of his offense: "¿Pregúntasme por qué estoy preso? Respondo que por lo que no sé."[147] Several critics have accepted the explanation that Quevedo was reprehended because of a poem which he wrote criticizing the government of Felipe IV.[148] Marañón, however, rejects this theory on the grounds that such an act was far too insignificant to merit the rigorous penalty which Quevedo suffered, and also because Quevedo, throughout his four years in prison, never made any reference to such a poem.[149] Whatever his crime might have been, Quevedo did not appear to hold any grudge against the Conde-Duque. He wrote two letters to the privado in 1641 and in 1642, and in both of them he addressed Olivares with words of praise and respect:

> Todo lo he perdido. La hacienda, que siempre fué poca, hoy es ninguna entre la grande costa de mi prisión y de los que se han levantado con ella. Mis amigos, mi adversidad los atemorizó. No me ha quedado sino la confianza en vuecelencia... La autoridad de vuecelencia ha de interceder con su majestad y su propia grandeza consigo.[150]

From these lines, it can be seen that Quevedo felt that it was the King not the privado whom he had angered. This is born out by the fact that when the Conde-Duque was dismissed in January of 1643, all of his enemies were pardoned and liberated.[151] Quevedo,

---

[147] "Epístolas a imitación de las de Séneca" (1640-1641), *Obras* II (1964), 967.

[148] Se A. Fernández Guerra, "Vida de Don Francisco de Quevedo y Villegas" in *Obras de Quevedo*, Tomo I. Madrid: Biblioteca de Autores Españoles, 1876, pp. LXXI-LXXII.

[149] See Marañón, pp. 132-133.

[150] "Memorial al Conde-Duque Don Gaspar de Guzmán" (1641), *Obras* II (1964), 973-974.

[151] Marañón, p. 136.

however, remained in León until June of that year when, after several dignitaries pleaded with the King on his behalf, he was finally set free.

The mystery surrounding Quevedo's imprisonment has given rise to several legends which have been perpetuated by historians, one of these being the belief that it was the Conde-Duque who imprisoned Quevedo as an act of personal vengeance. Because of this legend, it has been thought that they became bitter enemies, and, consequently, numerous works in opposition to Olivares have been falsely attributed to Quevedo.[152] One of these, *Vida caída y muerte del Conde-Duque de Olivares* (1643), a virulent attack on the privado, was analyzed by a modern German critic, Ernst Werner, and found to be the work of an Italian named Guidi.[153] As Werner comments: "Das Quevedo als Verfasser der *Caída* in Betracht gezogen wurde, lag bei der ziemlich grossen Anzahl seiner Streitschriften gegen Olivares eigentlich nahe."[154] It has long been assumed that Quevedo despised Olivares and wrote numerous diatribes against him. The evidence to support this belief is slight, and it is time to expose the frailty of this contention.

When the Conde-Duque fell from power in 1643, Quevedo began writing a message to the King which, in all its known copies, remained unfinished. In this *Panegírico,* he expressed his approval of the King's decision to reclaim the role of single and supreme ruler. Not once, however, does Quevedo make a direct reference by name to the Conde-Duque, as this quote exemplifies:

> ... por muerte de vuestro glorioso y piadoso padre, solevastéis la capacidad de un vasallo a compañero de las resoluciones del gobierno; y cumplidos éstos, habéis empezado a hablar y obrar por vos. Veinte y un años ha estado detenida la lumbre de vuestro espíritu esclarecido, para

---

[152] See "Indice de Obras Apócrifas," *Obras* II (1964), 1362-1370. The only direct personal insults to Olivares found in Quevedo's works are in four letters written to personal friends a few months before Quevedo's death in 1645. See "Epistolario," *Obras* II (1964), 1009-1012. The bitterness shown in these remarks may have been sincere or they may simply have been the innocent words of a disillusioned, dying man.

[153] See E. Werner, "Caída del Conde-Duque de Olivares," (Nach vershiedenen Handschriften in Müenchen, Dresden und Stuttgart.) *Revue Hispanique,* Tome LXVI, 1927, p. 3.

[154] Ibid., p. 5.

que se conozca los años que podéis restaurar en una hora.[155]

Rather than insult the former privado, Quevedo mixes his enthusiasm for this change with a discreetly veiled tone of criticism of the Monarch's own failure to assert himself at the beginning of his reign. In these pages, Quevedo tries to express the same optimism he felt in 1621 when there was a similar purge of privados and the prospect of a fresh start. However, he is too old and too experienced not to realize that the possibility of improvement is slight, and thus his enthusiasm in the *Panegírico* appears forced and reveals the growing disillusionment of his last years.

It is interesting to observe that the final paragraph of the *Panegírico* regarding Olivares' dismissal contains a statement which seems to be conciliatory toward the Conde-Duque. Quevedo writes to Felipe IV:

> El apartar semejantes personas no presupone culpa suya, siempre suele ser conveniencia forzosa, y no sólo puede haber inocencia en el que apartan, sino en el que justician. Conviene que uno muera por el pueblo, porque toda la gente no perezca.[156]

Basically, Quevedo did not approve of a privado possessing greater influence than a monarch, and this explains his impersonal criticisms of privanza during this period. However, Quevedo was mature and practical enough to understand that, given Felipe IV's irresponsibility, Olivares was an authoritative leader with a desirable program for Spain, one which coincided with many of his own aspirations. In essence, the Conde-Duque was the lesser of the evils at that time and certainly a better privado than his predecessors. Quevedo's words in the above quote seem to be admitting the necessity of Olivares' privanza and mitigating his blame for Spain's tragic situation.

In 1637, Quevedo wrote a short commentary to a Spanish translation of Thomas More's *Utopia* in which he made the following assertion:

---

[155] *Panegírico a la majestad de Felipe IV* (1643), *Obras* I (1964), 948.
[156] *Obras* I (1964), 950.

Yo me persuado que fabricó aquella política contra la tiranía de Inglaterra, y por eso hizo isla su idea, y juntamente reprehendió los desórdenes de los más príncipes de su edad. Fuérame fácil verificar esta opinión; empero no es difícil que quien leyere este libro la verifique con esta advertencia mía: quien dice que se ha de hacer lo que nadie hace, a todos los reprende; esto hizo por satisfacer su celo nuestro autor. [157]

What Quevedo has written about More could also be said about his own *Política*. The same spirit of dissatisfaction and criticism which he observed in More is found in his own writing. Quevedo knew, perhaps better than most writers of his time, the critical significance of Spain's political situation, and he could not stand idly by while his nation suffered. To satisfy his patriotic zeal and to express his concern, he wrote the *Política de Dios* and numerous other works which have been discussed in this chapter. The defense of political traditions was more important to Quevedo than any other aspect of his traditionalism because he realized that the success or failure of the Spanish monarchy would determine the future of the nation as a whole.

---

[157] *Noticia, juicio y recomendación de la "Utopía" de Tomás Moro, Obras* I (1964), 476. That Quevedo chose to write this commentary is further evidence of his political traditionalism. In the history of Renaissance ideas, More, the conservative "moralist", has often been contrasted with Machiavelli, the anti-traditional "realist". See E. Harris Harbison, "Machiavelli's *Prince* and More's *Utopia*," in *Facets of the Renaissance*, ed. William H. Werkmeister, New York: Harper Torchbooks, 1963, pp. 41-71.

CHAPTER THREE

RELIGIOUS TRADITIONALISM

SPANISH CATHOLICISM

To speak of a national religious tradition in Spain is, of necessity, to speak of Christianity, and more particularly, of Catholicism. The roots of this tradition extend back into the first century A. D. when the evangelist, St. Paul, is said to have come to Spain to spread the new religion of Christ.[1] Christianity offered a unique spiritual orientation to the new Hispano-Roman converts, one which would shape the future destiny of the Spanish nation:

> ... la religión cristiana suponía una nueva universalidad, muy superior a la del mundo romano, y un nuevo modo de ser de los hombres, centrado ahora en la intimidad del individuo, capaz por sí mismo de realizar por la fe y la conducta el fin sobrenatural al que le destinaba el Dios que le había creado... Estos hombres nuevos, estos cristianos, harán de España un país que seguirá siendo romano durante mucho tiempo por su cultura, su lengua y sus instituciones, pero que además será cristiano por ese nuevo modo de ser espiritual de sus habitantes, que transformará sustancialmente las costumbres y las concepciones éticas y sociales.[2]

The close alliance between Church and State in Spain was officially established with the conversion of Recaredo in 587 at the

---

[1] See Luis García de Valdeavellano, *Historia de España de los orígenes a la baja Edad Media*. Madrid: Revista de Occidente, S. A., 1952, p. 231.
[2] Ibid., pp. 228-229.

Third Council of Toledo and solidified during the Moorish occupation when the Hispanic realms fought to reconquer their land as well as to preserve their faith. By the end of the fifteenth century, the Spanish religious tradition was more firmly entrenched than that of any other European power, and Spain's national goals mirrored the aims of the Christian religion:

> Fué España la única que, prolongando su inveterada decisión medieval, identificó sus propios fines nacionales con los fines universalistas de la Cristiandad, tomando éstos como propios a partir de Fernando el Católico, quien, como Gracián dice, "supo juntar la tierra con el cielo." [3]

When in the sixteenth century Martin Luther and other reformers proclaimed their opposition to the dogma of the Church of Rome and the Papacy, Spain initiated the Counter-Reformation, reaffirming her adherence to the traditional creeds of the Church of Rome. Throughout the Golden Age, Spain maintained the spirit of the Holy Roman Empire and shouldered the burden of defending Catholicism, seeking to establish its supremacy in Europe and in the New World.

Despite the penalties inflicted upon disbelievers by the Inquisition, Spain was not free of non-Catholic and "heretical" sects. To varying degrees, such groups as Jews, Moslems, Lutherans, and the fanatical "iluministas" coexisted with the overwhelming majority of orthodox Catholics. The common Spaniard of this time accepted Catholicism as a matter of fact and faith, never doubting his beliefs: "Para el español de los siglos XVI y XVII, a no ser que fuera teólogo o erudito, el dogma cristiano no constituía un objeto especial del entendimiento sino más bien del corazón." [4]

---

[3] Ramón Menéndez Pidal, *Los españoles en la historia* in *España y su historia*, Vol. I. Madrid: Ediciones Minotauro, 1957, p. 36.

[4] Ludwig Pfandl, *Introducción al estudio del Siglo de Oro*. Barcelona: Casa Editorial Araluce, 1929, p. 159.

QUEVEDO'S RELIGIOSITY

Quevedo, like most of his fellow countrymen, was a devout Catholic. His first biographer, Tarsia, describes the nature of Quevedo's piety on several occasions:

> Frecuentaba las iglesias con mucha devoción, asistiendo todos los días a los Santos Sacrificios con tal compostura y silencio, que jamás le vieron divertir la atención con otro cualquiera, aunque fuese de los mayores por sangre o dignidad; pues en lo que obraba estaba todo, ya fuese aplicando al espíritu, ya a los estudios, procurando siempre que lo exterior sirviese al interior y más perfecto.[5]
>
> Cuán inclinado fué a la devoción y obras de religión cristiana, indicion con las limosnas que hacía, los buenos consejos que daba, los libros espirituales que sacó y la frecuencia de los santos sacramentos de la penitencia y eucaristía. Guardaba un cuaderno en que tenía asentadas todas las confesiones que había hecho, así generales como particulares, desde que tuvo uso de razón...[6]

The sincerity and constancy of his faith in Catholicism was founded upon more than emotional and environmental influences. In contrast to the ordinary Spaniard of his day, Quevedo was an educated theologian who possessed an intimate knowledge of the history and traditions of the Church and the works of the Church Fathers.[7] Thus, for Quevedo, religion was not only a matter of the heart, but also of the mind.

In spite of his religiosity, Quevedo has been called a skeptic by more than one critic.[8] Although his skepticism was philosophical rather than religious in orientation, it still raises the question of

---

[5] Don Pablo Antonio de Tarsia, *Vida de Don Francisco de Quevedo y Villegas* (1658-1662) in *Obras* II (1952), 878.

[6] Ibid., p. 893.

[7] He obtained a degree in theology at the age of twenty-five after studying at the Universities of Alcalá de Henares and Valladolid. See L. Astrana Marín, ed. *Obras* II (1952), 857 (Note I).

[8] See Américo Castro, "Escepticismo y contradicción en Quevedo" in *Semblanzas y estudios españoles*. Princeton: 1956, pp. 391-396. Also Constantino Láscaris Comneno, "Senequismo y agustinismo en Quevedo," *Revista de Filosofía* (Madrid), núm. 34, julio-sept. de 1950, p. 467.

whether Quevedo was ever considered unorthodox in the eyes of the Church, for, as Américo Castro explains,

> El filósofo escéptico, que niega la posibilidad de la certeza no ha sido nunca bien visto por la ortodoxia. La Iglesia aspira a que la creencia religiosa no esté en pugna con la razón; se esfuerza en todo caso, en utilizar los medios racionales para llegar a las verdades divinas. Si se niega valor al conocimiento humano de modo absoluto, las verdades de la fe corren peligro de verse también arrastradas en esa duda torrencial. [9]

According to Castro, Quevedo's skepticism is based upon an unnatural attitude toward reality: "El ascético siente despego hacia la vida y la naturaleza, mas no la odia ni duda de su realidad. Quevedo hace ambas cosas, ninguna de las cuales está muy en armonía con una actitud religiosa clara y transparente." [10] Further on, he says:

> El escepticismo de Quevedo no arranca de la convicción de que sólo tengan valor las verdades reveladas y de que el hombre no pueda llegar más que a éstas, sino de un supuesto metafísico según el cual la actividad racional no puede llegar a ninguna meta. A lo sumo (como Quevedo es un mero aficionado a la filosofía, su pensamiento no es riguroso ni metódico), a lo sumo se salvan las verdades matemáticas de esa quiebra general de la ciencia humana, lo que demuestra otra vez que la actitud escéptica no se debe a fe exclusiva en las verdades reveladas y desprecio de todo lo demás, por el hecho de ser realidad subcélica. Más metódica y consecuente es su actitud respecto de la sensibilidad y la emoción; el mundo carece para él de todo valor moral y estimable. Nada es; y si es, no vale. Y el humano hacer, además, no lleva a ninguna parte. [11]

Thus far I have presented only Castro's analysis of Quevedo's skepticism and his implication that Quevedo's religious attitude was not entirely orthodox. Let us now examine what Quevedo has writ-

---

[9] Castro, "Escepticismo y contradicción...", p. 392.
[10] Ibid., p. 391.
[11] Ibid., pp. 392-393.

ten to elicit this commentary. In 1627, in the prologue to *El mundo por de dentro,* he wrote the following:

> Es cosa averiguada, así lo siente Metrodoro Chío y otros muchos, que no se sabe nada y que todos son ignorantes. Y aun esto no se sabe de cierto: que, a saberse, ya se supiera algo; sospéchase. Dícelo así el doctísimo Francisco Sánchez, médico y filósofo, en su libro cuyo título es *Nihil Scitur.* No se sabe nada. En el mundo hay algunos que no saben nada y estudian para saber, y estos tienen buenos deseos y vano ejercicio: porque, al cabo, sólo les sirve el estudio de conocer cómo toda la verdad la quedan ignorando. Otros hay que no saben nada y no estudian, porque piensan que lo saben todo. Son déstos muchos irremediables. A éstos se les ha de envidiar el ocio y la satisfacción y llorarles el seso. Otros hay que no saben nada, y dicen que no saben nada porque piensan que saben algo de verdad, pues lo que es, no saben nada, y a éstos se les había de castigar la hipocresía con creerles la confesión. Otros hay, en éstos, que son los peores, entro yo, que no saben nada, ni quieren saber nada, ni creen que se sepa nada y dicen de todos que no saben nada. Y todos dicen dellos lo mismo y nadie miente.[12]

From this brief discourse on the folly of the human quest for knowledge, one receives the impression that Quevedo was less interested in the philosophical and religious repercussions of his statements than in the manipulation of words in an engaging and skillful manner. However, a few years later, in 1633, he returned to the same subject in *La cuna y la sepultura,* this time with gravity and in greater detail. In the fourth chapter of this work which discusses the nature of death and the vanity of human existence, Quevedo describes man's search for wisdom as one of the supreme human vanities:

> La mayor hipocresía y más dañosa y sin fundamento, es la de la sabiduría; porque la del dinero fúndase en que la hay, y que tiene alguno el que se trata como si tuviera mucho. La de la virtud hayla también y la del valor; pero la de la sabiduría, como no hay ninguna, no se funda sino sólo en presunción.

---

[12] *Obras* I (1964), 163-164.

> Parece que se han concertado los hombres, y por consolarse desta ignorancia se creen unos a otros lo que dicen que saben. Y dejando esto al voto de cada uno, si quieres averiguar por su boca de todos y por la tuya que nadie sabe nada, cree a esos mismos sabios lo que dijeren, y verás cómo nadie sabe nada; que en persuadiéndose ellos a que saben lo que piensan y otros dicen, afirman que los otros no saben nada, y creen que con ellos ha de morir la sabiduría. [13]

Like Francisco Sánchez whose *Quod nihil scitur* (1581) he had read and cited in *El mundo por de dentro,* Quevedo found a solution in religion for his philosophical skepticism. Man is not granted the capacity to know all the truths of the universe because that power is reserved only for God: "... la sabiduría verdadera está en la verdad, y la verdad es una sola, y esa verdad una es Dios solo, que por eso le llaman Dios verdadero; y fuera dél, todo es opinión y los más cuerdos sospechan." [14] In spite of man's inability to acquire true wisdom, there is a way which he can fulfill his existence and approach the truth:

> Preguntarásme que, supuesto esto, cuál es la cosa que un hombre ha de procurar aprender. No me parece que el trabajo y el estudio del hombre se logrará en nada fuera de la consideración y ejercicio de las virtudes, que es sólo lo que a un hombre pertenece: procurar persuadirte a amar la muerte, a despreciar la vida, a conocer tu flaqueza y la vanidad de las cosas que fuera de aquel solo Señor son; pues sólo el buen uso de todas, ordenado a aquel fin, está a tu cargo. [15]

---

[13] *La cuna y la sepultura, Obras* I (1964), 1207. Quevedo's words are reminiscent of the "Admonitions" of Thomas à Kempis' *The Imitation of Christ* when he says: "Our own judgment and feelings often deceive us, and we discern but little of the truth. What doth it profit to argue about hidden and dark things, concerning which we shall not be even reproved in the judgment because we knew them not? Oh grievous folly, to neglect the things which are profitable and necessary and to give our minds to things which are curious and hurtful! Having eyes, we see not." Book I, Chapter III, *The Imitation of Christ,* trans. Rev. William Benham. London: George Routledge & Sons, Ltd., 1905, p. 6.

[14] *La cuna y la sepultura, Obras* I (1964), 1208.

[15] *La cuna y la sepultura, Obras* I (1964), 1208.

Acaba de persuadirte a que dentro de ti mismo tienes que hacer tanto, que aun, por larga que sea tu vida, te faltará tiempo, y que no puedes saber nada bueno para ti, si no fuere lo que aprendieres del desengaño y de la verdad; y que entonces empezarás a ser sabio, cuando no temieres las miserias, ni codiciares las honras, ni te admirares de nada, y tu mismo estudiares en ti; que leyéndote está tu naturaleza introducciones de la verdad. Cada día y cada hora que pasa es un argumento que precede para tu desengaño a la conclusión de la muerte. *Y está cierto, así lo dice el predicador hijo de David, "que sabiduría, ciencia y alegría, solamente la da Dios al bueno, y en su presencia;" y que sin él, y ausente y desterrado, la ciencia y sabiduría que tuvieres será la que te fingieres a ti mismo*; y el contento, el que el engaño del mundo te persuadiere a tenerle por tal. [16] (Emphasis added)

These words of advice from Quevedo recall those of another great humanist who is remembered for his philosophical skepticism, Michel de Montaigne:

C'est assez vescu pour autruy, vivons pour nous au moins ce bout de vie. Ramenons à nous et à nostre aise nos pensées et nos intentions. Ce n'est pas une legiere partie que de faire seurement sa retraicte; elle nous empesche assez sans y mesler d'autres entreprinses. Puis que Dieu nous donne loisir de disposer de nostre deslogement, preparons nous y; plions bagage; prenons de bonne heure congé de la compaignie; despetrons nous de ces violentes prinses que nous engagent ailleurs et esloignent de nous. Il faut desnouer des obligations si fortes, et meshuy aymer cecy et cela, mais n'espouser rien que soy. C'est à dire: le reste soit à nous, mais non pas joint et cole en façon qu'on ne le puisse desprendre sans nous escorcher et arracher ensemble quelque piece du nostre. La plus grand chose de monde, c'est de sçavoir estre à soy. [17]

The solution for the doubt which Quevedo expresses in the powers of human reasoning finds a precedent in both Francisco Sánchez and Montaigne:

---

[16] *La cuna y la sepultura, Obras* I (1964), 1209-1210.
[17] Michel de Montaigne, Livre Premier, Chapître XXXIX, "De la solitude" in *Trois essais de Montaigne*, ed. G. Gougenheim and P. Schuhl. Paris: Librairie Philosophique de J. Vrin, 1951, pp. 14-16.

> El resultado de esta duda no será el encaminarse hacia un idealismo tipo cartesiano, sino el emplear la introspección como método en la especulación filosófica. Este método tiene para Quevedo dos precedentes: Montaigne y Francisco Sánchez. Francisco Sánchez dejó un solo camino para la ciencia, el de la *visio interna,* el camino de la contemplación de la inferioridad del hombre, pues sostenía que sólo cada cosa concreta y singular puede ser objeto de ciencia, para terminar afirmando que la sola ciencia posible es la del hombre real e individual. [18]

The tendency toward philosophical skepticism within Spain itself was evident during the Golden Age. However, as Otis Green points out, the skeptic was also a fideist:

> If one should ask why Spaniards were users rather than creators of philosophy, he would find the answer, perhaps, in the typically Spanish lack of confidence in the merely human, which manifests itself... in the general preference for religious solutions. This distrust of the Goddess Reason is expressed countless times, in countless works, during Spain's age of greatest intellectual activity. Though Etienne Gilson has observed that the combination of skepticism and fideism is "classical and characteristic of all ages," its presence appears — with unusual strength and persistence — in writings of Spaniards many of whom are not genuine philosophers but rather Christian humanists, moralists, or ascetics. [19]

If we now refer back to the allegations made by Américo Castro in regard to Quevedo's skepticism and its supposedly unorthodox overtones, we may conclude that Castro has exaggerated the extent of Quevedo's doubts. [20] Quevedo, like other Spaniards before him, was skeptical of the powers of human reasoning. In effect, the skepticism which he expresses is a traditional Spanish attitude nurtured by the Christian conviction that God is the Truth and the source of all knowledge. Quevedo's skepticism did not lead him to

---

[18] C. Láscaris Comneno, "Senequismo y agustinismo en Quevedo," pp. 468-469.

[19] Green, *Spain and the Western Tradition,* Vol. III. Madison: University of Wisconsin Press, 1965, pp. 301-302.

[20] See Chapter V for a further discusion of Castro's belief that Quevedo was a "negativist".

question the dogma of the Church or to doubt his own faith in Catholicism. On the contrary, it convinced him of the necessity of establishing a more intimate approach to religion:

> No admitas otra declaración a las palabras de Cristo que la de la Iglesia romana, que es sola y verdadera iglesia. Y haciendo esto, verás que las cosas con que fueres bueno y agradable a Dios, y hijo de su ley, te darán salud y vida en el cuerpo y paz y gozo en el alma. Y sobre todo, atesora en tu pecho el temor de Dios, que ése te dará valentía en las demás cosas, asegurará los sucesos de tu amor y el premio dél, pues en el temor de Dios empieza la sabiduría, crece el amor y se deshace el miedo de las demás cosas que nos hacen terribles las opiniones recibidas. [21]

Following the tradition of religious militancy initiated by his distant ancestors during the reconquest of northern Spain, Quevedo was not content to assume the role of a passive Christian. All of his ethico-religious works reveal the urgency of his desire to defend the Catholic faith and the spirit behind this faith which had sustained and preserved the Spanish nation. One of these works, *Providencia de Dios* (1641), was inspired by his hope to illuminate the shadowed minds of atheists by endeavoring to prove certain fundamental Christian concepts such as the immortality of the soul and the existence of God. His awareness of the limitations of the powers of human reason does not deter him, for he is convinced that this is merely an indication of men's indulgence in sin and vice:

> En ninguna cosa se echa de ver con tanta infamia del entendimiento humano la torpeza bestial, y la noche que derrama e introduce en el hombre el pecado y el vicio, como en haber necesitado de que se escriba y defienda que hay Dios, que su providencia gobierna el mundo, y que las almas son inmortales. [22]

As a final proof of Quevedo's orthodox religious attitude, it may be pointed out that none of his works were ever censored by the Inquisition. The reason for this has been aptly stated by Fernández-Guerra:

---

[21] *La cuna y la sepultura, Obras* I (1964), 1214.
[22] *Providencia de Dios, Obras* I (1964), 1388.

Pero, ¿cómo la Inquisición, tan suspicaz, tan nimia, severa y escrupulosa, no vejó, no molestó, no persiguió jamás a Quevedo? ¿Cómo no hizo alto en desenfados muy censurables de algunos de sus escritos? ¿Cómo se limitó a indirectas y corteses amonestaciones? ¿Cómo fué siempre considerada, afectuosa y atenta con el agrio, desvergonzado e implacable censor de las corrompidas costumbres en todas las clases y estados de los hombres? Esta es la grande prueba del mérito del autor de los *Sueños* y de *la Política de Dios y gobierno de Cristo*; el más solemne testimonio de la importancia del escritor popular, de que estaba el reino entero en favor suyo, y de que le miraba España como el predilecto, si no el mejor de sus hijos. El tribunal de la Fe respetó la fe pura, ardiente, del gran teólogo y escriturario, la ciencia del varón ilustre enriquecido con los tesoros de los Santos Padres, el cristiano valor y libertad evangélica de quien era sostén de la religión, amparo de la moral y defensor de la causa de todo un pueblo.[23]

His Idea of Heresy and his Attitude toward the Jews

Quevedo's highly orthodox and traditional religious convictions caused him to be an implacable critic of heretics.

According to Raúl del Piero, there were two notions of heresy in Spain during the time Quevedo wrote.[24] One, more generalized and more traditional, defined heresy as any belief in dissonance with the dogma of the Church, either before or after Christ's time. The other, as was held by Melchor Cano following Thomist precepts, was more restricted and more modern, as it sustained that a heretic could only be someone who had once been baptized; in other words, the term "heretic" could not be applied to pre-Christian idolaters or to those belonging to a non-Christian faith.

It will be evident that Quevedo did not subscribe to the latter, more modern notion of heresy if we turn to the final pages of the *Sueño del infierno* (or *Zahurdas de Plutón*) written in 1608. Dream-

---

[23] A. Fernández-Guerra, "Vida de Don Francisco de Quevedo y Villegas" in *Obras de Quevedo,* Tomo I. Madrid: Biblioteca de Autores Españoles, 1876, LXX.

[24] Raúl del Piero, "Algunas fuentes de Quevedo," *Nueva Revista de Filología Hispánica,* Vol. 12, núm. 1, enero-marzo de 1958, pp. 36-37.

ing he is visiting hell, the author describes all the heretics he finds agonizing there. Beginning with pre-Christian pagans, Quevedo proceeds to enumerate a long list of heretics, concluding with such names as Mohammed, Calvin, Luther, Melanchthon and other figures of the reform movement.[25] In another *Sueño* recently discovered by James O. Crosby, Quevedo writes with obvious relish:

> Tras la Ambición y Soberbia, entró la maldita canalla de Lutero, Mahoma y sus secuaces, con toda la maldita canalla de herejes y apóstatas que, como indignos de la misericordia de Dios, provocaban contra ellos los cielos y la tierra; blasfemos, perjuros, de las navajas de sus lenguas despedazados; los bárbaros idólatras, semejantes a sus dioses en las culpas y castigos.[26]

In Quevedo's eyes, all these disbelievers were equally guilty, for he did not recognize the distinctions of the more restricted notion of heresy, but rather defended the traditional view that had been popularized over several centuries in Spain.

During the first centuries of the Arabic invasion of Spain, isolated communities of Jews flourished under the atmosphere of Islamic tolerance. When this tolerance ceased in the eleventh century, the Jews sought protection among the Christians, and Spanish culture was enriched by their presence. Nevertheless, a current of anti-Semitism existed in the Christian attitude of the Middle Ages, as exemplified by the "Raquel e Vidas" episode in the *Poema de Mío Cid*. This feeling reached a peak in Spain in 1492 when the Jews who refused to convert to Christianity were expelled from the country for reasons of political and religious unity.

In keeping with this tradition of anti-Semitism in Spanish literature, Quevedo wrote a satire of the Jews in a famous passage from *La fortuna con seso y la hora de todos* (1635) called "La isla de Monopantos."[27] It is commonly accepted that this satirical sketch

---

[25] See *Obras* I (1964), 160-162.
[26] Cited by Crosby, "Un sueño desconocido," *Nueva Revista de Filología Hispánica*, Vol. 14, núm. 3-4, julio-dic. de 1960, p. 304.
[27] See *Obras de Quevedo*, ed. A. Fernández-Guerra. Tomo I, pp. 414-419. This edition contains the most complete editorial notes and interpretation of the Monopantos episode.

was meant to burlesque the Conde-Duque de Olivares, since he had supported a plan to bring some Jews back to Spain.[28] The Monopantos episode satirizes the Jews as being materialistic money-seekers, betrayers of the Christian faith, and followers of Machiavelli in their quest for power in Europe. In the words of one of the rabbis of Monopantos:

> De la ley de Moisen sólo guardamos el nombre, sobrescribiendo con él y con ella las excepciones que los talmudistas han soñado, para desmentir las Escrituras, deslumbrar las profecías, y falsificar los preceptos, y habilitar las conciencias á la fábrica de la materia de estado; doctrinando para la vida civil nuestro ateismo en una política sediciosa, prohijándonos de hijos de Israel á hijos del siglo. Cuando tuvimos ley no la guardábamos; hoy, que la guardamos, no es ley sino en la breve pronunciación de las tres letras.[29]

From the emphasis Quevedo places upon their social and political as well as their religious traits, it is understandable how his dislike of Machiavellian power-politics heightened his intolerance of the Jewish religion.

Another example of Quevedo's disdain for the Jews is a short work written in 1619 under the pseudonym, "El Maestro Toribio de Armuelles," entitled *La primera y más disimulada persecución de los judíos contra Cristo Jesús y contra la iglesia en favor de la sinagoga*.[30] Why Quevedo used a pseudonym is not known; it may have been that he wanted to disguise his anti-Semitism for some political or social reason. In any event, his condemnation of the Jews' denial of Christ is stated with vehemence:

---

[28] To be granted entry to Spain, the Jews would be required to pay a certain sum of money, thus aiding the faltering economy of the nation.

The Conde-Duque's biographer, Marañón, disagrees with the opinion of critics like Fernández-Guerra who believe that Quevedo's attack on Olivares in this episode was a "sátira sangrienta." He also rejects the idea that this satire may have been the cause of Quevedo's final imprisonment. See *El Conde-Duque de Olivares: La pasión de mandar*, 4th ed. Madrid: Espasa-Calpe, S. A., 1959, p. 132.

[29] *Obras de Quevedo*, ed. Fernández-Guerra, Tomo I, p. 417.

[30] See *Obras* I (1964), 1130-1135.

Frecuentemente se lamenta David de la perfidia, idolatría, ceguedad y dureza de los judíos. Y habiendo cargado yo la consideración sobre los sucesos que del pueblo hebreo escribe Moisés... hallo que son tan exquisitamente detestables, que en tanto que Dios los hablaba y gobernaba y defendía... le despreciaban, dejándole por simulacros y dioses ajenos, mentirosos y ridículos; y estando esperando la venida suya en el Mesías, cuando vino y le vieron, le crucificaron... De que se colige que los judíos no permanecen en la verdad, y que obstinados perseveran en duración, que compite con la eternidad en la mentira y en el error. [31]

Quevedo's indignation in his opposition to heretics and to the Jews is motivated by his conviction that the only true religion is Catholicism. There was, however, one non-Christian for whom he held the greatest respect and upon whom he did not look as a heretic.

QUEVEDO AND SENECA

Quevedo's overt admiration of the writings of the Stoic philosopher, Lucius Annaeus Seneca, has been discussed by many literary critics. In Seneca's works, Quevedo discovered the epitome of Christian morality, although this first-century native of Cordoba was not a professed or baptized Christian. Despite this, Quevedo wrote: "De Dios grandes cosas dijeron los filósofos, y más y mayores que todos, Séneca." [32] Time and again, he refers with affection to "mi Séneca." In my opinion, the rapprochement between these two great minds is a firm indication of Quevedo's traditionalism.

Evidences of Stoicism in the literature of Spain had multiplied progressively since the fourteenth century. In the later Middle Ages, writers such as Don Juan Manuel, Pero López de Ayala, Jorge Manrique and el Marqués de Santillana followed the current of Stoic morality; and in the Golden Age, many others joined their ranks, among them, Fray Luis de León, José Luis Vives, Antonio

---

[31] *Obras* I (1964), 1130-1131.
[32] *Homilía a la Santísima Trinidad, Obras* I (1964), 1165.

de Guevara and Cervantes.[33] Of all those authors of neo-Stoic tendencies, Quevedo has been called "el escritor más conscientemente estoico de cuantos brillaron en su edad";[34] he has earned the reputation of being a "second Seneca," for he was not only an advocate of Stoic morality, but also a frequent imitator of Seneca's style.[35]

The tradition of Senequism in Spain has been pointed out by many native historians and critics. According to García de Valdeavellano,

> La moral de Séneca es una moral práctica al modo español y el pensamiento senequista se reviste para expresarse, con formas características del genio hispánico... no es de extrañar la huella que el "Senequismo" deja en el espíritu hispánico y en sus modalidades expresivas con una reiteración que no puede sorprendernos.[36]

In the words of Menéndez y Pelayo, "En Séneca están apuntados ya los principales caracteres del genio filosófico nacional."[37] And Ángel Ganivet writes in *Idearium español*:

> El espíritu español tosco, informe, al desnudo, no cubre su desnudez primitiva con artificiosa vestimenta; se cubre con la hoja de parra del senequismo; y este traje sumario queda adherido para siempre y se muestra en cuanto se ahonda un poco en la superficie o corteza ideal de nuestra nación...[38]

---

[33] See Chapter IV of Manuel de Montoliu, *El alma de España y sus reflejos en la literatura del Siglo de Oro*. Barcelona: Editorial Cervantes, 1942, pp. 355-553.

[34] Ibid., p. 486.

[35] See Pierre Delacroix, "Quevedo et Sénèque," *Bulletin Hispanique*, Vol. LVI, Num. 3, 1954, pp. 305-307. Also Menéndez y Pelayo has compiled a detailed list of "Imitaciones y reminiscencias de Séneca en Quevedo," in *Biblioteca de Traductores Españoles*, Vol. IV, in *Edición Nacional de las Obras Completas*. Madrid: Consejo Superior de Investigaciones Científicas, 1953, pp. 109-118.

[36] García de Valdeavellano, p. 208.

[37] Menéndez y Pelayo, *La Ciencia Española*, Vol. I, in *Edición Nacional de las Obras Completas*. Madrid: Consejo Superior de Investigaciones Científicas, 1953, p. 306.

[38] Ganivet, *Obras completas*, Vol. I. Madrid: Aguilar, 1943, p. 90.

Menéndez Pidal sees in the common Spaniard a quality of "senequismo espontáneo" which is evidenced by a lack of concern for material necessities:

> El español, duro para soportar privaciones, lleva dentro de sí el *sustine et abstine,* resiste firme y abstente fuerte, norma de la sabiduría que coloca al hombre por cima de toda adversidad; lleva en sí un particular estoicismo instintivo y elemental; es un senequista innato. Por eso el pensamiento filosófico español, en el curso de los siglos, se inspiró siempre en Séneca como en autor propio y predilecto. [39]

One contemporary critic, however, takes exception to the view of the majority of his colleagues regarding Senequism in Spain. Américo Castro, in *La realidad histórica de España,* expresses the opinion that "Séneca no era español, ni los españoles son senequistas." [40] He says that if the Spaniards were true Senequists, they would be more critical in their attention to the world around them, rather than being complacent in their religious beliefs:

> Bien o mal, Séneca usa un método crítico que los españoles, en lo que se refiere a la ciencia natural, no han usado sino modernamente y como aplicación de lo hecho antes por sus vecinos europeos, no por Séneca. Si los españoles hubieran sido senequistas, todo en ellos habría sido diferente de como ha sido y es; su interés se hubiera centrado en este mundo, no en el otro de la creencia. [41]

Moreover, says Castro, Seneca was a dualist in that he separated his thinking from the reality of the material world surrounding him, a dichotomy which is impossible for a Spaniard to accept: "Lo malo, lo feo y lo sucio aparecen en la obra de Séneca en la zona de las 'tinieblas exteriores', pues son lo que existe fuera de la personalidad del filósofo." [42] These two statements (made consecutively by Castro) are somewhat contradictory, and actually do not prove

---

[39] Menéndez Pidal, *Los españoles en la historia* in *España y su historia,* Vol. I, p. 15.

[40] A. Castro, *La realidad histórica de España.* México: Editorial Porrúa, 1954, pp. 642-646 (Apéndice I).

[41] Ibid., p. 642.

[42] Ibid., p. 643.

the point he wishes to make. First he says that Seneca, unlike the Spaniards, was more critical in his interest in the world around him; then he states that disagreeable material reality had no immediate bearing upon Seneca's thinking. Castro dwells upon generalities and ignores an explanation of the doctrines of Seneca's philosophy. At one point he does make the following statement: "El ser sobrio, valeroso y paciente sufridor de cualquier mal es independiente de la filosofía estoica en la cual adquirían sentido aquellos comportamientos morales. ..."[43] But are not these moral virtues the foundation for the achievement of the goal of Senequism, i.e., the serene and unanguished acceptance of man's mortality? As one critic has written of this philosophy:

> Es la mayor conformidad con la muerte que haya existido jamás; su aceptación más completa, su justificación más descarada y total. Pasa el hombre por la vida como la luz por un cristal, y sólo hay que cuidar de que nuestro paso no deje empañada su transparencia, ni marcada su huella. [44]

It is precisely this practical moral application of the doctrine of Seneca, not its metaphysical implications, which has been kept alive in Spain and which has become a tradition in Spanish philosophy:

> De todos los sistemas filosóficos de la antigüedad clásica, el estoico es el que ha alcanzado mayor difusión atravesando las fronteras de la pura filosofía para llegar a la masa culta que de un modo formal no se ha entregado a la especulación filosófica. Se podría afirmar tal vez con alguna precipitación, que el estoico ha alternado con las distintas modalidades del platonismo en ser el alimento filosófico de mayor consumo entre los no filósofos de oficio. Pero mientras que el platonismo ha enlazado a menudo con la religión y con frecuencia por vías de heterodoxia, especialmente con la forma mística, el estoicismo por el contrario, ha sido el pensamiento laico, la zona que pudiéramos llamar más neutral.
> En España, tendremos que separar inmediatamente el estoico consciente, definido, manifiesto, del popular; el

---

[43] Ibid., p. 644.
[44] María Zambrano, *Pensamiento y poesía en la vida española*. México: Fondo de Cultura Económica, 1939, p. 101.

estoicismo, en suma, sabio, del estoicismo popular, que parece correr en una tradición honda a veces analfabeta.[45]

It must be remembered that Spain is first and foremost a Catholic country, and that it was within this atmosphere that Senequism flourished as a practical moral philosophy, not as a philosophy of religion.

In the same work, Américo Castro states that Quevedo was not a Senequist because he rejected the insensitivity of the Stoics.[46] However, in making this assertion, Castro overlooks Quevedo's own explanation of Stoic "insensibilidad." Rather than interpret it as a denial of all human emotions, as did St. Thomas Aquinas, Quevedo preferred to understand it as an active effort *not to be overcome by these emotions*:

> Santo Tomás, doctor angélico, y con él todos, condenan esta insensibilidad católicamente, sin que pueda ser lícita alguna respuesta. Yo, para mostrar que no se me ha cansado la afición con los estoicos, confesando ser hoy herejía afirmarlo, y error en la antigüedad, como lo prueban todos, me esforzaré a interpretarlos.
> Ellos dicen que no se han de sentir algunos afectos, y esto enseñan y esto mandan. Persuádome que algunos, por la palabra sentir, entendieron dejar vencer de los afectos, puesto que de sentirlos nacen las virtudes, como la clemencia, piedad y conmiseración, y de vencerse dellos procede de la pusilanimidad para poder producir las virtudes. No es cortesía descaminada entender bien lo que dijeron algunos de aquellos que encaminaron todas sus acciones al bien; muchas cosas los debemos; débannos una.[47]

Again, Castro says that Quevedo was not a Senequist because he could not agree with Seneca's theory that suicide was admirable.[48] It is true that Quevedo opposed suicide as any orthodox Catholic would, and he lamented Seneca's stand on this subject. However,

---

[45] Ibid., pp. 86-87.
[46] See Castro, *La realidad...*, p. 644. Castro also errs in equating the Stoic "insensibilidad" with "apatía"; the Stoic philosopher, to achieve his goal, must avoid apathy at all costs.
[47] *Nombre, origen, intento, recomendación y descendencia de la doctrina estoica, Obras* I (1964), 977.
[48] See Castro, *La realidad...*, p. 644.

he emphasized the fact that Seneca was one of the few Stoics who supported this theory, and therefore it should not be considered a Stoic idea, but rather a personal opinion of Seneca's:

> ¿Cómo, ¡oh grande Séneca, no conociste que es cobardía necia dejarse vencer del miedo de los trabajos; que es locura matarse por no morir?... Y es de advertir que no porque Séneca tenga opinión de que es lícito darse la muerte, es opinión estoica; no lo es sino de un estoico. [49]

Castro's allegations fall short of their intended impact when one sees Quevedo's conciliatory attitude and his desire to interpret Seneca, and Stoicism in general, in a way that is most in harmony with Catholicism. In addition to these points, it is interesting to note that, although Castro says "Séneca no era español," [50] Quevedo did consider him a Spaniard. [51] Certainly Castro's statement may be substantiated from a purely objective historical viewpoint. Nonetheless, the fact that Quevedo and so many other Spaniards, both before and after him, believed that Seneca was a Spaniard is an equally cogent historical truth. It is, in my opinion, a far more important factor in determining the extent of Seneca's influence in Spain. Julián Juderías has expressed the impact of this influence and Quevedo's support of it in the following way:

> Como otros muchos pensadores de nuestra tierra fue Quevedo un senequista convencido y ferviente, lo cual demuestra además cuán genuinamente español es, lo mismo en sus cualidades que en sus defectos, en sus tendencias que en su manera de pensar, pues si fuera necesario aducir alguna prueba fehaciente de la continuidad del pensamiento español, de la íntima trabazón que existe entre los que en épocas diversas lo manifestaron, ninguna mejor ni más evidente que el entusiasmo que siempre despertaron en nuestra patria las doctrinas del insigne maestro de Nerón y el crecido número que tuvo de imitadores y discípulos. [52]

---

[49] *Nombre, origen...*, *Obras* I (1964) 974.
[50] Castro, *La realidad...*, p. 642.
[51] "Desquitéme de un español con otro," says Quevedo, referring to Seneca. *Nombre, origen...*, *Obras* I (1964), 974.
[52] Julián Juderías, *Don Francisco de Quevedo y Villegas: La época, el hombre, las doctrinas*. Madrid: Estab. tip. de J. Ratés, 1923, p. 176.

Throughout the Middle Ages, Seneca's works were read in Spain. The close affinity between his moral teachings and those of Christian evangelists often led to confusion when works by Christian writers were mistakenly attributed to Seneca.[53] Both Stoicism and Christianity valued the virtues of patience and resignation in the face of adversity, temperance of worldly appetites, love of poverty and acceptance of death. In the Golden Age, the influence of Renaissance ideals of Humanism and the Erasmian current which penetrated Spain brought about a revival of Stoicism, and more particularly, of an admiration for Seneca. It was primarily due to Erasmus that the concept of morality in the minds of Spanish writers became autonomous after many centuries of subjugation to the dogma of the Catholic religion.[54] The Erasmian and Humanistic emphasis on the feedom of man's reason and individual will, totally divorced from his religious beliefs, opened up a new field of interest in literature, for it freed morality from the shackles of religion. In this sense, Senequism was reinstated as a viable moral philosophy in its own right without dependence upon Christianity to sustain it in Spain. It thus became possible, in Montoliu's words, "aceptar la nueva corriente estoica, no para desencadenarla como una ofensiva racionalista contra el dogma tradicional, sino como una confirmación puramente humana de los grandes valores éticos del cristianismo. ..."[55]

Shortly after this revival of Stoicism became popular in Spain, Quevedo completed his education at Alcalá and began corresponding with Justus Lipsius, a noted Belgian humanist. Lipsius, a onetime defender of the Protestants, later an avowed Catholic and friend of Erasmus and Montaigne, exchanged several letters with the young Spanish scholar before dying in 1606. Lipsius was a great admirer of the philosophy of Seneca, and in one of his letters dated October of 1604 he told Quevedo that he was preparing an edition of Seneca's works: "Nunc Seneca vester me totum habet, ad quem *Stoicae doctrinae* excerpta praemisi."[56] Inspired by the example of this venerable Belgian, Quevedo studied Seneca in greater depth,

---

[53] See Menéndez y Pelayo, *La Ciencia Española*, Vol. I, pp. 212-213.
[54] See Montoliu, p. 426.
[55] Ibid., p. 419.
[56] "Epistolario," *Obras* II (1964), 818.

thus developing an interest which would grow more intense as he matured. Many years later, Quevedo exclaimed, "¡Oh mi Lipsio, grande honra de Francia! Tanto como España debe a Córdoba porque le dió a Séneca, te debe España porque se le resucitas y se le defiendes." [57]

Quevedo cherished the teachings of Seneca and defended Stoicism with as much tenacity as his Catholic beliefs would permit. References to Seneca are found in his humorous satirical works as well as in his serious political and moral essays. His most fervent period of Senequism was during the years of 1630 to 1635 when he wrote several works inspired by his admiration of Stoicism, among them, *Nombre, origen, intento, recomendación y descendencia de la doctrina estoica.* [58] In this essay, Quevedo selects Epictetus as the principal expounder of the Stoic moral doctrine and offers his personal theory that Epictetus derived his philosophy from the book of Job in the Old Testament. [59] Pointing out a rapport in the spirit of these two works, Quevedo suggests that the virtues espoused by the Stoics must have been inspired by the Scriptures from whence, he implies, come all great truths: "No pudieron verdades tan desnudas del mundo, cogerse limpias de la tierra y polvo de otra fuente que de las sagradas letras." [60] This interpretation of the origin of Stoicism betrays Quevedo's invincible adhesion to the traditional doctrines of the Christian religion. His devotion to the beliefs of his own creed lead him to impose his concept of the unique truth of Christianity upon an essentially pagan philosophy. In his deep admiration for the Stoic teachings, he seems unable to accept the fact that they might be classified as heretical. By proposing this theory, Quevedo is trying to rationalize the affinity between Christianity and Stoicism which had been accepted as a fact in Spain for centuries. [61]

---

[57] *Epístolas de Séneca, Obras* I (1964), 1722.
[58] See *Obras* I (1964), 970-991.
[59] *Obras* I (1964), 971.
[60] *Obras* I (1964), 971.
[61] See Montoliu, p. 374. It is also interesting to note that Américo Castro in *La realidad histórica de España*, p. 644, contends that in promoting this theory, Quevedo falsified the foundations of Stoicism, thus proving that he was not a Senequist. It is my belief that Quevedo's effort to establish this theory is greater proof of his devotion to Senequism, albeit he was first and foremost a devout Catholic.

It is not surprising that Quevedo should have felt much in common with Seneca. In many aspects their lives were much alike. Both were of distinguished backgrounds, both lived in the court and both participated in affairs of state as advisers, Seneca with Nero in Rome, and Quevedo with Osuna in Naples. Both of them knew the misfortunes of exile, and yet both enjoyed the admiration of their contemporaries. However, more important than all these parallels, Seneca and Quevedo shared a common dismay as witnesses of the decadence of their respective eras. They saw the social and political corruption that surrounded them and offered similar warnings to their fellow men. The vexation expressed in Seneca's Epistle XVI on "A General Dissolution of Manners," [62] for example, is a product of the same type of concern that Quevedo felt for the future of Spanish society when he wrote his famous satirico-moral essays. The fundamental problem to be dealt with, as both Seneca and Quevedo envisaged it, was a moral one. In this sense, beyond any barrier of religion, the two writers were dedicated to the same task of improving human moral conduct. The letters in imitation of Seneca which Quevedo wrote while in prison from 1639 to 1643 are evidence of their oneness of purpose:

> ¡Oh mi Lucilio!, el negocio principal del hombre es vivir, y acabar de vivir de manera que la buena vida que tuvo y la buena memoria que deje le sean urna y epitafio. El acierto está en desnudarse bien deste cuerpo, no en cubrirle con la fanfarria de los jaspes ni la soberbia de las pirámides...
> Ahora, porque la muerte acaba también la carta, te digo que debemos morir, y nada a la muerte; mas debemos saber morir. Esto sabe quien a la muerte no le deja otra cosa que le quite sino el postrer aliento... [63]

Even before this final imprisonment, during which time Quevedo endured the most difficult test of his Stoic qualities, he wrote:

> Yo no tengo suficiencia de estoico, mas tengo afición a los estoicos. Hame asistido su doctrina por guía en las dudas,

---

[62] See *Seneca's Morals*, ed. Sir Roger L'Estrange. New York: National Book Company, 1890, pp. 970-971.
[63] Epístola XXXIX, *Obras* II (1964), 970-971.

por consuelo en los trabajos, por defensa en las persecuciones, que tanta parte han poseído de mi vida. [64]

His Attitude toward Erasmus of Rotterdam

In the first half of the sixteenth century, the influence of Erasmus in Spain was considerable. [65] His followers were prevalent in the court of Carlos I as well as at the University of Alcalá de Henares. His books were extremely popular in Spain, and his fame as a humanist was widely acclaimed.

Erasmus' "philosophia Christi," as outlined in his *Enchiridion Militis Christiani* (1503), was aimed at a revitalization of pure Christian spiritualism free of the rhetoric of scholasticism. As Erasmus explained: "Theologiam minimum ad sophisticas artutias delapsam, ad fontes ad priscam simplicitatem revocare conatus sum." [66] He sought a revival of the simple virtues expounded in the Bible, and he hoped for a more intimate relationship between man and God.

His vast knowledge of the classics led Erasmus to recognize the virtue of Seneca's works, of which he published a critical edition in 1529. He saw in Senequism, as did Quevedo several decades later, the same asceticism found in Christian moral doctrine, and through his influence, there appeared a renewed interest in Seneca in Spain. [67]

Because of certain ecclesiastical reforms which Erasmus had suggested, many orthodox Spanish Catholics accused him of heresy. His prestige was further diminished when the "iluministas" adopted his *Enchiridion* as their guide to spiritual reform. [68] This peripheral religious sect, characterized by pseudo-mystics called "beatas," was persecuted by the Inquisition. However, Erasmus himself did not suffer persecution since the Inquisitor General was one of his admirers. Following the death of the leading Erasmists in the court

---

[64] *Nombre, origen...*, *Obras* I (1964), 978.

[65] See Marcel Bataillon, *Erasmo y España*, 2 Vols. México: Fondo de Cultura Económica, 1950.

[66] ("I have endeavored to recall theology that has fallen into sophisticated squabbling back to its source and original simplicity.") Cited by John Dolan, ed. *The Essential Erasmus*. New York: The New American Library, 1964, p. 25.

[67] See Montoliu, pp. 424-426. Quevedo does not acknowledge this contribution as he did J. Lipsius'. See quote corresponding to footnote 57.

[68] See Bataillon, Vol. I, p. 244.

of Carlos I and the death of Erasmus in 1536, his influence in Spain began to decline. Many of those who had tried to vindicate his religious philosophy were no longer alive to defend his reputation, and the air of suspicion surrounding his work became more apparent. [69]

Several generations later when Quevedo lived, the influence of Erasmus was far less potent in Spain. From Quevedo's comments, it is evident that he had read the works of the great humanist and that he admired his vast learning. [70] Nonetheless, in each reference he makes to Erasmus, Quevedo finds faults to criticize, i. e., he accuses him of mocking Spanish pronunciation, [71] of being excessively proud, [72] and of maliciously defending an unorthodox view of marriage of saints and clergymen. [73] Judging purely from his references to Erasmus by name, it must be concluded that Quevedo felt a basic antipathy toward Erasmus' personality and that he mistrusted his orthodoxy as a Catholic, although he does not specifically refer to him as a heretic.

Quevedo's religious traditionalism caused him to criticize Erasmus and consciously to avoid any overt and unconditional praise of his ideas. However, a close reading of Quevedo's work proves that subconsciously, or at least silently, he himself was a follower of the Erasmian approach to spiritual reform and moral revitalization. One critic, Luis Astrana Marín, has called Quevedo "enamorado de Erasmo," [74] while another, D. W. Bleznick, has merely referred to "un esfuerzo erasmista por volver a los preceptos cristianos originales" in Quevedo's writing. [75] In my opinion, the latter of these two critics has made the correct analysis of his relationship with Erasmism. Quevedo was too much of a conservative in matters of religious orthodoxy to approve of Erasmus himself. However, Que-

---

[69] Ibid., p. 503.
[70] For example, Quevedo calls Erasmus "doctísimo" in *España defendida y los tiempos de ahora, Obras* I (1964), 518.
[71] *España defendida..., Obras* I (1964), 518.
[72] See *Virtud militante, Obras* I (1964), 1263.
[73] See *Vida de San Pablo Apóstol, Obras* I (1964), 1471.
[74] L. Astrana Marín, ed. *Obras* II (1952), Apéndice I, 1347.
[75] D. W. Bleznick, "La Política de Dios de Quevedo y el pensamiento político en el Siglo de Oro," *Nueva Revista de Filología Hispánica*, Vol. IX, 1955, p. 392.

vedo's own writing demonstrates a distinctly Erasmian tendency to bring practical Christian mores back to their purest state. Long before Quevedo wrote the *Política de Dios,* Erasmus expressed the idea that princes should rule in the image of Christ:

> I pray the true Christian prince to behold the image of his chief Prince. If he observes how Christ entered His Kingdom and how He departed the earth, he will understand how He would have them rule. [76]

Quevedo's affinity with Erasmus is best portrayed in *La cuna y la sepultura,* a work written by Quevedo in 1633. [77] As Antonio Alatorre has discovered, in the second part of this work (entitled *Doctrina para morir*) Quevedo has paraphrased sections of Erasmus' *Praeparatio ad mortem* and Constantino Ponce de la Fuente's exposition of *Beatus vir.* [78] This discernible use of Erasmian texts confirms their relationship and Alatorre's conclusion reiterates the same:

> Erasmo y el Doctor Constantino... sirven casi un siglo más tarde a Quevedo para expresar, en una obra en que puso algunas de sus más hondas preocupaciones, el mismo anhelo erasmista de una religión menos recargada de ceremonias externas, menos farisaica y más íntima. [79]

THE DEFENSE OF SANTIAGO'S PATRONAGE OF SPAIN

In the year 1617, the Carmelite Order launched a campaign in the Cortes of Castilla to obtain official recognition of Santa Teresa de Jesús as the "santa patrona" of Spain alongside Santiago who had been the nation's "santo patrón" since the Middle Ages. This proposal precipitated open discord between the supporters of San-

---

[76] *The Complaint of Peace* (1517) in *The Essential Erasmus,* ed. John Dolan, p. 25.

[77] See *Obras* I (1964), 1190-1226.

[78] See Antonio Alatorre, "Quevedo, Erasmo y el Doctor Constantino," *Nueva Revista de Filología Hispánica,* núms. 3-4, julio-dic. de 1953, pp. 673-685. Constantino was a follower of Erasmus, and was incarcerated and died in the jail of the Inquisition.

[79] Ibid., p. 685.

tiago and the Carmelites which was only heightened by an apostolic brief from Pope Urban VIII in 1627 sanctioning the co-patronage. From that date until 1630, the polemics between the opposing factions motivated a long series of written and oral protests.

A central figure in this dispute was Francisco de Quevedo, who ardently defended the sole patronage of Santiago. In 1627, Quevedo wrote a lengthy *Memorial por el patronato de Santiago*,[80] sent to the Consejo de Castilla; and the following year he reinforced his position with another paper entitled *Su espada por Santiago* which he addressed to the King, Felipe IV.[81] In addition, he wrote a poem in favor of Santiago and a letter pleading his cause to the Pope in 1628.[82] Although Quevedo's participation in this national dispute gained him the admiration of many "santiaguistas," it also brought upon him the disfavor of Olivares, who may have been influential in having him exiled to La Torre de Juan Abad from April to December of 1628.[83] His *Memorial* also evoked the vindictive response of Francisco Morovelli, a dedicated opponent who attacked Quevedo's defense of Santiago and criticized his capabilities as a writer.[84]

Undeniably, this altercation brought persecution and discomfort to Quevedo. Why did he assume the burden of defending Santiago's patronage, and why did he persist in his efforts? Among other hypotheses, it has been suggested that Quevedo disagreed with the Carmelites' teachings and disdained their mysticism.[85] Then too, it must be acknowledged that Quevedo thrived on polemics and actively stimulated controversies in other relationships with his contemporaries. This aspect of his nature, however, can only be pointed out as a minor impetus behind a greater motivation. It is also known that Quevedo vigorously pursued his appointment to the Order of Santiago in 1617. Though he was justifiably proud of this

---

[80] See *Obras* I (1964), 765-787.
[81] See *Obras* I (1964), 400-445.
[82] See *Obras* II (1964), 449-453. The letter to the Pope has since been lost.
[83] Fernández-Guerra, ed., "Vida de Don Francisco de Quevedo y Villegas," in *Obras de Quevedo*, Tomo I, p. LXII. The Conde-Duque was a supporter of Santa Teresa since his son-in-law's uncle, Fray Pedro Madre de Dios, was a principal Carmelite in the polemics with Quevedo and other "santiaguistas."
[84] See Morevelli's response to Quevedo in *Obras* II (1952), 1129-1170.
[85] See Castro, *La realidad*..., pp. 198-199.

achievement, it cannot be considered sufficient reason for his desire to defend the patron of his Order.

It is my opinion that Quevedo's primary motivation may be found in his personal conviction that the sole patronage of Santiago was more than a religious tradition; it was also a national tradition which had to be conserved for the benefit of the nation. For Quevedo, sharing the patronage with Santa Teresa would be tantamount to negating Santiago's value as a symbol of national cohesion, not to mention the implied insult to Christ whose will it was that Santiago help deliver Spain from Moorish domination in the Middle Ages. This reasoning is expressed in the following lines from *Su espada por Santiago* which Quevedo sent to Felipe IV:

> Señor, Santiago apóstol, primo de Jesucristo, pariente de su Santísima Madre, restaurador de las Españas, redentor de los españoles dándoles la verdadera fe, único y solo patrón nuestro, pudiendo pedirnos cuanto tenéis, pues se le debéis todo vos y el reino... se contenta hoy con que no le quitéis lo que ni le distes ni pudistes dar. Y esto no porque el Santo pierda nada en el patronato; sólo porque la memoria de mil seiscientos años no os acuse por contradicción de tantos reyes y gentes como con ellos han reverenciado y agradecido, la elección de Cristo y beneficios y maravillas suyas, obradas en exaltación de vuestra corona. [86]

Quevedo's defense of the solitary patronage of Santiago is based not only upon established custom, but also upon a unique juridico-political factor. According to Quevedo's reasoning, the patronage of Spain was granted to Santiago through divine will, by Christ himself, not by the will of any secular power: "... Santiago no es patrón de España porque entre otros santos le eligió el Reino, sino porque cuando no había reino, le eligió Cristo nuestro Señor para que él lo ganase y le hiciese, y os le diese a vos." [87] Having stated this fact, Quevedo proceeds to demonstrate that the Cortes of Castilla have no jurisdiction over the patronage of Spain, since they are unable to take away, limit or diminish what is not in their power to alter: "¿... cómo, Señor, quitará o limitará o disminuirá el Reino a Santiago lo que no le dió, y le debe lo que es suyo por

---

[86] *Obras* I (1964), 436.
[87] *Memorial por el patronato de Santiago, Obras* I (1964), 771.

expresa voluntad de Cristo?" [88] Thus, the granting of a co-patronage to Santa Teresa was without any legal foundation or precedent, nor could there be one, for Christ alone is the judge and jury in such a cause:

> Ni se ha visto otra vez en el mundo pedir patronato de las naciones a tribunal alguno, rey o república, por haber sido ese repartimiento de la disposición de Cristo y cosa encargada por él, y no pretendida por alguno, donde la negociación hasta ahora no ha tenido entrada. [89]

Throughout the *Memorial*, Quevedo points out this logic to the Consejo Supremo de Castilla, emphasizing the necessity of reversing the decision of the Cortes, or "el Reino," as he calls them. [90] A year later, Quevedo appealed directly to the King, asking him to revoke the unjust ruling of the "Reino" since "es lícito a los reyes revocar las cosas que ordenaron por mala información y defectuosa y en perjuicio de tercero." [91] In this argument, Quevedo has assumed the role of a lawyer presenting a brief in defense of his client. He has based his case not only upon the force of precedent, but also upon the injustice of a procedural error.

Time and again in his defense, Quevedo reiterates the value of Santiago's sole patronage as a national tradition, "la costumbre tan anciana y venerable destos reinos." [92] Quevedo, who had repeatedly demonstrated his capacity as a realist in his social satire, accepted as a matter of fact as well as faith Santiago's visible participation in the battles against the Moors during the Reconquest. Almost fanatical in his adherence to the traditional belief in Santiago's appearance in the midst of battle, Quevedo writes:

---

[88] *Memorial...*, *Obras* I (1964), 772.

[89] *Memorial...*, *Obras* I (1964), 769.

[90] José Antonio Maravall draws attention to Quevedo's reference to the Cortes as "el Reino" or "todo lo que no es el Rey" as a traditional concept since the Middle Ages in Spain. However, he points out that in 1627, the Cortes were made up only of the bourgeoisie from the cities, as the clergy and nobility were dependent upon the King. Maravall sees in Quevedo's recognition of the Cortes as an independent political entity the emergence of the "estado llano" or "tercer estado" concept of modern government. See "Quevedo y la teoría de las Cortes," *Revista de Estudios Políticos*, vol. XV, núms. 27-28, 1946, pp. 145-149.

[91] *Su espada por Santiago*, *Obras* I (1964), 410-411.

[92] *Memorial...*, *Obras* I (1964), 777.

> ...en las historias y annales antiguos hallaréis que se han dado en España cuatro mil setecientas batallas campanales a los moros. ...Hallaréis que el santo Apóstol, peleando y visiblemente, ha dado las victorias y la muerte a tan inumerables enemigos. [93]

A similar unswerving faith in Santiago's military exploits was felt by the majority of Spaniards in the Golden Age. Devotees had carried this faith to the New World in the sixteenth century, and there Santiago reportedly appeared in several battles against the indians. [94] However, after Spain had extended the horizons of her power in the latter 1500s, the authenticity of the Santiago legend began to be questioned. Supporters of the proposed co-patronage of Santa Teresa as well as other writers of the early seventeenth century voiced their skepticism both through serious attempts at refuting the myth and by mocking or burlesquing it. [95]

To Quevedo, this willful attempt to subvert the faith in Santiago was a symptom of the general infirmity of the day. In a poem defending Santiago he says:

> ... ...
> Con Santiago en la boca solía España
> salir a la campaña,
> diciendo en todo estrago:
> "¡España, cierra! ¡A ellos, Santiago!"
> Mas ya que le hacen guerra,
> también Santiago con España cierra.
>   Tú, inventora de trajes y de voces,
> España, no conoces
> los que causas ultrajes
> pues a ejemplo de voces y de trajes,
> después de lo que abonas,
> inventarás patrones y patronas. [96]
> ... ...

This passion for novelty and change bothered Quevedo, for he saw no new faiths replacing those which were discarded, no sincerity

---

[93] *Su espada por Santiago, Obras* I (1964), 423.
[94] See R. Heliodoro Valle, "Santiago en la imaginación de América." *Cuadernos Americanos*, vol. XX, 1945, pp. 153-154.
[95] See Castro, *La realidad...*, p. 190.
[96] "De viento y de bronce labios," *Obras* II (1964), 453.

or constancy to support innovations. Against "novedades" in general, he writes:

> ...debéis reparar en que si mudanzas de trajes y novedades en divisas han sido a los reinos indicio ejecutado de grandes pérdidas, en las materias de la devoción y religión se puede y debe desvelar más el cuidado en la observancia de lo que siempre ha sido. [97]

The concept expressed in the foregoing statement is fundamental to Quevedo's traditionalistic philosophy. In the case of Santiago's patronage, Quevedo was defending not only a historico-religious legend, but also a traditional moral attitude that had flourished alongside the cult of Santiago. This attitude, developed over a period of centuries, has been described by García de Valdeavellano in this way:

> Y es que la circunstancia de que la España cristiana, aquella España que lentamente renacía por la feliz conjunción del esfuerzo ideal con el político y el militar, apareciese abrigando en tierra propia el cuerpo del Apóstol que le había evangelizado, fue así convertida desde el siglo IX por los Cristianos independientes del al-Andalus en una garantía y en una promesa de victoria, en la seguridad de una protección celestial, de la que era Santiago el instrumento; en una creencia nacional viva y fecunda, nacida de las entrañas mismas de la conciencia colectiva y enraizada en ella como una realidad indestructible... [98]

What Quevedo objected to, above all else, was the conscious destruction of the national ideal, personified by Santiago, which had given Spain the impetus to unite and conquer. For him, the loss of this tradition signified a diminution of the spirit of confidence and unity which was essential to the survival of the Spanish nation.

In deference to the uproar created by this dispute of the patronage of Spain, Pope Urban reversed his decision of 1627 in another brief of 1630. After this, the polemic slowly ceased and the problem did not recur until 1812 when the co-patronage was again reinstated by the Cortes.

---

[97] *Memorial...*, *Obras* I (1964), 771.
[98] García de Valdeavellano, p. 693.

Quevedo and the Spanish Society of his Time

Most readers of Spanish literature remember Quevedo as the master of social satire. Their first contact with his writing is usually through his short and witty *Vida del Buscón* and his ingenious *Sueños*. In these works, Quevedo employs an intriguing narrative framework to convey what is esentially a panoramic satire of contemporary society. Critics have written many pages analyzing the style and content of these and other of Quevedo's satirico-moral works. My purpose in this discussion is not to repeat this, but rather to comment upon the motivation behind their composition as it may apply to Quevedo's traditionalism.

In the course of Spanish history, there have been several eras characterized by abnormal moral decadence. Such periods have provoked famous literature of social criticism, for example, Pero López de Ayala's *Rimado de Palacio* and the anonymous *Coplas de Mingo Revulgo* in the late Middle Ages, and Mariano José de Larra's *Artículos de costumbres* in the early nineteenth century. Of all these eras, the seventeenth century was perhaps the most notoriously decadent. As Gregorio Marañón writes:

> Aún cuando los textos de cualquier época de la historia de los pueblos abundan en testimonios de que, los contemporáneos, invariablemente, la creían la más pecaminosa de cuantas existieron, es evidente que estos testimonios se redoblan en número y expresividad durante los reinados que pusieron fin a la Casa de Austria. [99]

It is often true that social immorality becomes more rampant in times of political and economic crisis. During the reigns of Felipe III and Felipe IV, Spain lacked effective leadership. Both monarchs set poor examples for their subjects, as they ignored official duties in their concern for satiating their own respective sensual and spiritual needs. The lavish spending on the part of the elite court society brought about a long period of uncontrollable inflation, and the ordinary Spaniard was overwhelmed by unreason-

---

[99] Marañón, p. 223.

able taxes and corrupt government bureaucracy. Understandably, the consequence was an increase in petty crimes, prostitution and vagrancy, all of which has been described at length in an interesting study by José Deleito y Pinuela.[100] The indifferent attitude of the Monarch appeared to filter down through the various social levels of court life, and the result was a growing rate of adultery and sexual libertinage, accompanied by an increase in venereal diseases. All of Spanish society seemed to lapse into a state of lethargy and indulgence; no longer was the noble spirit of adventure and sacrifice evident in Spain. What had come to pass was, as one writer has described it, "la muerte ... del quijotismo."[101]

Many Spaniards have endeavored to define the traditional qualities of their own national character. An interpretation of this nature is necessarily influenced by the subjective viewpoint of the individual who attempts it, nonetheless, such a definition is possible and valid since historical and cultural facts may vindicate it. With the exception of certain moments in history, the quality which Menéndez Pidal considers most basic to the Spanish character is "sobriedad" (sobriety or abstemiousness), from both a material and ethical standpoint:

> Muchas veces se ha puesto en relación el complejo del carácter español con el suelo habitado. Unamuno insiste en ello: el espíritu áspero y seco de nuestro pueblo, sin transiciones, sin términos medios, está en conexión íntima con el paisaje y el terruño de la altiplanicie central, duro de líneas, desnudo de árboles, de horizonte ilimitado, de luz cegadora, clima extremado, sin tibiezas dulces. Pero esa relación no es válida respecto a cualidades que se dan fuera del paisaje de ambas Castillas. La sobriedad física se halla igualmente en la risueña y fértil Andalucía, y, para mí, la sobriedad es la cualidad básica del carácter español, que no depende de un determinismo geográfico castellano, y es tan general que, partiendo de ella, podemos comprender las demás características...[102]

---

[100] See Deleito y Pinuela, *La mala vida de la España de Felipe IV*. Madrid: Espasa-Calpe, S. A., 1959.
[101] Marañón, p. 221.
[102] Menéndez Pidal, *Los españoles en la historia* in *España y su historia*, Vol. I, p. 14.

As Menéndez Pidal explains, this "sobriedad" is closely linked with the tradition of Senequism in Spain, and he speaks of a "senequismo espontáneo" of the national spirit. [103]

In a foregoing section of this chapter, I have discussed Quevedo's defense of Seneca and of the virtues espoused by that philosophy which coincided with the ideals of Christian morality. As I have pointed out, it was precisely the quality of moral fortitude or "sobriedad" which Quevedo admired most in Seneca and which he wanted to preserve in the spirit of Catholic Spain. The degenerate atmosphere of Spanish society in the first decades of the seventeenth century was anything but "sobrio." Thus, Quevedo dedicated himself to the task of protesting against the current of immorality and apathy which seemed to engulf the society around him. His primary and most appealing vehicle of protest was the satirization and burlesque mockery of social types and customs.

Knowing court society as intimately as any writer of his time, Quevedo was well equipped with material for his attacks. Between 1600 and 1639 he wrote numerous short works burlesquing current fads and weaknesses. In each of them, there is an implied or overt reference to the absence of "sobriedad." One of his earliest works, *Capitulaciones matrimoniales* (c. 1600), is an amusing list of qualities desirable in a wife, as enumerated by a certain "Juan" of the Court. [104] It is in many ways a burlesque counterpart to Fray Luis de León's *La perfecta casada*. To this, Quevedo adds a description of the "vida de corte y oficios entretenidos en ella." [105] Here is an example of one type of court figure which he burlesques:

> Hay figuras artificiales que usan bálsamo y olor para los bigotes, copete, guedejas y aladares, de que usan mucho jaboncillo de manos y pelotilla de cera de oídos. Su conversación es damas, caballos y caza, visten y platican degenerando de la plebe y tal vez se tientan de poesía, a que se inclinan los enamorados, a quienes no satisface menos talento que el de Lope de Vega o don Luis de Góngora, por lo que han oído. Lo superior llaman bonito; lo bueno, razo-

---

[103] Ibid., p. 15.
[104] *Obras* I (1964), 50-52.
[105] *Obras* I (1964), 52-59.

nable, y a lo malo, pésimo; nada les contenta; la causa nunca la dan por ser inferioridad. [106]

Quevedo's criticism in this sketch is aimed at the vanity, artificiality and emptiness of court dandies whose only concern is in making themselves appear elegant and blasé.

Another work of the same period entitled *Epístolas del Caballero de la Tenaza* constitutes a lesson in frugality. [107] A daily routine is involved:

> En levantándose lo primero persignará su dinero y santiguaráse de los que se lo pidieron, y dará gracias a nuestro Señor que le han dejado amanecer, diciendo: "Señor mío Jesucristo yo te doy muchas gracias, aunque soy caballero de la Tenaza, porque has permitido que me hayan dejado dormir los embestidores y pedigones; y ofrezco firmemente de no dar, ni prestar ni prometer, por palabra, obra ni pensamiento. [108]

Quevedo's satire in this work can be taken in two ways: he mocks the type who is stingy to the point of being ridiculous, and he also attacks the mercenary attitude of the women who pursue men for their money more than for love. As money became more scarce, those who had it became more powerful, a fact of life which Quevedo develops in the poem, "Poderoso caballero es don dinero." [109]

The prevalence of adultery was a well-known fact in Quevedo's time, and this also became the butt of one of his short satires called *Carta de un cornudo a otro*. [110] Making fun of the immorality which fostered this custom, Quevedo writes: "... realmente nosotros conforme a buena justicia siempre tenemos razón para ser cornudos; porque si la mujer es buena, comunicarla con los próximos es caridad y si es mala, es alivio propio." [111] Quevedo's experience with marriage came late in life and was exceedingly brief. He may have been a fancier of women, but his opinion of their morals and

---

[106] *Capitulaciones matrimoniales, Obras* I (1964), 52.
[107] *Obras* I (1964), 77-86.
[108] *Epístolas del Caballero de la Tenaza, Obras* I (1964), 78.
[109] See *Obras* II (1964), 213-214.
[110] See *Obras* I (1964), 91-93.
[111] *Carta de un cornudo a otro, Obras* I (1964), 92.

their tactics in trapping men was very low. Time and again, he criticizes them in his satire:

> Pues sábete que las mujeres lo primero que se visten, en despertando, es una cara, una garganta y unas manos, y luego las sayas. Todo cuanto ves en ellas es tienda y no natural. ¿Ves el cabello? Pues comprado es y no criado. Las cejas tienen más ahumadas que de negras; y si como se hacen cejas se hicieran las narices, no las tuvieran. Los dientes que ves y la boca era, de puro negra, un tintero, y a puros polvos se ha hecho salvadera... Dígote que nuestros sentidos están en ayunas de lo que es mujer y ahitos de lo que le parace. [112]

In yet another short satire entitled *Lo más corriente en Madrid,* Quevedo compiles a dictionary of the people and things indigenous to court life. [113] Here are some of his entries:

> A. *Alcahuetas,* más que picadoras a respecto de lo que se gasta más su caballería.
> *Amigos* como treguas, mientras duran las comodidades.
> *Agravios* limosneros que siempre dan a pobres.
> B. *Barbas* y cabellos dominicos; sobre blanco capas negras.
> *Banderas* por la razón de estado, sobre las almenas de la justicia.
> *Barrigas* de algodón como pantorrillas, nuevo modo de hidropesía. [114]

Virtually no element of Spanish society, except the poor man and the soldier, [115] escapes Quevedo's satire. His condemnation of society in general is clear in this notable reference to the once respected virtue of honor:

> Todos tienen honra, y todos son honrados, y todos lo hacen todo caso de honra. Hay honra en todos estados, y la honra se está cayendo de su estado, y parece que está ya siete

---

[112] *El mundo, por de dentro, Obras* I (1964), 172.
[113] See *Obras* I (1964), 116-118.
[114] *Lo más corriente en Madrid, Obras* I (1964), 116.
[115] He did not include the soldier in his attacks because, most likely, Quevedo felt that he represented the spirit of valor and adventure which Spain was lacking in her society.

estados debajo tierra. Si hurtan, dicen que por conservar esta negra honra, y que quieren más hurtar que pedir, y que es mejor pedir que no hurtar... y al fin en el mundo todos han dado en la cuenta, y llaman honra a la comodidad, con presumir de honrados y no serlo se ríen del mundo. [116]

Not only in prose, but also frequently in verse, Quevedo lamented the loss of "sobriedad" and fortitude. One of his most fervent poetic diatribes against society was written in 1624 and dedicated to the Conde-Duque de Olivares to whom Quevedo then looked for Spain's salvation. Entitled "Epístola satírica y censoria contra las costumbres presentes de los castellanos," this long poem is characterized by the poet's nostalgia for better days:

... ...
Señor Excelentísimo, mi llanto
ya no consiente márgenes ni orillas;
inundación será la de mi canto.
... ...
Yace aquella virtud desaliñada,
que fué, si rica menos, más temida
en vanidad y en sueño sepultada. [117]

The same sentiment is expressed in another poem, a romance which begins in this manner:

Cansado estoy de la corte,
que tiene en breve confín
buen cielo, malas ausencias,
poco amor, mucho alguacil.
Ahito me tiene España,
provincia, si antes feliz,
hoy tan trocada, que trajes
cuida y olvida la lid. [118]
... ...

In the space of a few decades, the way of life in Spain had changed, and the effects of inflation had fallen most heavily upon the poor.

---

[116] *El sueño de la muerte, Obras* I (1964), 184.
[117] *Obras* II (1964), 447.
[118] *Obras* II (1964), 298-299.

In one of his poems, Quevedo describes the conversation between four drunkards who analyze this situation.

> ... ...
> ¿En qué ha de parar el mundo?
> ¿Qué fin tendrán estos tiempos?
> Lo que hoy es ración de un paje,
> de un capitán era sueldo,
> cuando eran los hombres más
> y habían menester menos.
> ... ...
>
> Andaba entonces el Cid
> más galán que Gerineldos
> con botara colorada
> en figura de pimiento.
> Y hoy si alguno ha de vestirse
> le desnudan dos primero:
> el mercader de quien compra
> y el sastre que ha de coserlo.
> ... ...
>
> Todo se ha trocado ya,
> todo al revés está vuelto:
> las mujeres son soldados
> y los hombres son doncellas.
> ... ...
>
> Si yo reinara ocho días,
> pusiera en todo remedio
> y anduvieran tras nosotros
> y nos dijeran requiebros. [119]
> ... ...

And finally, this famous sonnet in which Quevedo looks about him with despair, remorse and regret:

> Miré los muros de la patria mía,
> si un tiempo fuertes, ya desmoronados,
> de la carrera de la edad cansados,
> por quien caduca ya su valentía.
>
> Salíme al campo, vi que el sol bebía
> los arroyos del hielo desatados;

---

[119] "Gobernando están el mundo," *Obras* II (1964), 241-242.

> y del monte, quejosos, los ganados,
> que con sombras hurtó su luz al día.
>
> Entré en mi casa, vi que amancillada
> de anciana habitación era despojos;
> mi báculo más corvo y menos fuerte,
>
> vencida de la edad sentí mi espada,
> y no hallé cosa en que poner los ojos
> que no fuese recuerdo de la muerte. [120]

Although many of the social evils of Spain could be traced to the political and economic programs of the government, a large part of them were fomented by the mental attitude of the people themselves. Their discontent and their vanity caused them to lead an artificial life, always seeking the new and the different. Such an existence could only become a vicious circle, as Quevedo points out:

> Perdió el mundo el querer ser otro, y pierde a los hombres el querer ser diferentes de sí mismos. Es la novedad tan mal contenta de sí, que cuando se desagrada de lo que ha sido, se cansa de lo que es. Y para mantenerse en novedad ha de continuarse en dejar de serlo, y el novelero tiene por vida muertes y fallecimientos perpetuos. Y es fuerza, u que deja de ser novelero, u que siempre tenga por ocupación el dejar de ser. [121]

In his opinion, a healthy and productive society cannot exist if its members are continually searching for novelty. There is no virtue or satisfaction in living like a cork, bobbed by every current of change. The ultimate challenge for man is that of establishing his own values and fighting for their survival. The tragedy of Spanish society, as Quevedo understood it, was that the strong moral fiber, or "sobriedad," which had once been its mainstay, was giving way to vanity and affectation. As René Bouvier has aptly stated:

---

[120] *Obras* II (1964), 42. R. M. Price advances the opinion that the word "patria" in this poem means "village," and that Quevedo was looking inside himself, not at Spain. See "A Note on the Sources and Structure of 'Miré los muros de la patria mía'," *Modern Language Notes,* Vol. LXXVIII, 1963, p. 198. Even if this is true, the poem reflects Quevedo's disillusionment with what he sees and with his own efforts to arrest corruption.

[121] *Marco Bruto, Obras* I (1964), 827.

> En réalité, Quevedo rêve... d'une Espagne grandiose et hiératique, figée dans les traditions du passé et cristallisée dans sa foi, et il ne souhaite que le retour aux anciennes mœurs et aux vieilles coutumes. Pour lui, l'origine des malheurs du siècle n'est point dans l'insuffisance de la constitution, ni dans l'affaiblissement du commerce, de l'industrie, de l'agriculture, mais dans la médiocrité, dans la platitude morale. [122]

Although I have devoted a separate chapter to the analysis of Quevedo's religious traditionalism, I should emphasize that his religious attitude is actually the crux of his traditionalism. As Bouvier notes in the above quote, Quevedo dreams of revitalizing the traditional Spain "cristallisée dans sa foi." The essence of Spanish traditionalism, whether it be considered from a juridico-political or socio-moral viewpoint, is the Catholic religion; in the words of Francisco Puy:

> ...la esencia de nuestra constitución, de nuestro ser como unidad jurídico-política, es el servicio de la catolicidad, el servicio de Dios en la forma más inmediata en que cualquier sociedad humana, salvo la misma iglesia... puede hacerla. Esa es la esencia de nuestra tradición, ése el ser de España. Los demás pueblos pueden buscar su razón de ser donde les plazca. La nuestra es ésta: servir a Dios, difundiendo su fe y defendiendo su Iglesia. [123]

---

[122] René Bouvier, *Quevedo, "Homme du diable, homme de Dieu."* Paris: Chez Honoré Champion, 1929, p. 151.

[123] Francisco Puy, *El pensamiento tradicional en la España del siglo XVIII (1700-1760)*. Madrid: Instituto de Estudios Políticos, 1966, p. 137.

CHAPTER FOUR

LITERARY AND CULTURAL TRADITIONS DEFENDED

THE LITERARY CRITIC

Quevedo's works in the field of literary criticism constitute the key to an understanding of his position in the literary world of the seventeenth century.¹ The critical works which are of most significance to this study and which have established Quevedo's fame as a literary polemicist are those expressing his opinion of "culteranismo" or "cultism" in poetry.² This literary phenomenon finds native antecedents in earlier Spanish poets such as Alfonso X (1226-1284), Juan de Mena (1411-1456), Juan de Padilla (1468-1522) and Fernando de Herrera (1534-1597), and it reflects a Baroque tendency

---

¹ As would be expected of a man of his public stature and literary reputation, Quevedo wrote brief criticisms of publications by his contemporaries; the following is a list of the works for which he prepared prologues: *El buen repúblico* by Agustín de Rojas; *Don Felipe el Prudente, segundo de este nombre, rey de las Españas y Nuevo-Mundo* by Lorenzo van der Hamen y León; *Historia de la prosperidad infeliz de Felipe de Catanea* by Pedro Mateo; *Panegírico al Sol* by Claudio Flavio Juliano el Apóstata (trans., Vicente Mariner, 1633); *Milicia evangélica para contrastar la idolatría de los gentiles...*, by Manuel Sarmiento de Mendoza; *Eternidad del rey don Felipe III...*, by Doña Ana de Castro Egas; *Eufrosina*, a play attributed to Jorge Ferreira de Vasconcelos; *Utopia* by Thomas More (trans., J. de Medinilla y Porres, 1637); and *Arte de ballestería y montería* by Alonso Martínez de Espinar. These short prologues, however, are generally formal and flattering in tone and do not offer any new insight into Quevedo's attitude toward literary expression.

² Unlike modern critics of Baroque poetry who employ the terms "culteranismo" and "gongorismo", Quevedo referred primarily to "poesía culta" or to "poetas cultos."

towards artificiality and affectation in the arts.[3] Its counterpart in France was called "préciosité," in England, "euphuism," and in Italy, "marinismo." It has been said that "el culteranismo aspira a crear un mundo de belleza absoluta, atendiendo sobre todo a los valores sensoriales."[4] To achieve this end, the cultist poet made frequent use of obscure metaphors, neologisms, mythological allusions, latinized syntax and extravagant and ornamental figures of speech. The result was a new poetic sect which one irate contemporary called "ciega, enigmática y confusa, engendrada en mal punto y nacida en cuarta luna."[5] Whether or not one has such an adverse opinion of "culteranismo," it is a fact that it represented a departure from the traditional classic style of verse-writing.

Quevedo's denunciation of "culteranismo" is found not only in his satiric essays *Aguja de navegar cultos, Cuento de cuentos,* and *La culta latiniparla,* but also in the *Sueños, El discurso de los diablos, La fortuna con seso, La vida del Buscón,* various satiric poems,[6] and the burlesque *Premáticas.*

In his merciless satire of contemporary "poetas cultos," Quevedo repeatedly criticizes the loss of purity and clarity of expression in their verse. As one of his biographers has written,

> El extravío literario más censurado por don Francisco fue el oscurecimiento de la idea, originado unas veces por las dicciones impropias y otras por el morboso deseo de originalidad, el cual como en el caso de Góngora y los demás culteranos, entierra el pensamiento bajo voces exóticas, metáforas extravagantes y varias otras forzadas figuras.[7]

From the date of the first national literary masterpiece, *Poema de Mío Cid* (c. 1140), until the advent of the seventeenth century,

---

[3] See E. Kent Kane, Chapters V and VI of *Gongorism and the Golden Age.* Chapel Hill: University of North Carolina Press, 1928, pp. 84-127.

[4] J. García López, *Literatura española,* 5th ed., Barcelona: Editorial Teide, 1959, p. 222.

[5] Francisco de Cascales, Epístola VIII in *Cartas Filológicas,* ed. Justo García Soriano, Vol. I. Madrid: Espasa-Calpe, S. A., 1930, p. 176.

[6] See: "¡Qué preciosos son los dientes," Obras II (1964), 264-265; "Leí los rudimentos de la aurora," p. 384, and "Con tres estilos alanos," pp. 405-406.

[7] Lucio Pabón Núñez, *Quevedo: Político de la oposición.* Bogotá: Editorial Agra, 1949, p. 30.

Spanish literature had favored a tradition of unaffected and realistic expression, exemplified by such works as *El Libro de Buen Amor, La Celestina, El Lazarillo de Tormes* and the poetry of Fray Luis de León. The most outstanding literary critics and interpreters of literary precepts in the sixteenth century maintained the value of clarity and verisimiltude in artistic composition. Quevedo's reaction to the artificiality of "culteranismo" was thus a reaffirmation of traditional literary principles.

The best example of the traditional exposition of literary precepts during the Golden Age is found in the writing of Alonso López Pinciano, a well-known interpreter of Aristotle. Pinciano's principal work, *Philosophia Antigua Poética* (1596) expounds the theories of Aristotle's *Poetics* and adapts them to the Renaissance mentality.[8] During this period, as Amezúa y Mayo points out, there were accepted rules of composition which were imposed upon all writers, and they in turn were accustomed to such norms of procedure:

> Todavía el imperio del "magister dixit" pitagórico sobrevive e impera; la autoridad de los clásicos es acatada casi por todos, y singularmente en materia literaria la de Aristóteles, a cuyos dictados se someten poetas y dramaturgos con sumisa docilidad.[9]

The sixth "epístola" of Pinciano's *Philosophia* discusses the precepts of poetic language. There are, according to the author, certain "vocablos peregrinos" which ought to be used with the greatest caution by the poet: they consist of those words which are borrowed from another language and those which the poet invents on his own.[10] The poet must be careful not to abuse his freedom by employing these "vocablos peregrinos" too frequently and in a manner which might obscure his verse:

> Confiesso que tiene necesidad de la templanca y prudencia esta mezcla de vocablos propios y muchos de los peregrinos

---

[8] See Sanford Shepard, *El Pinciano y las teorías literarias del Siglo de Oro*. Madrid: Editorial Gredos, 1962, p. 27.

[9] Agustín González de Amezúa y Mayo, *Cervantes, Creador de la novela corta española*, Vol. I. Madrid: Consejo Superior de Investigaciones Científicas, 1953, p. 127.

[10] López Pinciano, *Philosophia Antigua Poética,* ed. A. Carballo Picazo, Vol. II. Madrid: Consejo Superior de Investigaciones Científicas, 1953, p. 127.

> metaphóricos para que la frasi [sic] poética sea la que debe, porque de tal manera se podria hazer la mezcla, que quedasse muy fea y abominable, no sólo no emendada. Tenga, pues, la frasi [sic] poética muchos vocablos propios y, de los peregrinos metafóricos, más, de los forasteros, hechos y absoletos [sic], digo, de los ya olvidados y de los alterados en cuerpo, sean muy pocos. De los demás alterados en el ánima, dichos tropos, medianamente, y con mucha variedad dellos, porque no cansen; y assí quedará la oración y frasi [sic] poética no sólo no bárbara, pero emendada y muy agradable con la novedad que trae consigo. Desto mismo que acabo de dezir resultará también la claridad de la oración, la qual dicha claridad dize Aristóteles que es la principal virtud de la oración, porque, siendo pocos, los forasteros vocablos y los hechos y absoletos [sic], no serán parte para escurecerla; que los demás vocablos peregrinos no la hazen escura, si son bien traydos, pues ni las alteraciones de los vocablos en el cuerpo ni en el ánima suelen hazer escuridad, antes las metháphoras, cuyo uso es más necesario y más orna y menos cansa, aclaran mucho lo oración. [11]

In spite of the vagueness of his statements, Pinciano is explicit in his emphasis on the importance of clarity as the first virtue to be sought in writing. He recognizes, however, that there are certain excusable reasons for obscurity in poetry, either when a poet does not wish to be understood or when a reader is not knowledgeable enough to understand the poet. [12] The one unpardonable source of obscurity is the lack of skill on the part of the poet:

> La tercera escuridad es mala y viciosa, que nunca buen poeta usó, la qual nace por falta de ingenio de invención o de elocución, digo, porque trae conceptos intricados y difíciles, o dispone, o por mejor dezir, confunde los vocablos de manera que no se deja entender la oración. [13]

Could Pinciano have been thinking of the "cultists" who were just gathering force as a poetic movement when he wrote the *Philoso-*

---

[11] Ibid., pp. 159-60.
[12] Ibid., pp. 161-162.
[13] Ibid., p. 162.

phia?[14] Whether or not this was the case, Pinciano's theories are significant to the study of Quevedo's critical attitude toward "culteranismo" as they represent the tradition of adherence to classical literary precepts which reached its peak during the Golden Age.

Quevedo's allegiance to the classical tradition of literary norms is apparent in his satiric jabs at "poetas cultos." In *La fortuna con seso y la hora de todos* (1636), he mocks the obscurity of a poet whose verses defy understanding:

> Estaba un poeta en un corrillo, leyendo una canción cultísima, tan atestada de latines y tapida de jerigonzas, tan zabucada de cláusulas, tan cortada de paréntesis, que el auditorio quedó en ayunas. Cogióle la Hora en la cuarta estancia, y a la oscuridad de la obra, que era tanta que no se vía la mano, acudieron lechuzas y murciélagos, y los oyentes, encendiendo linternas y candelillas, oían de ronda la musa, a quien llaman "la enemiga del día que el negro manto descoge." Llegóse uno tanto con un cabo de vela al poeta... que se encendió al papel por en medio. Dábase el autor a los diablos, de ver quemada su obra, cuando el que la pegó fuego le dijo: "Estos versos no pueden ser claros y tener luz si no los queman; más resplandecen luminaria que canción."[15]

This amusing sketch aptly reveals Quevedo's attitude toward the cultist poet to whom he also referred as "vuestra diabledad, príncipe de las tinieblas."[16]

Quevedo's aversion to cultism was based upon practical and esthetic criteria. This bizarre form of poetry was not only intellectually puzzling, but also devoid of the simple beauty which accompanies clarity of thought. Primarily, however, Quevedo resented the effect that cultist poetry was having upon the Castilian language. In order to give a more esoteric tone to their poetry, the cultists had borrowed words from Latin and contrived their own special lexicon, avoiding the use of common vocabulary whenever possible. In the following excerpt from one of his romances, Quevedo parodies this technique and mocks its adherents:

---

[14] Sanford Shepard thinks that this "tercera escuridad" may have been a veiled reference to cultism. See *El Pinciano y las teorías literarias...*, p. 68.
[15] *Obras* I (1964), 233.
[16] *Discurso de todos los diablos*, *Obras* I (1964), 214.

... ...
Si bien el palor ligustre
desfallece los candores,
cuando muchos esplendores
conduce a poco palustre,
construye el aroma ilustre
víctima de tanto culto,
presintiendo de tu bulto
que rayos fulmina horrendo.
Ni me entiendes, ni me entiendo.
Pues cátate, que soy culto. [17]
... ...

The poets who espoused "culteranismo" were not writing for the enjoyment of the masses: "El escritor evita todo aquello que pueda ser comprendido por el vulgo, porque sólo le interesa despertar la admiración de un público selecto, lo que le lleva a la creación de un tipo de arte únicamente accesible a unos pocos." [18] In contrast to the plays of Lope de Vega which were written expressly for the general public, cultist poetry represented a conscious effort to avoid contact with the average mentality. It is not surprising, therefore, that the pedantry and affectations which characterized the cultist literary style soon became part of the speech habits of snobs and social climbers in the Court. Quevedo was particularly critical of the multitude of females who adopted this habit and, burlesquing their inane affectations, he wrote *La culta latiniparla* (1629). In this short work, his cryptic humor reaches an apogee:

> Al moño en culto llamará *herencia,* pues queda de las difuntas; y en plusquamculto dirá: Traigo el eco del malo rizado, o el enemigo sin di" (pues *dimoño* es el enemigo, y en quitándole el *di,* es moño, diablo mudo); y también le llamará el *casi-diablo*; y advierta no resbale, y le llame el cachidiablo de pelo. [19]

Another common custom among "poetas cultos" was the frequent use of mixed metaphors, so incongruous that their meaning was obscured. Quevedo's response to this was again satirical:

---

[17] "Con tres estilos alanos," *Obras* II (1964), 405.
[18] García López, p. 220.
[19] *Obras* I (1964), 375.

> ... ...
> Eran las mujeres antes
> de carne y de huesos hechas,
> ya son de rosas y flores,
> jardines y primaveras.
> Hortelano de facciones,
> ¿qué sabor queréis que tenga
> una mujer ensalada
> toda de plantas y hierbas?
> ¿Cuánto mejor te sabrá
> sin corales una jeta,
> que con claveles dos labios,
> mientras no fueres abeja?
> ¡Oh cultos de Satanás,
> que a las facciones blasfemas
> con que piden, con que toman,
> andáis vistiendo de estrellas! [20]
> ... ...

The beauty of the woman, obscured by the poet's choice of ridiculous metaphors, may be compared by inference to the beauty of the Castilian language sullied by cultist impurities. Quevedo's verses here are reminiscent of Cervantes' *El Licenciado Vidriera* in which the protagonist, Tomás Rodaja, expounds a similar judgement of contemporary poets:

> Otra vez le preguntaron qué era la causa de que los poetas, por la mayor parte, eran pobres. Respondió que porque ellos querían, pues estaba en su mano ser ricos, si se sabían aprovechar de la ocasión que por momentos traían entre las manos, que eran las de sus damas, que todas eran riquísimas en extremo, pues tenían los cabellos de oro, la frente de plata bruñida, los ojos de verdes esmeraldas, los dientes de marfil, los labios de coral y la garganta de cristal, transparente, y que lo que lloraban eran líquidas perlas; y más, que lo que sus plantas pisaban, por dura y estéril tierra que fuese, al momento producía jazmines y rosas; y que su aliento era de puro ámbar, almizcle y algalia; y que todas estas cosas eran señales y muestras de su mucha riqueza. [21]

---

[20] "¡Qué preciosos son los dientes," *Obras* II (1964), 265.
[21] Miguel de Cervantes Saavedra, *Novelas ejemplares,* ed. F. Rodríguez Marín, Vol. II. Madrid: Espasa-Calpe, S. A., 1957, pp. 48-49.

Quevedo professed a conservative attitude toward the use of the Castilian language much like that of Cervantes. His own lexical dexterity must have made it difficult for Quevedo to accept neologisms which were unnecessary and often absurd substitutes for traditional vocabulary. He had little patience with those who sought novelty for its own sake, as this quote from *Origen y definición de la necedad* (1624) makes clear: "Se declara y desde luego se da por necio de todos cuatro costados, al que por su lengua y autoridad quiere introducir nuevos modos de hablar y ser vocabulario de su tiempo." [22]

For the same reasons, Quevedo was equally critical of another contemporary fad, the use of popular expressions of the "germanía," or lower classes, by educated Spaniards. [23] In his opinion, this form of bastardization was as reprehensible as the cultist affectation, and to express his scorn for these tedious and vulgar impurities he wrote *Cuento de cuentos donde se leen juntas las vulgaridades rústicas que aun duran en nuestra habla* (1626). In the prologue-dedication which precedes the satiric "cuento," Quevedo describes the varied origins of the Spanish language which, he says, is like a poor man's cloak, "que son tantos los remiendos, que su principio se equivoca con ellos." [24] He admits that certain studies have been made of the origin of contemporary vocabulary, but he disdains their findings as "cosa más entretenida que demostrada." [25] Apparently overlooking Nebrija's *Arte de la lengua castellana* (1492), Quevedo laments the lack of grammatical texts in Castilian: "Ninguno ha escrito gramática; y hablamos la costumbre, no la verdad, con solecismos." [26] He then offers a long list of examples of verbal impurities which had become accepted as correct usage in Castilian; some of them are as follows:

> El *alma* decimos; y supuesto que *el alma bueno* no se puede decir, *el*, que es artículo masculino, ha de ser *la*, y pronunciar *la alma*.

---

[22] *Obras* I (1964), 68 (Variantes).
[23] For a description of the "germanía," see José Deleito y Pinuela *La mala vida en la España de Felipe IV*. Madrid: Espasa-Calpe, S. A., 1959, p. 123.
[24] *Obras* I (1964), 366.
[25] *Obras* I (1964), 366.
[26] *Obras* I (1964), 366.

No quiero nada peca en lo de las dos negaciones, y debe decirse *quiero nada*.

Bien considerable es el entremetimiento desta palabra *mente*, que se anda enfadando las cláusulas y paseándose por las voces *eternamente, ricamente, gloriosamente, altamente, santamente*, y esta porfía sin fin. ¿Hay necedad tan repetida de todos, que cursa cosa que algún letor se me quiera excusar de no haberla dicho?

Mal hablado llaman al que habla mal, habiéndole de llamar *mal hablador*.

Mire lo que le digo, decimos todos por *óigame*; pues no se parecen los ojos y las orejas. *Aqueste,* por *este*; *agora,* por *ahora*. Son infinitas las veces que, pudiendo escoger, usamos lo peor.[27]

Quevedo's criticism of "vulgaridades rústicas" recalls Don Quijote's censure of Sancho Panza's peculiar manner of speech: "Mira, Sancho, no te digo yo que parece mal un refrán traído a propósito; pero cargar y ensartar refranes a troche moche hace la plática desmayada y baja."[28] Like Don Quijote, however, Quevedo himself indulged in the use of popular expressions in his satire, thereby unwittingly condoning their existence and adding to their perpetuity. Moreover, as E. Mérimée has noted: "Par cette crainte de la vulgarité, Quevedo se rapprochait des cultistes."[29]

Although his opposition to both the pedantic and the vulgar may seem hypercritical, it is strong evidence of Quevedo's preference for the traditional, well-established norms of speech and writing. In theory, if not always in practice, he condemned the innovations which threatened to undermine the clarity and purity of the Castilian language.

His Attack against Góngora

In the words of Quevedo's first biographer, Pablo Antonio de Tarsia, "Toda la vida de don Francisco fué una milicia continua-

---

[27] *Obras* I (1964), 366.
[28] Miguel de Cervantes Saavedra, *El ingenioso hidalgo Don Quijote de la Mancha,* eds. J. García Soriano and J. García Morales, Madrid: Aguilar, 1957, p. 1457.
[29] E. Mérimée, *Essai sur la vie et les œuvres de Francisco de Quevedo 1580-1645.* Paris: 1886, p. 340.

da." [30] As has been seen in the course of this study, Quevedo's life was marked by frequent changes of fortune often caused by his own belligerence. He was not an easy man to deal with, and his literary contemporaries were constantly at odds with him. [31] The most notorious manifestation of his pugnaciousness, however, was the long feud which Quevedo had with Luis de Góngora y Argote, the Cordoban poet who became the leader of the cultist movement.

The first evidences of this rivalry date back to 1603 when Quevedo, Góngora's junior by nineteen years, wrote a scathing poetic attack against one of Góngora's recent compòsitions, "¿Qué lleva el señor Esgueva?" an exceedingly coarse letrilla about a river which flowed through Valladolid. [32] This is a portion of Quevedo's initial attack:

> Ya que coplas componéis,
> ved que dicen los poetas
> que, siendo para secretas,
> muy públicas las hacéis.
> Cólico dicen tenéis,
> pues por la boca purgáis;
> satírico diz que estáis,
> a todos nos dais matraca;
> descubierto habéis la caca
> con las cacas que cantáis.
>
> De vos dicen por ahí
> Apolo y todo su bando
> que sois poeta nefando,
> pues cantáis el culo así.
> Por lo cual me han dicho a mí
> que desde hoy en adelante
> diga que obras vuestras cante,
> por el mandato de Apolo,
> con el son de un rabel solo,
> un rabadán ignorante.
>
> ... ...

---

[30] *Vida de Don Francisco de Quevedo y Villegas* (1658-1662) in *Obras* II (1952), 885.

[31] See M. Romera-Navarro, "Querellas y rivalidades en las academias del siglo XVII," *Hispanic Review*, Vol. IX, 1941, pp. 494-499.

[32] See Góngora, *Obras completas*, ed. J. Millé y Giménez and I. Millé y Giménez. Madrid: Aguilar, 1956, pp. 327-329.

> Vuestros conceptos alabo,
> pues de puro buena pesca,
> los hacéis a la gatesca,
> pues los hacéis por el rabo.
> Tenéis un ingenio bravo,
> hacéis cosas peregrinas,
> vuestras coplas son divinas;
> sino que dice un doctor
> que vuestras letras, señor,
> se han convertido en letrinas. [33]
> ... ...

Góngora lost no time in returning Quevedo's hostilities with equally shocking insults; addressing his reply to "Miguel Musa," one of Quevedo's pseudonyms, he wrote the following in the same year, 1603:

> Musa, que sopla y no inspira,
> y sabe que lo traidor
> poner los dedos mejor
> en mi bolsa que en su lira,
> no es de Apolo (que es mentira)
> hija Musa tan bellaca,
> sino de él que hurtó la vaca
> al pastor. A tal persona
> pongámosle su Helicona
> en las montañas de Jaca. [34]
> ... ...

From this date until Góngora's death in 1627, the two poets continued their feud.

What actually precipitated Quevedo's attack is still a matter of conjecture. In view of his own frequent sallies into the foul and the obscene,[35] he must have had more motivation than his opposition to a similar indiscretion on Góngora's part. Nor is Quevedo's combative nature enough cause to explain the outbreak of hostility. A

---

[33] *Obras* II (1964), 443-444.

[34] Góngora, *Obras completas,* pp. 417-418.

[35] This is evident by 1603 in parts of Quevedo's *Capitulaciones matrimoniales* and in his *Premáticas y aranceles generales.* Later, in 1620, he wrote *Gracias y desgracias del ojo del culo,* undoubtedly his most vulgar composition. See *Obras* I (1964), 95-100.

more plausible explanation is found when one understands the extent of Góngora's development of cultist techniques by the year 1603. As E. K. Kane not without prejudice points out, the *Polifemo* and *Soledades*, written around 1613, are the best known, but not the first works of cultism by Góngora: "... the germ of Góngora's revolting malady is almost congenital, and while it incubates progressively, it does so with such rapidity and completeness that before 1600, or at most 1605, every symptom of Góngora's grotesque poetry had fully developed." [36] It is possible that Quevedo witnessed this development and decided to make known his opposition to Góngora's bizarre innovations at a time when his own popularity in the Court was growing and his opinions were meriting respect. [37] Why then did Quevedo choose to attack one of Góngora's traditional-style poems rather than a cultist poem? Perhaps the reason for this was that Quevedo wished to discredit Góngora, but not at the expense of jeopardizing his own recently established literary position in the Court. By ridiculing him, he might be able to arrest the growth of Góngora's cultist retinue without openly attacking cultism itself which was very popular in court circles.

Quevedo's poem of 1603 attacking Góngora was not the first time which he expressed concern for current trends in Castilian poetry. In a burlesque *Premática* which he wrote in 1600, he declared, "En los poetas hay mucho que reformar y lo mejor fuera quitarlos del todo." [38] Quevedo had reason to be worried. The art of writing poetry was no longer cultivated exclusively by a small minority of serious and well-educated poets. A surfeit of leisure time had brought about an unusual phenomenon: "La manía de componer versos se hizo epidémica: príncipes y condes, guerreros y hombres de Estado, abogados y médicos, sacerdotes y frailes se dedicaron a esta tarea, y hasta los jornaleros y campesinos no se quedaron atrás." [39] This situation could only signify an increase in

---

[36] Kane, p. 72. Kane enumerates these symptoms as follows: neologisms, hyperbates, apostrophes, puns, pedantry, altisonance, obscurity, oxymoron, mythological allusions and grotesque metaphors. See pp. 74-80.

[37] Quevedo had gone to the Court in Valladolid in 1600 where his poetry was praised. In 1604, eighteen of his poems were included in Pedro de Espinosa's *Flores de poetas ilustres*, a tribute to his success.

[38] *Premática que este año de 1600 se ordenó*, Obras I (1964), 59.

[39] Adolfo F. Schack, *Historia de la literatura y del arte dramático en España*, Vol. II. Madrid: Imprenta y fundición de M. Tello, 1886, p. 151.

mediocre verse and a more widespread search for stylistic novelties. As E. K. Kane has suggested, Góngora was unable to achieve recognition for his poetry in the traditional style, so he decided to satisfy the public thirst for novelty with something entirely different.[40] A departure from the mainstream of traditional Spanish poetry, Góngora's innovations supplied an outlet for many aspiring poets who sought to avoid the contagion of the masses. If Quevedo realized the full nature of Góngora's background, it evidently did not diminish his animosity toward him.

If we accept the fact that Quevedo began his campaign against cultist poetry in 1603, then he must be recognized as the first of a sizeable group of impugners of Góngora's cultism. According to Menéndez y Pelayo, the opposition was led by the following authors: Pedro de Valencia in *Censura de Las Soledades, Polifemo y obras de don Luis de Góngora* (1613); Francisco de Cascales in *Cartas Filológicas* (1627); Juan de Jáuregui in *Discurso poético* (1623); Lope de Vega in *De la nueva poesía* (1611); Francisco de Quevedo; and Manuel de Faria y Sousa in his Commentary of 1639 to Luis de Camões *Lusíades*.[41] With the exception of Quevedo, the earliest date of any formal criticism of cultism by these writers is Lope's short discourse of 1611 which was published with *La Philomena*.[42] It is my contention that Quevedo anticipated this opposition by several years. In 1603, and again in 1609, he wrote several poems attacking Góngora's poetry.[43] The following verse

---

[40] Kane, p. 81.

[41] See Menéndez y Pelayo, *Historia de las ideas estéticas en España*, Vol. II in *Edición Nacional de las Obras Completas*. Madrid: Consejo Superior de Investigaciones Científicas, 1962, p. 330. I have used the dates supplied by Menéndez y Pelayo for the works of Valencia, Lope de Vega and Faria y Sousa. See pp. 330-350.

[42] See Lope de Vega, *De la nueva poesía* in *Colección escogida de obras no dramáticas*. Madrid: Ediciones Atlas (BAE), 1950, pp. 137-142.

[43] These poems are:
"Ya que coplas componéis" (1603)
"En lo sucio que has cantado" (1603)
"Yo te untaré mis versos con tocino" (1609)
"Poeta de '¡Oh qué lindico!'" (1609)
"Vuestros coplones, cordobés soñado" (1609)
The dates are those established by L. Astrana Marín, ed. in *Obras* II (1952), 173-178.

written in 1609 illustrates Quevedo's vehement objection to the style of his adversary:

> Poeta de "¡Oh, qué lindico!,"
> verdugo de los vocablos,
> que a puras vueltas de cuerda
> los hacéis que digan algo;
> ... ...
> Poeta de bujarrones
> y sirena de los rabos,
> pues son de ojos de culo
> todas tus obras o rasgos;
> ... ...
> no es posible que seas hijo
> de ciudad a cuyos partos
> debe Roma y todo el mundo
> los Sénecas y Lucanos.
> Córdoba no te parió,
> si no es que se hizo preñado
> algún arrabal de ti,
> y que naciste en el campo.
> Racionero dicen que eres,
> mas yo irracional te hallo,
> aunque en la cola y lo sucio
> canónigo eres del Rastro.
> Góngora te llaman todos,
> ilustre apellido y claro,
> mas viénete como al Potro
> el Manrique, por su amo.
> ¿Quién te mete con los griegos
> aun no siendo tú troyano?
> ¿Por qué de lo que no has visto
> hablas como papagayo?
> ... ...
> Gongorilla, Gongorilla,
> de parte de Dios te mando
> que, en penitencia de haber
> hecho soneto tan malo,
> andes como Juan Garín,
> doce años como gato,
> y con tu soneto al cuello,
> por escarmiento y espanto.
> Y advierte que si respondes
> a estos versos, mentecato,
> que te aguarda por respuesta
> otro romance más largo.

> Y que desde aqueste punto
> toda mi vida consagro
> a decir mal de tus cosas,
> aun entre sueños hablando. [44]
> ... ...

The fact that these poems, and those which followed for many years thereafter, are so crude and libelous in tone may account for the relative lack of attention given to them in comparison to Quevedo's prose criticism of cultism. And yet, these verses, most of them in sonnet form, are the ultimate mockery of the Cordoban poet's style because they are often more "gongoristic" than Góngora. [45] To burlesque the technique of his rival, Quevedo once wrote his own satiric counsel on how to be a "poeta culto" which is found in his *Aguja de navegar cultos* (1625):

RECETA

> Quien quisiere ser Góngora en un día
> la jeri (aprenderá) gonza siguiente:
> *fulgores, arrogar, joven, presiente,*
> *candor, construye, métrica, armonía;*
> *poco, mucho, sí, no, purpuracía,*
> *neutralidad, conculca, erige, mente,*
> *pulsa, ostenta, librar, adolescente,*
> *señas, traslada, pira, frustra, harpía,*
> *cede, impide, cisuras, petulante,*
> *palestra, liba, meta, argento, alterna,*
> *si bien, disuelve, émulo, canoro.*
> Use mucho de *líquido* y de *errante,*
> su poco de *noturno* y de *caverna,*
> anden listos *lívor, adunco* y *poro*;
> que ya toda Castilla
> con sola esta cartilla
> se abrasa de poetas babilones,
> escribiendo sonetos confusiones;
> y en la Mancha pastores y gañanes,
> atestadas de ajos las barrigas
> hacen ya soledades como migas. [46]

---

[44] *Obras* II (1964), 445-446.
[45] See Manuel Durán, "Algunos neologismos en Quevedo," *Modern Language Notes,* Vol. LXX, February 1955, pp. 117-119.
[46] *Obras* I (1964), 362.

One of Quevedo's sonnets written to Góngora in 1619 constitutes the ultimate parody of cultist neologisms. In this intentional mockery of Góngora's style, Quevedo joins the ranks of what he calls "poetas babilones,/ escribiendo sonetos confusiones":

> Sulquivagante, pretemor de Estolo,
> pues que lo expuesto al Noto solificas
> y obtusas speluncas comunicas,
> despecho de las musas a ti solo,
>
> huye no carpa de tu Dafne Apolo
> surculus slabros de teretes picas,
> porque con tus per-versos damnificas
> los institutos de tu sacro Tolo.
>
> Has acabado aliundo su Parnaso;
> adulteras la casta poesía,
> ventilas bandos, niños inquietas,
>
> parco ceruleo, veterano vaso:
> pía-culos perpetro tu porfía,
> estrupando neotéricos poetas. [47]

Manuel Durán has said of his poem and another similar to it: "No conocemos otro ejemplo de libertad en la creación semejante a estos en toda la literatura española clásica. El sentido de las palabras queda subordinado a la impresión caótica y artificial del conjunto, en violenta mueca contra el culteranismo." [48] Quevedo's imagination and ingenuity in creating new words did not, however, divert him from his primary purpose of insulting Góngora. Not only does he rebuke his adversary by saying, "adulteras la casta poesía," but he also injects the entire sonnet with disguised profanity. [49]

In a conscious effort to ridicule Góngora, Quevedo had invented a sonnet which could not be more alien to his traditionalistic taste. Unfortunately, these poems were more amusing than edifying, and his bizarre imitation of Góngora was, in itself, so obscure

---

[47] *Obras* II (1964), 440.

[48] Manuel Durán, "Algunos neologismos en Quevedo," p. 119.

[49] Quevedo's profanities in this poem are what might be called "bathroom humor," evident in such words as "surculus" and "pía-culos." It is the continuation of the same insults found in his first poems to Góngora.

that the message of censure has been lost in a complex of fabricated absurdities. The fate which he later predicted for those who followed his instructions for being "culto" in *Aguja de navegar cultos* was verified: "... serás culto, y lo que escribieres oculto, y lo que hablares lo hablarás a bulto. Y Dios tenga en el cielo el castellano y le perdone." [50]

From 1603 until Góngora's death in 1627, Quevedo's animosity did not diminish in intensity. During this same period, Góngora continued to write sporadically in the cultist manner, but by far the majority of his poetic output was traditional in style. [51] Quevedo appears to have been blind to the dual nature of Góngora's poetry, for his poems never praise the traditional style of his rival. Then again, perhaps the very fact that he thought that Góngora betrayed his own talents and capitalized upon the popularity of cultism in the Court made Quevedo disdain him all the more. Whatever the precise reason, Quevedo portrayed Góngora as an anathema to poetry. The final lines of an epitaph he wrote to the Cordoban poet aptly express this sentiment:

> ....
> Fuése con Satanás, culto y pelado:
> ¡mirad si Satanás es desdichado! [52]

THE EDITOR

When Góngora died in 1627, Quevedo did not stop his war against cultism. His personal feud was terminated, but he adopted other measures of combatting the poetry which Góngora had come to represent. As E. K. Kane laments, cultist poetry did not die with Góngora: "As the century wore on, gongorism seemed to increase rather than diminish, the only decline being in the quality, if indeed such a thing can be imagined." [53]

---

[50] *Obras* I (1964), 363.
[51] Less than one-fifth of Góngora's poetry was cultist in style, according to Kane, p. 69.
[52] "Este que en negra tumba rodeado," *Obras* II (1964), 443.
[53] Kane, p. 51.

Unlike other opponents of this poetic movement, Quevedo did not limit his attack to negativistic criticism and satire. He took a positive step toward counteracting cultism by seeking previously unpublished models of the traditional style of poetry which he favored to offer to the public. In 1629, Quevedo edited and published for the first time the poetry of Fray Luis de León and, in 1631, the poetry of Francisco de la Torre. [54]

Quevedo's selection of Fray Luis' poetry as an antidote to cultism is understandable for several reasons. Like Quevedo, Fray Luis was a humanist who knew the Greek and Latin classics and imitated them frequently. His poetry, in contrast to the verse "al itálico modo" of Garcilaso's generation, was essentially religious in tone and revealed a moral preoccupation similar to that of Quevedo. A current of Stoicism pervaded Fray Luis' poetry, "... el estoicismo tradicional del alma española, aquel sentido moralista que ya había sido elemento esencial y permanente en la lírica castellana de los siglos precedentes hasta la revolución petrarquista, y que ahora va a cobrar nueva vida en la obra de Fray Luis de León. ..." [55] Not only in his poetry, but also in his life as a scholar and theologian, Fray Luis set an example of the highest moral and intellectual standards. Like Quevedo, Fray Luis knew the discomfort of imprisonment and he endured this persecution with Stoic fortitude. Aside from these factors which Quevedo must have admired as would a kindred spirit, Fray Luis' poetry was his chosen model because it was unencumbered by rhetoric or obscure vocabulary and syntax. It was, as one can see in a poem like "Noche serena," an expression of the poet's desire to flee from the darkness of material reality to the luminosity of the heavens. As Pedro Salinas has written:

> Heaven is light. But beside that, heaven is the revelation of truth, the explanation of the universe. Fray Luis was a platonist, and for him heaven is the kingdom of ideas

---

[54] I shall limit my discussion to the edition of Fray Luis de León's poetry as it is more significant for present purposes. Francisco de la Torre's poetry is not as well-known; indeed, at one time, it was thought that Quevedo himself was the author, but this theory has since been discredited. See E. Mérimée, pp. 316-323.

[55] Manuel de Montoliu, *El alma de España y sus reflejos en la literatura del Siglo de Oro*. Barcelona: Editorial Cervantes, 1942, p. 452.

and pure spirits. In his poetry the Christian ideal and platonic clarity form an ideal world that is unequaled in our lyric. We said luminosity, light. This is the impression of the senses. But we would add now: clarity, that is, the light of the intelligence. The luminous in him has two phases: seeing and understanding. Heaven is supreme light and supreme intelligence. The joy of the soul is to be saved in the comprehension of the world, which from below could not be understood, was all confusion. [56]

The style and content of Fray Luis' verse, which harmonized so closely with Quevedo's ideals, were the appropriate rebuttal to the poetry of cultism.

Quevedo expressed his preference for this classic and traditional style in a letter to the Conde-Duque de Olivares to whom he dedicated his edition of Fray Luis' work. [57] The fact that he singled out the Conde Duque for this particular dedication is significant. Quevedo says that he chose Olivares because of his fame as a protector of the arts:

> ...le dedico estos escritos de tanto precio, señor... porque no conozco otro que con tal afecto y estimación haya admitido autores desta nota, ni quien deje de molestar la atención ajena, hablando o escribiendo, con estas demasías mendigadas, si no es vuestra excelencia. [58]

In yet another part of the dedication, Quevedo praises Olivares' literary style: "... pues siempre ha escrito tan fácil nuestra lengua, y tan sin reprehensión. ..." [59] However, the Conde-Duque's biographer, Gregorio Marañón, feels that Quevedo's flattery was exaggerated. The Conde-Duque was a moving orator, but his prose style in written documents was less polished:

> ...a pesar de su erudición, ...la cualidad más característica de su estilo epistolar es ese descuido, como de conversación,... impuesto sin duda, por la tremenda prisa de sus quehaceres. Con el tiempo, este descuido se fue acrecen-

---

[56] Pedro Salinas, *Reality and the Poet in Spanish Poetry*. Baltimore: The Johns Hopkins Press, 1940, p. 111.
[57] See "Al Excelentísimo Señor Conde-Duque," *Obras* I (1964), 466-473.
[58] *Obras* I (1964), 473.
[59] *Obras* I (1964), 467.

tando, así como la incongruencia del pensamiento, que siempre tuvo. [60]

In the same dedication, Quevedo continues his praise of Olivares' style by saying: "Ni ha mostrado vuestra excelencia afición a otro estilo." [61] The falsehood of this statement is evident when one discovers that the Conde-Duque protected Góngora and treated him with particular affection in the Court; and as Marañón writes, "En sus dichos y en sus hechos, Don Gaspar fué uno de los más conspicuos personajes del gongorismo. ..." [62]

Why did Quevedo attribute qualities to the Conde-Duque which he did not possess? Quevedo knew from experience the importance of obtaining the privado's favor for the ultimate success of his project. Moreover, he must have thought that Olivares might be influenced by a certain amount of discreet flattery. It is also likely that Quevedo hoped that this would help to attenuate the Conde-Duque's cultist tendencies and convince him of the need to set an example of clarity and purity of spoken and written Castilian in the Court.

His letter of dedication to Olivares is, in itself, a lengthy condemnation of cultism and a defense of the traditional style of poetry as characterized by Fray Luis de León, "... el mejor blasón de la habla castellana." [63] In this letter, Quevedo is obsessed by the desire to praise and to justify clarity of thought and expression. He says that throughout history, those who wrote "artes de poesía" maintained this standard which is universally accepted:

> Y en todas lenguas aquellos solos merecieron aclamación universal, que dieron luz a lo oscuro, y facilidad a lo dificultoso; que oscurecer lo claro, es borrar, y no escribir; y quien habla lo que otros no entienden, primero confiesa que no entiende lo que habla. [64]

This precept of good style as expressed by Quevedo recalls the following words from *Diálogo de la lengua* (1535) of another Spanish humanist, Juan de Valdés:

---

[60] G. Marañón, *El Conde-Duque de Olivares: La pasión de mandar*, 4th ed. Madrid: Espasa-Calpe, S. A., 1959, p. 144.
[61] "Al Excelentísimo...," *Obras* I (1964), 467.
[62] Marañón, pp. 152-153.
[63] "Al Excelentísimo...," *Obras* I (1964), 466.
[64] *Obras* I (1964), 466.

> ...todo el bien hablar castellano consiste en que digáis lo que queréis con las menos palabras que pudiéredes, de tal manera que, esplicando bien el conceto de vuestro ánimo y dando a entender lo que queréis dezir, de las palabras que pusiéredes en una cláusula o razón no se pueda quitar ninguna sin ofender o a la sentencia della o al encarecimiento o a la elegancia.[65]

Although almost a century separates these two writers, they both upheld the same precepts and were motivated by similar reactions against affectation and obscurity.[66]

It is interesting to note, with reference to the previous discussion of Pinciano, that in this letter, Quevedo's most oft-quoted authority of literary precepts is Aristotle. He is aware of the fact that his cultist contemporaries had tried to justify their outlandish style by citing the following words from Aristotle's *Poetics*:

> La virtud de la dicción ha de ser perspicua, no humilde: la que constare de nombres propios será perspicua; sea ejemplo de la humilde poesía de Cleofonte y de Stenelo. Aquélla es venerable y excluye todo lo que es plebeyo, que usa de vocablos peregrinos; peregrino llamo la variedad de lenguas, translación, extensión, y todo lo que es ajeno de lo propio.[67]

Quevedo says that those who have done this are in error: "... son hombres que despiden el estudio en llegando a la cláusula que desean. Aclaman estos renglones por texto expreso, en disculpa de los barbarismos y solecismos que escriben, de que resulta la enigma."[68] If they had read further in the *Poetics*, they would have noticed this qualification (the same one pointed out by Pinciano):

> Empero si alguno rebuja todas estas cosas juntas, o hará enigma u barbarismo; enigma, si amontona traslaciones: barbarismo, si lenguas.[69]

---

[65] Juan de Valdés, *Diálogo de la lengua*, ed. J. F. Montesinos. Madrid: Ediciones de "La Lectura," 1928, p. 155.

[66] Valdés opposed "los frívolos latinizantes del siglo xv," according to J. F. Montesinos, ed. in "Introducción," *Diálogo de la lengua*, p. LXIX.

[67] Cited by Quevedo, "Al Excelentísimo...," *Obras* I (1964), 466.

[68] *Obras* I (1964), 467.

[69] Cited by Quevedo, "Al Excelentísimo...," *Obras* I (1964), 467. It

Quevedo has little patience with the cultists. To him, they are the primary offenders against the Castilian language:

> De buena gana lloro la satisfacción con que se llaman hoy algunos *cultos,* siendo temerarios y monstruosos; osando decir que hoy se sabe hablar la lengua castellana, cuando no se sabe donde se habla, y en conversaciones aun de los legos tal algarabía se usa, que parece junta de diferentes naciones, y dicen que la enriquecen los que la confunden. [70]

He refers to cultism as "esta cizaña de nuestra habla." [71]

In direct contrast to cultist poets, Quevedo presents the poetry of Fray Luis de León, a model of purity and elegance:

> No tienen en nuestra España, en los grandes y famosos escritores de aquel tiempo, comparación las obras de fray Luis de León, ni en lo serio y útil de los intentos, ni en la dialéctica de los discursos, ni en la pureza de la lengua, ni en la facilidad de los números; ni en la claridad... [72]

Reiterating the supreme importance of clarity in writing, Quevedo cites Antonio Lullo's *De oratione*: " 'Ac de claritate quidem principio dicendum videtur: quae prima semper et maxima virtus existimata est orationis. ...' (Lo primero diremos de la claridad, que siempre es la primera y la mayor virtud de la oración. ...)" [73] In this regard, Fray Luis receives Quevedo's fullest admiration.

In effect, Quevedo's dedicatory letter to the Conde-Duque has served one purpose: not that of explicating the poetry of Fray Luis, but that of proving the virtue of clarity in poetry. The edition he compiled and published, therefore, was not an end in itself, but a means to an end. The ultimate, or perhaps ulterior, motive was, once again, to fortify the traditional values of Castilian poetry which were threatened by the captivating delirium of cultism.

---

should be noted that Quevedo refers directly to Aristotle, not mentioning Pinciano.

[70] *Obras* I (1964), 472.
[71] *Obras* I (1964), 473.
[72] *Obras* I (1964), 472.
[73] *Obras* I (1964), 472.

His Defense of Spanish Culture

Spain has had many critics of her culture, some motivated by feelings of inferiority, others by a conviction of superiority.[74] The stimulus for such commentary often arises from contact with other nations, as in the case of Juan de Valdés' *Diálogo de la lengua* (1535) or Miguel de Unamuno's *En torno al casticismo* (1895). This is also true of Quevedo's *España defendida y los tiempos de ahora* (1609), inspired by "... el ver maltratar con insolencia mi patria de los extranjeros, y los tiempos de ahora de los propios, no habiendo para ello más razón de tener a los forasteros invidiosos, y a los naturales que en esto se ocupan despreciados."[75]

In the prologue of this work, written in his youthful years, Quevedo laments two things:

> Tenemos dos cosas que llorar los españoles: la una lo que de nuestras cosas no se ha escrito, y lo otro que hasta ahora lo que se ha escrito ha sido tan malo, que viven contentas con su olvido las cosas a que no se han atrevido nuestros cronistas, escarmentadas de que las profanan y no las celebran.[76]

Spaniards have not written enough about their own country, and what little that has been written has done more harm than good. Quevedo was not ignorant of the wide acclaim given throughout Europe to Padre Bartolomé de las Casas' *La destruición de las Indias* (publ. 1552), an attack against the conduct of Spanish explorers and "encomenderos" toward the Indians of America. The "leyenda negra" originated by Las Casas was joyfully received by Europeans who resented Spain's political and religious hegemony; Las Casas' works were translated into every major European language and reprinted numerous times.[77] Upon concluding his prologue to *España defendida,* Quevedo makes specific reference to

---

[74] See Otis Green, Chapter IX, *Spain and the Western Tradition,* Vol. III. Madison: University of Wisconsin Press, 1964, pp. 250-279.

[75] *Obras* I (1964), 489. Quevedo left this work unfinished.

[76] *Obras* I (1964), 490-491.

[77] See Ramón Menéndez Pidal, *El Padre Las Casas: Su doble personalidad.* Madrid: Espasa-Calpe, S. A., 1963, p. 364.

Giról amo Benzoni who was the first Italian to echo Las Casas' accusations of Spanish cruelty in the New World: [78]

> Pues aún lo que tan dichosamente se ha descubierto y conquistado y reducido por nosotros en Indias, está disfamado con un libro impreso en Ginebra, cuyo autor fue un milanés, Jerónimo Bezón, cuyo título, porque convenga con la libertad del lugar y con insolencia del autor, dice: *Nuevas historias del Nuevo Mundo, de las cosas que los españoles han hecho en Las Indias occidentales hasta ahora y de su cruel tiranía entre aquellas gentes...* [79]

The time has come, says Quevedo, to counteract this type of slander and to rectify the mistaken impressions of Spain abroad: "Ya, pues, es razón que despertemos y logremos parte del ocio que alcanzamos en mostrar lo que es España y lo que ha sido siempre. ..." [80]

The first three chapters of *España defendida* are dedicated to (1) a description of Spain's topography and climate, (2) an investigation of ancient inhabitants and rulers of Spain, and (3) an analysis of the origin and etymology of the name "España."

Of the first topic he discusses, Quevedo says:

> ...es tal la tierra, fertilidad, sitio y clima de España, que tenemos en ella por güéspedes, olvidados de sus patrias, a todas las naciones, haciéndose en nuestra comunicación ricos y dejándonos con la suya pobres y engañados; que como dice Marcial, *semper (homo) bonus tiro es.* [81]

His obvious inference here is that Spaniards should be the ones to profit from their land, not foreigners.

In the second chapter, Quevedo examines an opinion valued as historical truth by some Spanish authors, [82] namely the opinion that the first rulers of Spain were descendants of Noah because Noah

---

[78] Ibid., p. 361.

[79] *Obras* I (1964), 491. Quevedo refers here to a later French edition (1579) of Benzoni's original Italian work, published in Venice in 1565. See Menéndez Pidal, *El Padre Las Casas...*, p. 361.

[80] *Obras* I (1964), 490.

[81] *Obras* I (1964), 492.

[82] Quevedo mentions the names of Florián de Ocampo, Padre Juan de Mariana, Mosén Diego de Valera and Fray Domingo de Baltanas as being among the guilty parties. *Obras* I (1964), 494-495.

came to Spain. After having enumerated the foundations (mostly linguistic analogies of names and places) presented for this opinion, Quevedo declares that he can find no valid historical proof to support them:

> Yo confieso que, aunque a parecer de los religiosos y observantes de la antigüedad, parecerá que quito en esto maliciosamente mucha honra a mi patria, que tengo por sospechosa y mal fundada ésta que usurpa el nombre de historia siendo fábula... [83]

In Quevedo's opinion, such false beliefs have originated from a desire to add glory to the national heritage by linking it to biblical history:

> Hay algunos que, así a su nobleza como a su ser, acogiéndose a la antigüedad, lo engrandecen y aumentan; y ciudades de los tiempos apartados hacen en sí y en sus cosas todo lo que les falta, confundiéndolo con los días, pues queda burlada cualquiera diligencia que pretenda examinar cosa que huyó a sagrado, donde no alcanza la memoria. [84]

Quevedo cannot agree with those who say that Noah came to Spain "porque hay un lugar que se llama Noela en Galicia y otro que se llama Noega en Asturias." [85] If such analogies are considered valid, he says, then by similar reasoning, Adam must have been in Spain too and founded the hamlet of Odom near Madrid, since in Syriac the Hebrew name "Adam" is written "Odom." [86] All of this, according to Quevedo, is "fábula," the fruit of vivid imaginations. Actually, the first historically authenticated event in Spain's antiquity was the Carthaginian occupation. [87]

Throughout this discussion, Quevedo is aware of the fact that he is willfully destroying a myth sustained by some of his compatriots. He contends, however, that revealing its fictional bases is not jeopardizing Spain's honor, for it is better to establish honor

---

[83] *Obras* I (1964), 495.
[84] *Obras* I (1964), 492.
[85] *Obras* I (1964), 494.
[86] *Obras* I (1964), 494.
[87] *Obras* I (1964), 495.

upon bases of historical truths than to invent stories which may disguise the truth: "... la antigüedad que tanto estiman los extranjeros, es por las muchas infamias que les disimula y desculpa." [88]

Why, one might ask at this point, does Quevedo attack this myth because of its weak historical backing while he defends the existence of Bernardo del Carpio [89] and the battle exploits of Santiago el Apóstol, patron saint of Spain? The criterion which Quevedo employed in choosing which myths to defend appears to be more than that of historical accuracy, for there is no reliable historical evidence to support any of the ones which have been mentioned. A closer look will show that Quevedo preferred to defend myths which had become traditional among the Spanish people as national myths, either in relation to their religious faith or in support of their political values. Such myths, like those connected with Santiago or Bernardo del Carpio, made up for their lack of historical foundation by having added moral substance to the Spanish spirit, by having contributed to the nation's ideals of political and religious unity. In Quevedo's words: "Más me enojó ver ... que salió otro, atreviéndosenos a la fe y a las tradiciones y a los santos, y no quiso que Santiago hubiese sido patrón de España ni venido a ella." [90] In contrast, the myth of the original rulers of Spain being descendants of Noah had no comparable value. It had not captured the imagination of the Spanish people, nor had it contributed to their ideals. According to Quevedo it was founded purely upon the egotistic aim of reinforcing Spain's antiquity and prestige, guided by a weak effort to trace the national history back to biblical times.

An additional reason for destroying this myth was that Quevedo had established what he considered a more valid proof of Spain's antiquity. In the third chapter of *España defendida,* he explains:

> No porque conmigo puedan algo las etimologías, que las más veces son obra del ingenio y no testimonios de la verdad, gasto en la razón del nombre de España este capítulo, sólo, porque en el origen vario de ése le recompensa mucha

---

[88] *Obras* I (1964), 492.
[89] See *Obras* I (1964), 490.
[90] *Obras* I (1964), 490.

de la antigüedad que en el capítulo pasado no he admitido, por mal deducida de los sueños de Anio. [91]

From his study of the origin of the word "España," Quevedo concludes that it came from the Greek "Pania" (meaning "land of the god, Pan," and also meaning "fortune") and the Hebrew "is" (meaning "man"), together forming "men of Pania." [92] The word "iberos" is, according to Quevedo, of Asiatic origin, "cosa que, ni nos quita gloria, ni nos ofende la antigüedad con que nacimos, que es igual con el tiempo. ..." [93]

After this introductory linguistic discussion, Quevedo turns in the fourth chapter to an analysis of the Castilian language, its antecedents, its grammar and its literary works. His underlying purpose, to prove the antiquity of Spain, is constant. However, he says that he has been further motivated to this defense by a statement made by the Flemish cartographer, Gerardus Mercator, which imputed severe shortcomings to the Spanish language and to Spanish scholars. [94] Quevedo's indignation at this insult is somewhat attenuated by his reasoning that foreigners cannot find fault with Spanish deeds, so they express their envy by unfounded criticism of Spanish culture. What they refuse to notice is that "... no sólo en todo género de letras no nos han excedido ningunos pueblos del mundo; pero que son pocos los que en copia y fama y elegancia de autores en el propio idioma y en el extranjero nos han igualado. ..." [95] He thus sets the stage for his subsequent defense of the cultural superiority of Spain over the rest of Europe.

With regard to the origin of the Castilian language, Quevedo enumerates the admixture of influences which have produced modern Spanish: Latin, Greek, Gothic ("godo"), Hebrew, Arabic and Syriac. In each case, he analyzes characteristic morphological and phonological changes, all the while demonstrating his own knowledge of these languages, in itself a refutation of Mercator's

---

[91] *Obras* I (1964), 496.
[92] *Obras* I (1964), 498.
[93] *Obras* I (1964), 500.
[94] See *Obras* I (1964), 502.
[95] *Obras* I (1964), 502.

insults to the ability of Spanish scholars. [96] As he mentions the influence of each language, Quevedo voices his disdain for foreign words incorporated into the original vocabulary of the ancient Spanish language. In reference to the Jewish influence, his anti-Semitism is evident in this comment: "¡Maldita inundación!" [97] Speaking of the Arabic and Carthaginian influences on Spanish vocabulary, he uses, respectively, the words "corrupción" and "detrimento." [98] Quevedo looks upon these borrowings as impurities, and he regrets the disappearance of the original mother tongue caused by centuries of linguistic change:

> Así que, siendo tanta con los días la mudanza de las lenguas, que ayer decían en España, vuestra señoría, y luego dijeron vueseñoría, y luego vuesia y ahora vusa, y toda esta mudanza he alcanzado yo en menos de veinte años, mal hace quien procura defender que desde el tiempo de Nuestra Señora se hablaba así como ahora, si apenas vocablo antiguo se conoce ya en las voces castellanas. [99]

The most interesting and original part of this chapter is Quevedo's effort to establish the antiquity of the Castilian tongue. In examining its alphabet and grammar, he finds that Spanish has more in common with ancient Hebrew than with Latin or Greek, thus proving "... que tiene nuestra lengua más antigüedad que la latina y griega en que no se diferencian sus letras ni gramática de las lenguas originales, como la griega y latina, que hablan con casos y tienen diferentes conjugaciones." [100] Moreover, to prove the ancient tradition of a Castilian vernacular apart from Latin, Quevedo states of ancient Latin writers: "... dijeron expresamente no sólo que eran diferentes [las dos lenguas] sino que en la suya admiraban la dureza de la nuestra." [101] As Raimundo Lida has pointed out, Quevedo's

---

[96] Quevedo has at hand, however, Bernardo de Alderete's *Origen de la lengua castellana* (1600) to substantiate his own statements. See *Obras* I (1964), 502.
[97] *Obras* I (1964), 506.
[98] *Obras* I (1964), 508-509.
[99] *Obras* I (1964), 512. Quevedo does not specify what he considers to be the original mother tongue in Spain.
[100] *Obras* I (1964), 507.
[101] *Obras* I (1964), 512.

primary motive in this defense is to establish the connection, broken by him in the second chapter, between the original Spanish inhabitants and the ancient Hebrew peoples of the Bible:

> El propósito está claro. Las gentes que hoy llamamos españolas partieron un día de las proximidades del Paraíso terrenal. Marcharon hacia occidente, evitaron los fríos de Alemania, Flandes, Escandinavia y Francia y vinieron por fin a establecerse en el país más tibio y abundante: España. Contemplado desde las alturas de la genealogía, el hilo central de la historia pasa por Judea y España. Testimonio vivo de ese enlace es hoy la lengua española. Lengua supereminente que por sí ennoblece todo lo que toca. [102]

The difference is that Quevedo accomplishes this connection through a rather limited practice of historical linguistics, not by vague linguistic analogies of names and places which he criticized in the second chapter.

Also defending Castilian literature in the fourth chapter, Quevedo suggests that perhaps Mercator is incapable of appreciating its great value "... porque la materia de los libros y la pureza de su verdad no es manjar de tu entendimiento, arrastrado de vicios torpes y criado a pechos de la herejía rebelde; que, por huir del cielo, tratas sólo de cosas de la tierra. ..." [103] Whether he meant it to be serious or not, this insult to Mercator reveals an underlying truth which was self-evident to Quevedo: Spanish literature of the Golden Age was predominantly Catholic in sentiment. Unlike other European countries, the Renaissance in Spain did not bring about a general secularization of religious values: "Even when Spain was fully 'open' to the light, even when the Inquisitor General and the emperor's secretary for Latin letters were Erasmists, Spain gave no evidence of wishing to convert religious values into secular values." [104] Spanish literature, like the Spanish State in the sixteenth and seventeenth centuries, was essentially theocentric in nature:

> ...toda el alma de la nación y todo el sentido de su política interior y exterior, toda su cultura renacentista quedó

---

[102] Raimundo Lida, "La *España defendida* de Quevedo y la síntesis pagano-cristiana," *Imago Mundi* (R. Argentina), vol. II, núm. 9, 1955, p. 6.
[103] *Obras* I (1964), 515.
[104] Green, *Spain and the Western Tradition*, Vol. III, p. 229.

impregnada de este espíritu religioso, que fué el verdadero conductor y polarizador de todas las fuerzas creadoras de España a partir del siglo XVI, de suerte que bien puede decirse que en España no hubo interrupción, como en otros países, sino superación o sublimación de la Edad Media, cuyos ideales teocéntricos se adaptaron en forma original a las nuevas corrientes renacentistas. [105]

Without an understanding and appreciation of this traditional religious inspiration, Castilian literature loses much of its value.

In order to show Mercator the emptiness of his accusations against Spanish literature, Quevedo lists famous authors and works of the fifteenth and sixteenth centuries. Here, his love of the Greek and Latin classics gives way to his patriotism as he lauds the excellence of Spanish writers: "¿Qué Horacio, ni Propercio, ni Tibulo, ni Cornelio Galo, excedió a Garcilaso y Boscán? ¿Qué Terencio a Torres Naharro?" [106] In the manner of a final reproach, he reminds Mercator that "... los españoles, más se precian de hacer cosas dignas de ser escritas, que no de escribir sueños o lo que otros hicieron." [107]

Throughout *España defendida,* Quevedo alternates between defending Spain against foreign allegations of inferiority and exhorting his compatriots to follow his example. In the fifth chapter, he makes known his fears that Spaniards are resting on their laurels and that the nation is "viuda en parte del antiguo vigor." [108] Continuing his reminiscent tone, he writes: "Las ciencias que se aprendieron para vivir bien, por la mayor parte se estudian para sólo vivir." [109] Quevedo's hope for Spain's future is that Felipe III will inaugurate a spirit of rejuvenation, what has been termed by one critic, "el retorno a lo castizo, un volver-sobre-sí nacional." [110] This work has served a double purpose for Quevedo: he has vigorously defended the traditions of his nation's culture and, at the same time,

---

[105] Montoliu, pp. 568-569.

[106] *Obras* I (1964), 515.

[107] *Obras* I (1964), 517. Could Quevedo have been referring to himself when he wrote "escribir sueños"? He had already written three *Sueños* by 1609.

[108] *Obras* I (1964), 524.

[109] *Obras* I (1964), 524.

[110] Raimundo Lida, "Quevedo y su España antigua," *Romance Philology,* Vol. XVII, No. 2, Nov. 1963, p. 270.

he has sounded an alarm to his contemporaries to keep these traditions alive. When one realizes that Quevedo wrote this work, *España defendida y los tiempos de ahora,* at the age of twenty-nine, the early formation of his traditionalistic attitudes becomes apparent.

CHAPTER FIVE

TRADITIONALISTIC ASPECTS OF QUEVEDO'S STYLE

THE CHOICE OF THEMES AND GENRES

A Renaissance Spanish humanist, Sebastián Fox Morcillo, in his *De imitatione seu de informandi styli ratione* (1554), expressed the following opinion regarding literary style in relation to the writer: "Por el estilo es tan fácil conocer la naturaleza y costumbres de cada uno, como por su rostro y por su trato."[1] If this is true, then an analysis of Quevedo's style will help to elucidate his character about which so many contradictory studies have been written.

The exceptionally varied nature of Quevedo's works is the first quality which captures the reader's attention. In both prose and verse, Quevedo exploited many literary genres, styles and themes. He wrote with equal knowledge of the sublime and of the ridiculous, of the lives of saints and the meandering of picaros. Political doctrine, social satire, philosophy, theology, all of these subjects were treated by Quevedo. His poems were both serious and burlesque in tone, and he cultivated such verse forms as sonnets, romances, letrillas, jacaras, redondillas, quintillas and decimas. In every pursuit, Quevedo was a man of vast culture and talent. He was the embodiment of the intellectual, traditionally revered by ancient and modern society as the teacher of men.[2]

---

[1] Cited by M. Menéndez y Pelayo, *Historia de las ideas estéticas en España*, Vol. II, in *Edición Nacional de las Obras Completas*. Madrid: Consejo Superior de Investigaciones Científicas, 1962, p. 163.

[2] See Otis Green, *Spain and the Western Tradition*, Vol. III. Madison: University of Wisconsin Press, 1965, p. 391.

As Otis Green points out in *Spain and the Western Tradition*, literature has been looked upon since ancient times as "an instrument of power ... it was exercised for social, for civilizing ends: to induce men to live in harmonious secular association, or to educate them in the ways of holiness and salvation."[3] Literary works have traditionally been used for instructional purposes. The ancient apologues of Sanskrit origin which passed into Western literature were essentially didactic in nature.[4] So, also, were the works of religious import dating from the earliest biblical stories. Literary theorists and the majority of Spanish writers in the Middle Ages and the Renaissance upheld the Aristotelian-Horatian principle that poetry, or literature, should consist of delightful instruction.[5] That a work was pleasing or amusing was not enough; it must convey a message of instructive value to the reader.

Quevedo followed this literary tradition in the majority of his works. A constant moral preoccupation penetrates his prose and verse, whether they be serious or frivolous in tone. Although he knew that his satiric works were most often read for purposes of entertainment, he hastened to warn his audience that he was not inspired by a malicious intent to slander, but by a solemn desire to censure vices:

> Sólo te pido, lector, y aun te conjuro por todos los prólogos, que no tuerzas las razones ni ofendas con malicia mi buen celo, pues lo primero, guardo el decoro a las personas y sólo reprehendo los vicios; murmuro los descuidos y demasías de algunos oficiales, sin tocar en la pureza de los oficios.[6]

As Otis Green has commented, Quevedo "exploited the public interest in vice as a means of realizing himself artistically," this being, according to Green, Quevedo's "keenest satisfaction."[7] It is evident to the reader of the *Sueños* or the *Vida del Buscón* that Quevedo

---

[3] Ibid., p. 390.
[4] The apologues appeared in Spanish literature in the thirteenth century through translations from Arabic, i.e., *Calila e Dimna* (1251). Subsequent Medieval literature was strongly influenced by these short didactic works.
[5] See Green, pp. 432-439.
[6] "Prólogo" to *El sueño del infierno*, *Obras* I (1964), 141.
[7] Green, p. 428.

enjoyed writing satires much in the same way that the Arcipreste de Hita indulged his own sense of humor and fantasy in the *Libro de Buen Amor*. Quevedo's satiric talent in the *Sueños* might also be compared with the bizarre depictions of vice by the artist Hieronymous Bosch (d. 1516) whose paintings Quevedo had seen and admired.[8] Nonetheless, despite the pleasure which Quevedo took in creating his visions of hell, a concern for the public welfare was not merely incidental to his work. To substantiate this, we shall recall his words from *España defendida y los tiempos de ahora*, written at approximately the same time that he was working on the *Sueños*:

> Prolijo fuera y vanaglorioso en querer contar por menudo todas las cosas que nos sucedieron a los españoles gloriosamente en los días que han pasado, sin callar que ha habido hijo suyo que llora estos tiempos y el verla viuda en parte del antiguo vigor, y osa decir que la confianza de haberle tenido introduce descuido en conservarle.
> Han empezado a contentarse los hombres de España con heredar de sus padres virtud, sin procurar tenerla para que la hereden sus hijos ...¿A qué vicio no ha abierto la puerta con llave de oro la avaricia? ¡Muchos en este tiempo entierra la gula! ¡Qué cosa más fea y contra naturaleza, guisar muerte para sí del sustento natural! Otros, del juego, que fue a moderados ánimos entretenimiento, hicieron oficio... Y así, en España heredan hoy a los más sus desórdenes y sus vicios antes que sus hijos, mujeres ni hermanos.[9]

Quevedo wrote this in 1609, after he had already finished three of the *Sueños*. Even though he may have found artistic challenge and satisfaction in the satiric genre, his words in the above quote show that he was sincerely critical of the vices which he characterized. As B. Sánchez Alonso has described, Quevedo admired the early Latin satirists and sought to imitate them; yet his own artistic self-realization was not the primary motivation behind his satire:

---

[8] Bosch is mentioned by Quevedo in *El alguacil endemoniado* (1607) in the words of a devil who says: "Remediad esto que poco ha que fué Jerónimo Bosco allá, y preguntándole por qué había hecho tantos guisados de nosotros en sus sueños, dijo que porque no había creído nunca que había demonios de veras." *Obras* I (1964), 137.

[9] *Obras* I (1964), 524.

Los acentos burlescos y festivos, que con tanto donaire derramaba en su sátira, no hacen sino encubrir su fondo de amargura y descontento. No es un hombre superficial a quien fácilmente contenta el espectáculo del pueblo que le rodea. Escoge ese tono porque le parece el más eficaz para representar la realidad humana, o mejor, la realidad española, que es lo que plenamente le interesa en todas sus obras.[10]

Quevedo's intention to impart a moral lesson is more openly pronounced in his political and philosophical works and in a large body of poems which are inspired by a concern for Spain and, more generally, for the problems of human existence.

Within the framework of his preoccupation with morality, Quevedo treats a variety of traditional literary themes. Those to which he returns most frequently are topics relating to the philosophical nature of the human condition, i.e., time, death, solitude, the evils of self-indulgence and the relationship between the soul and the body.[11] He devotes relatively scant attention to the description of natural surroundings, a theme found in abundance in the works of his cultist adversary, Luis de Góngora.

In reference to Quevedo's choice of themes, Emilio Carilla has said, "Inútil es buscar en Quevedo el concepto del amor. ..."[12] This opinion has been shared by other critics in the past and it is a misconception which Otis Green has successfully attempted to combat in his study entitled *Courtly Love in Quevedo*.[13] He points out that even though the theme of love is often treated crudely in Quevedo's writing, there is a significantly large body of his verse which deals with this theme on a lofty and idealistic level.[14] These poems are primarily the ones dedicated to "Lisi," Quevedo's secret love for more than twenty-two years. Here is found a full development of the theme of courtly love, a love of chaste detachment

---

[10] B. Sánchez Alonso, "Los satíricos latinos y la sátira de Quevedo," *Revista de Filología Española*, vol. XI, Cuaderno I, 1924, p. 37.

[11] See Emilio Carilla, "Quevedo y 'el Parnaso Español'," in *Estudios de literatura española*. Rosario: Imprenta de la Universidad Nacional del Litoral, 1958, p. 159.

[12] Ibid., p. 165.

[13] See Green, *Courtly Love in Quevedo*. Boulder (Colorado): University of Colorado Press, 1952.

[14] Ibid., p. 4.

from the beloved. The poet realizes the impossibility of attaining the object of his desires, and he therefore takes refuge in the cult of "blessed suffering" wherein love assumes a sacred character, and becomes a religion in itself.[15] In terms of Christian morality, Renaissance courtly love was a "truancy" which did not exclude the love of God, the only love to which it would inevitably yield.[16] Although there are Platonic elements in Quevedo's love poetry, he remains closest to the concept of courtly love which admits an expression of sensual desires not accepted by Plato who sought, through love, the transcendence of all human desire.[17]

Quevedo's treatment of courtly love in his poems to Lisi represents the continuation of a traditional theme in Spanish poetry since the Middle Ages:

> Quevedo inherited from his Spanish predecessors an adapted and evolved form of the chivalric concept of love. Progressively purged of license and adapted to Christian courtship and marriage, it yet preserved in definitely recognizable shape the traditional pattern of courtly love.[18]

The following sonnet is an example of Quevedo's adherence to this tradition:

> Que vos me permitáis sólo pretendo,
> y saber ser cortés y ser amante,
> esquivo a los deseos y constante,
> sin pretensión a sólo amar atiendo.
>
> Ni con intento de gozar ofendo
> las deidades del garbo y del semblante;
> no fuera lo que vi causa bastante,
> si no se le añadiera lo que entiendo.
>
> Llamáronme los ojos las facciones;
> prendiéronlos eternas jerarquías
> de virtudes, y heroicas perfecciones.

---

[15] Ibid., p. 82.
[16] Ibid., p. 9.
[17] Ibid., p. 24.
[18] Ibid., p. 79.

> No verán de mi amor el fin los días:
> la eternidad ofrece sus blasones
> a la pureza de las ansias mías. [19]

Here, the poet assures his beloved that he only seeks the pleasure of "amour lointain" without any intention of physical satisfaction: "no con intento de gozar ofendo/ las deidades del garbo y del semblante." His love, he says, is pure: "la eternidad ofrece sus blasones/ a la pureza de las ansias mías." Another of the same group of sonnets is this one in which the poet echoes the ancient troubadour's lament of love:

> Lisis, por duplicado ardiente Sirio
> miras con guerra y muerte l'alma mía;
> y en uno y otro sol abres el día,
> influyendo en la luz dulce martirio.
>
> Doctas sirenas en veneno tirio
> con tus labios pronuncian melodía;
> y en incendios de nieve hermosa y fría,
> adora primaveras mi delirio.
>
> Amo y no espero, porque adoro amando,
> ni mancha al amor puro mi deseo,
> que cortés vive y muere idolatrando
>
> lo que conozco, y no lo que poseo;
> sigo sin presumir méritos cuando
> prefiero a lo que miro lo que creo. [20]

Otis Green has pointed out Quevedo's use of the familiar concept of "dulce martirio" from which the lover suffers and yet without which he could not exist. [21] The third stanza expresses the futility of his love and the fatalistic approach which he takes in rationalizing it. As Green notes, "The noblest and most poetic part of his love poetry is ... the expression of a chivalric passion which could not have existed as it did but for the pre-existing tradition of courtly love. [22]

---

[19] *Obras* II (1964), 120.
[20] *Obras* II (1964), 126.
[21] Green, *Courtly Love in Quevedo*, p. 32.
[22] Ibid., p. 81.

The sincerity of these poems to Lisi has been doubted on occasion because of Quevedo's frequent prose attacks against women.[23] However, it would be unfair to think of Quevedo as a misogynist purely because he expressed a mistrust of the female nature in his satire. He was readily disposed toward mocking female idiosyncrasies and affectations, but this does not prove that he was incapable of true love. Quevedo was, as Green and other critics have often pointed out, a man of moods, and equally adept at handling the serious and the burlesque as the situation warranted. His poems to Lisi deserve recognition as an example of noble and sincere lyric verse. The fact that he was one of the last Spanish poets to follow the tradition of courtly love in the Renaissance is significant in the history of Spanish literature as it indicates the last vestiges of idealism in an era which was moving toward the cult of reason.

Of all the literary themes we have mentioned, the one which Quevedo treats in most detail is the contemplation of death and how a good Christian should learn to accept his mortality. This theme, equally essential to the Stoic philosophy, has played an important role in Spanish literature since the Middle Ages.[24] The strong Catholic tradition of Spain has kept this theme alive; its doctrine teaches that death is only a stepping stone to a better life, and therefore, it must be welcomed as a release from worldly chains. As Otis Green writes:

> Vives and Erasmus and More, Quevedo and Boussuet, Gracián and Donne, nourished by the same tradition, stood firmly on the bedrock of Christian teaching on death: though our human frailty cringe before it and loathe its corruption; though the sense of sin compel us to fear God's justice, the passage from life to death is sweet to those who love the Lord, bitter and horrifying to those soon to be cast into outer darkness.[25]

---

[23] See Green, *Courtly Love in Quevedo*, p. 81.

[24] Among other medieval works, the most famous developments of the theme of death are Jorge Manrique's *Coplas por la muerte de su padre*, the anonymous *Danza de la muerte*, and Juan Ruiz's treatment of the death of Doña Urraca, the go-between (or "alcahueta") in *El libro de Buen Amor*.

[25] Green, *Spain and the Western Tradition*, Vol. IV (1966), p. 133.

In modern literature, the theme of death is often treated differently, partially because of the tendency to strip it of all Christian religious significance and consider death as complete annihilation. However, the original Spanish literary tradition of this theme is inextricably linked with Catholic doctrine as well as with the philosophy of Stoicism, and this is the tradition which Quevedo continues in his prose and in his verse.

The aspect of this theme which Quevedo repeats most frequently is the reversibility of life and death, that is, the concept that life is actually a form of dying and that death is the beginning of true life.[26] Santa Teresa de Jesús expressed this concept when she said, "Muero porque no muero."[27] Quevedo's essay, *La cuna y la sepultura* (1633), elaborates this theme:

> Empieza, pues, hombre, con este conocimiento, y ten de ti firmemente tales opiniones; que naciste para morir y que vives muriendo; que traes el alma enterrada en el cuerpo, que cuando muere, en cierta forma resucita; que tu negocio es el logro de tu alma...[28]

Again, in the following sonnet, he writes of the fallacious notion that life is more precious than death:

> ¿Qué otra cosa es verdad, sino pobreza,
> en esta vida frágil y liviana?
> Los dos embustes de la vida humana
> desde la cuna son honra y riqueza.
>
> El tiempo, que ni vuelve ni tropieza,
> en horas fugitivas la devana;
> y en errado anhelar, siempre tirana,
> la fortuna fatiga su flaqueza.
>
> Vive muerte callada y divertida
> la vida misma; la salud es guerra
> de su propio alimento combatida.

---

[26] See J. Lanza Esteban, "Quevedo y la tradición literaria de la muerte," *Revista de Literatura,* vol. IV, núm. 7, julio-sept. de 1953, pp. 367-380.

[27] "Vivo sin vivir en mí / y de tal manera espero, / que muero porque no muero./, reprinted in *Obras completas,* ed. Padre Isidoro de San José, C. D. Madrid: Editorial de Espiritualidad, 1963, pp. 1177-1178.

[28] *Obras* I (1964), 1195.

> ¡Oh, cuanto inadvertido el hombre yerra,
> que en tierra teme que caerá la vida,
> y no ve que, en viviendo, cayó en tierra! [29]

In typically Baroque fashion, Quevedo treats the theme of death in two contrasting ways: one, the serious contemplation of death in his ascetic and philosophical works, and the other, a burlesque of the dead in the *Sueños*. Even in his most humorous moments, however, he never forgets the true seriousness of his satire of death. Compare, for example, the similarity between these two paragraphs, the first from the satiric *Sueño de la muerte,* and the second from *La cuna y la sepultura*:

> [Death speaks to the author] La muerte no la conocéis, y sois vosotros mismos vuestra muerte. Tiene la cara de cada uno de vosotros, y todos sois muertes de vosotros mismos. La calavera es el muerto, y la cara es la muerte. Y lo que llamáis morir es acabar de morir, y lo que llamáis nacer es empezar a morir, y lo que llamáis vivir es morir viviendo. Y los huesos es lo que de vosotros deja la muerte y lo que le sobra a la sepultura. Si esto entendiérades así, cada uno de vosotros estuviera mirando en sí la muerte cada día y la ajena en el otro, viérades que todas vuestras casas están llenas della y que en vuestro lugar hay tantas muertes como personas y no la estuviérades aguardando, sino acompañándola y disponiéndola. [30]

> Es, pues, la vida un dolor en que se empieza el de la muerte, que dura mientras dura ella. Considéralo como el plazo que ponen al jornalero, que no tiene descanso desde que empieza, sino es cuando acaba. A la par empiezas a nacer y a morir, y no es en tu mano detener las horas; y si fueras cuerdo, no lo habías de desear; y si fueras bueno, no lo habías de temer. Antes empiezas a morir que sepas qué cosa es vida, y vives sin gustar della, porque se anticipan las lágrimas a la razón. [31]

When, in 1635, Luis Pacheco de Narváez wrote his libelous attack against Quevedo entitled *El tribunal de la justa venganza,*[32]

---

[29] *Obras* II (1964), 39.
[30] *El sueño de la muerte, Obras* I (1964), 178.
[31] *La cuna y la sepultura, Obras* I (1964), 1193-1194.
[32] Reprinted in *Obras* II (1952), 1248-1329.

he dedicated a section of invective to the *Sueños* trying to single them out as heretical so that the Inquisition might take notice and indict Quevedo. Narváez took exception to his satires of death and hell:

> Acuso a don Francisco de Quevedo de hombre supersticioso en afirmar, como afirma, que los sueños que él soñó son verdades que descubren abusos, vicios y engaños; y demás de esto, de locamente temerario y fiero enemigo del género humano, pues a todos los hombres (y mujeres), sin perdonar dignidad ni oficio, los pone en el Infierno; y, sobre todo, en decir que supo cuándo había de ser el Juicio final y por qué pecados se había de condenar cada uno, y esto no por revelación o espíritu profético, sino odio y rencor, como lo manifiesta su malicia en no referir que viese los de la mano derecha del supremo Juez Cristo nuestro Señor... [33]

His efforts to implicate Quevedo were ignored, for Quevedo was highly respected for his orthodox religious beliefs.[34] As I have indicated, Quevedo's satire is not meant to be irreverent, and within the *Sueños* he reiterates religious and philosophical themes which are found in his most serious compositions. To assume that satire is always based upon contempt felt for that which is satirized is an error which Otis Green points out in relation to Juan Ruiz's parody of the Canonical Hours of Our Lady in the *Libro de Buen Amor*:

> Gay and yet respectful parody of sacred ceremonies, persons, or texts characterizes, or has characterized, practically all human cultures. The greater the esteem in which certain mores are held, the more pleasurable the comic relief that the act of parody provides.[35]

A corollary to the theme of death in Quevedo's works is the question of whether he was a pessimist or an optimist in his attitude toward human existence. Quevedo is often referred to as a pessimist, but this statement cannot be made without qualification. Otis Green has analyzed thoroughly the problem of optimism and

---

[33] Narváez, *El tribunal*..., in *Obras* II (1952), 1280.
[34] See Chapter Three, "Quevedo's Religiosity."
[35] Green, "A Hispanist's Thoughts on *The Anatomy of Satire*," *Romance Philology*, Vol. XVII, 1963, p. 128.

pessimism in Spain from the fifteenth to the seventeenth centuries, and he makes a valid distinction between the circumstantial and radical types of optimism and pessimism.[36] As he makes clear, radical pessimism is un-Christian, and it is therefore alien to the Spanish spirit since it conceives of human life and the universe as absurd and without purpose.[37] As long as Spain has been Christian, her religious and moral traditions have been based upon the conviction that God's creation is essentially good and that there is a basic harmony and order in the universe.[38] Quevedo, in *Providencia de Dios* (1641), voices this conviction and offers it as a proof of God's existence:

> Si a la naturaleza llamas principio de todo sin principio, necesariamente confiesas que hay un Dios. Pónesle nombres, mas no lo niegas; llámasle como quieres, no como debes. Ni el necio que dijo en su corazón que no había Dios; ni el descarado Selio, que dijo con la boca que no había dioses, dejaron de conocer, por todas las criaturas y por el orden y concierto del universo, que había Dios.[39]

In the light of this belief, it would be incorrect to refer to Quevedo as a pessimist without making a clear distinction between radical and circumstantial pessimism. Basically, Quevedo was a radical optimist, as was the traditional attitude in Spain. He was pessimistic only in the circumstantial sense; that is, he held a dim view of the present, seeing it as morally decadent and politically degenerate.

I must therefore disagree with Américo Castro's assertion that Quevedo was a "gran nihilista"[40] who admitted no truths other than non-reality and death:

---

[36] See Chapter IX, *Spain and the Western Tradition*, Vol. III, pp. 337-388. "The first [circumstantial] concerns itself with the human condition in the ups and downs of the here and now; the second [radical] deals with *being* in the most general and philosophic sense of the word, i.e., with the least possible determination or qualification" (p. 338).

[37] Ibid., pp. 339-340.

[38] Ibid., p. 285.

[39] *Obras* I (1964), 1427.

[40] Castro, "Escepticismo y contradicción en Quevedo," in *Semblanzas y estudios españoles*. Princeton: 1956, p. 393.

> El valor de la vida es negado abiertamente [por Quevedo];
> y no como el místico hace, que no cree en la vida *ésta,* por
> la infinita importancia que concede a la *otra,* sino en absoluto, por dificultad intelectual y temperamental de percibir
> sus valores. [41]

Quevedo was not a nihilist in either the political or philosophical sense because he recognized that the source of ethical values and knowledge was man's faith in God; through this active and conscious faith, life has value and meaning:

> Y está cierto así lo dice el predicador hijo de David, "que
> sabiduría, ciencia y alegría, solamente la da Dios al bueno,
> y en su presencia"; y que sin él, y ausente y desterrado, la
> ciencia y sabiduría que tuvieres será la que te fingieres a ti
> mismo... Considera que un hombre que hubo sabio pidió
> la sabiduría a Dios, y él se la dió, como fuente de toda
> verdad; y que la perdió en llegándose a las cosas de la
> tierra. Sea, pues, tu estudio, oh hombre que deseas ser sabio,
> para merecer este nombre, cerca de las cosas espirituales
> y eternas. [42]

Nor is it possible to accept without reservation this statement of Castro's:

> Hallo como nota distintiva de Quevedo, frente al tradicional
> *contemptus mundi* de los ascetas, la atracción y el interés
> que le inspira el ser la vida así como es; se preocupa más
> por reflejar su conciencia de ella, por sentirla como es,
> que por desdeñarla a fin de enfrentarse con la vida futura. [43]

After saying this, Castro quotes a love sonnet by Quevedo and offers it as evidence to support his idea that Quevedo could not have been a true ascetic. The fact that Quevedo experienced worldly pleasures and wrote about them in his poetry or satire does not automatically prove that he was incapable of approaching asceticism

---

[41] Ibid., p. 395. M. Morreale shares Castro's opinion in "Luciano y Quevedo," *Revista de Literatura,* Tomo VIII, núm. 16, oct.-dic. de 1955, p. 224.
[42] *La cuna y la sepultura, Obras* I (1964), 1209-1210.
[43] Castro, *La realidad histórica de España.* México: Editorial Porrúa, S. A., 1954, p. 59 (Note).

in his attitude toward his milieu. Quevedo's asceticism was certainly not that of a cloistered monk; he lived in the midst of court society and was subject to the vices and temptations which surrounded him. Nonetheless, he sincerely disdained the overindulgent nature of seventeenth century Spanish society, and later in life he wrote several works which were primarily ascetic in inspiration, i. e., *La cuna y la sepultura* (1633), *Virtud militante* (1634-1635), *La constancia y paciencia del Santo Job* (1641), *Providencia de Dios* (1641) and *Vida de San Pablo Apóstol* (1643). Américo Castro does not mention these works. Moreover, he contradicts his own opinion of Quevedo's nihilism [44] by stating in the above quote that Quevedo was interested in reality and did not disdain or deny it.

Quevedo's asceticism is most evident in the final fifteen years of his life (1630-1645). Perhaps the first motivation for his ultimate moral denunciation of worldly temptations was his own intimate knowledge of reality. In his earlier satiric works, he follows the Spanish tradition of realism in literature. Since the *Poema de Mío Cid,* Spanish writing has been characterized by a close bond with historical reality, in contrast with the tendency toward the supernatural which is recurrent in the French epic, *La Chanson de Roland.* Quevedo was well acquainted with the society of his time, as portrayed in the *Sueños* and the *Vida del Buscón,* and historians have shown that his literary interpretations are not so exaggerated as to be considered out of proportion with reality. [45] Quevedo's sense of realism extends to his choice of language for his respective works. Whenever appropriate, he fashions the tone of speech to fit the character involved, thus demonstrating his familiarity with the jargon and popular expressions of a variety of social types, i.e., the picaros Pablos and Pero Vázquez Escamilla, el Licenciado Cabra, and a long procession of minor characters.

In his choice of literary genres, Quevedo employed the traditional as well as several newer forms of prose and verse. In his prose works, he followed the traditional forms of essays, letters,

---

[44] See the quote corresponding to footnote 41 above.

[45] See: Deleito y Pinuela, *La mala vida en la España de Felipe IV.* Madrid: Espasa-Calpe, S. A., 1959; Cánovas del Castillo, *Historia de la decadencia española,* 2nd ed. Madrid: 1911; or M. Hume, *The Court of Philip IV: Spain in Decadence.* New York: Brentano's [1927].

commentaries and biographies. The dream idea as a structure for his *Sueños* was inspired by Greek and Latin writers, principally Lucian of Samosata (d. 312). Quevedo exploited the genre of the novel in his *Vida del Buscón*, although it cannot be compared in length or fantasy with Cervantes' *Don Quijote*. The novel as a literary genre was not highly esteemed in the Golden Age, and there were no precepts governing its use.[46] In writing the *Buscón*, he did not imitate the novels of chivalry or those of pastoral setting, but rather the tradition initiated by the first picaresque novel, *El Lazarillo de Tormes* (c. 1554). Unlike Cervantes, Quevedo could not envision a protagonist who was not the embodiment of an actual social type. Pablos has none of the charming naïveté in his nature which we find in *El Caballero de la Triste Figura*. Pablos is a character copied from everyday life, as common in Spain as was the poverty and depravation amidst which he thrived. In this sense, Quevedo adheres more closely to the Aristotelian requirement of verisimilitude in literature[47] than does Cervantes.

Within the dramatic genre, Quevedo wrote several plays, entremeses, dialogues, loas, bailes and jacaras, many of which have since been lost. His theatrical works date primarily from 1623 to 1628, a period when he was particularly popular in the Court and contributing to its festivities. These dramatic compositions are based upon themes which Quevedo had treated previously in his prose, many of them being social satires of types such as students, picaros, doctors and drunkards. It appears that Quevedo looked upon his dramatic output as a diversion, a change of pace. He was undoubtedly aware of the predominance of Lope de Vega in this genre and did not feel capable of competing with his extraordinary talent and public appeal. There is no reason to believe that he opposed the changes which Lope brought about in his "comedia nueva." On the contrary, Quevedo admired Lope, and their friendship was

---

[46] See A. González de Amezúa y Mayo, *Cervantes, Creador de la novela corta española*, Vol. II. Madrid: Consejo Superior de Investigaciones Científicas, 1956, pp. 349-352. This author points out that Pinciano, for example did not pay much attention to novels. Indeed, the term "novela" was Italian in origin and not in popular use in Spain during the Golden Age.

[47] See Sanford Shepard, *El Pinciano y las teorías literarias del Siglo de Oro*. Madrid: Editorial Gredos, 1962, pp. 60-61.

unusually solid and long-lasting considering the numerous hostilities which existed between Quevedo and other writers.[48]

The only play by Quevedo which has survived the centuries intact is entitled *Como ha de ser el privado* (1627). It is an eclectic work, neither wholly traditional nor modern in terms of Lope's technique. It is neither a comedy nor a tragedy, but rather a restatement in verse of the fundamental doctrines of his *Política de Dios* with some incidental romantic scenes. What is most noticeable about this play is it straightforward reference to contemporary political events: the first years of the reign of Felipe IV and his minister, Olivares, whose name in the play is Valisero, an obvious anagram. Quevedo wrote this three-act play at a time when he was in the Conde-Duque's favor, and the play exudes admiration for the powerful privado. He is portrayed as a sincere, diligent and pious minister, a model privado in every way.

If one is to single out the most traditional aspects of this work, they are to be found in the content of the play's moral message: a good privado must be disinterested, impervious to the temptation of personal glory, a supporter of the Catholic faith and a seeker of justice. The following lines are spoken by Valisero when the King asks him why they should not be close friends:

Marqués [de Valisero].

> Sí. Señor, porque un privado,
> que es un átomo pequeño
> junto al rey, no ha de ser dueño
> de la luz que el sol le ha dado.
> Es un ministro de ley,
> es un brazo, un instrumento
> por donde pasa el aliento
> a la voluntad del rey.
> Si dos ángeles ha dado
> Dios al rey, su parecer
> más acertado ha de ser
> que el parecer del privado.
> Y así, se debe advertir
> que el ministro singular,

---

[48] Quevedo mentioned Lope more than a dozen times in his work and always in glowing terms. Their friendship may well have been aided by a mutual dislike of cultism and by a love of national traditions.

aunque pueda aconsejar,
no le toca decidir. [49]

The similarity between this play and the *Política* extends even to the preference for certain metaphors which Quevedo uses; though not always exactly alike, they express similar conceptual relationships. Compare the following words from the *Política de Dios* with the above quote from the play:

> Los ministros, muy poderoso Señor, han de ser tratados del príncipe soberano como la espada, y ellos han de ser imitadores de la espada con el príncipe. Este los ha de traer a su lado, ellos han de acompañar su lado. Y como la espada para obrar depende en todo de la mano y brazo dél que la trae, sin moverse por sí a cosa alguna, así los ministros no han de tener obras y acciones sino las que les diere la deliberación del señor que los tiene a su lado. [50]

Why Quevedo chose to repeat the politico-moral theme of the *Política* in his play is an interesting consideration, especially in view of the fact that the first part of the *Política* had just been published during the previous year (1626). Perhaps he wanted to insure the King's notice of his message and impress upon Olivares the gravity of his duties. Had he merely been trying to flatter the privado, this could have been accomplished without the philosophical and doctrinary overtones of the existing plot.

It is unfortunate that no more of Quevedo's plays have survived intact, as *Como ha de ser el privado* is a poor indication of his dramatic talent. It would seem that Quevedo, like Cervantes, was far more successful in his shorter dramatic works, such as the entremeses and jacaras recited on stage between the acts of longer plays. These works were destined to amuse the average playgoer, and their burlesque tone, witty dialogue and realistic characterizations are reminiscent of Quevedo's prose satire. For example, his entremes entitled *Los refranes del viejo celoso* contains the same satire of meaningless names used in popular expressions as is found in *El sueño de la muerte*; here, as in the *Sueño*, these imaginary names

---

[49] Acto primero, *Como ha de ser el privado, Obras* II (1964), 596.
[50] *Política* (Pt. II, Chapt. XXI), *Obras* I (1964), 667.

such as "el Rey Perico" and "Pero Grullo" become characters who speak for themselves.[51] The entremes traces its origin back to Lope de Rueda's "pasos," although similarities can also be seen between the entremes and the earliest medieval "debates," i.e., rapid dialogue, popular speech, burlesque tone. Quevedo, like Lope, followed a national literary tradition of close contact with the spirit of the people. It is significant that he returns to this popular style in every genre of his work.

VERSIFICATION IN QUEVEDO'S POETRY

Quevedo's poetry presents a complex problem for our analysis, as it encompasses a wide variety of metric forms and an equally broad range of themes. Since many of his poetic themes such as time, death, solitude, and social satire find their counterpart in his prose works, I shall devote my attention to his verse techniques.

Although he first achieved public acclaim for his poetic rather than his prose talent, Quevedo showed little interest in insuring the publication of his verses.[52] His poems circulated in manuscript form and became well-known in the Court. Nevertheless, it was his prose production which Quevedo sought to have published and for which he showed most concern.[53] This would lead us to believe that he looked upon his poetry as he did his drama, as an artistic diversion, knowing that his prose works contained the essence of his philosophy in a more comprehensible and complete idiom.

In the art of versification, Quevedo was the equal of any of his contemporaries. His poetic genius was exuberantly praised by his editor and friend, González de Salas, in *El Parnaso Español* (1648):

> La felicidad e ingenio de nuestro don Francisco fuera de toda duda que reinó en la Poesía. Pocos, creo, que le enten-

---

[51] See *Los refranes del viejo celoso, Obras* II (1964), 582-587, and *El sueño de la muerte, Obras* I (1964), 186-195.

[52] See Emilio Carilla, p. 147.

[53] Tarsia, Quevedo's biographer, writing just over ten years after Quevedo's death, made a list of the published and soon-to-be published works of Quevedo. Of the thirty works mentioned, only one, *El Parnaso Español*, contains some of Quevedo's poetry, and this was published by his friend, González de Salas in 1648, three years after the poet's death. See *Vida de Don Francisco de Quevedo y Villegas* in *Obras* II (1952), 863.

dieron así, por comunicarle íntimamente pocos; pero yo lo tuve bien advertido siempre, aun cuando más presumió de otras erudiciones, y ansiosa y afectadamente las profesó y se divirtió por mucha edad en ellas. Grande facultad tuvo poética, y más por su naturaleza digo, que por su cultura; pudiendo también asegurar que hasta hoy yo no conozco poeta alguno español versado más, en los que viven, de hebreos, griegos, latinos y franceses, de cuyas lenguas tuvo buena noticia y de donde a sus versos trujo excelentes imitaciones. [54]

The metric forms which Quevedo used may be divided for our purposes into two groups: [55] (1) traditional juglaresque forms such as romances, letrillas, seguidillas and bailes; and (2) more modern forms derived from the medieval "mester de clerecía" and from Italian verse, such as sonnets, decimas, silvas, tercetos, quintillas and redondillas.

It cannot be said that Quevedo was more traditional than modern in his choice of verse forms, for he cultivated all forms in abundance as did his contemporaries, Luis de Góngora and Lope de Vega. During the period in which Quevedo wrote, the art of poetic versification in Castilian was dedicated to assimilating and consolidating verse forms borrowed from Italy in the late fifteenth and early sixteenth centuries: "El Siglo de Oro se interesó menos en introducir nuevas invenciones métricas que en reelaborar y ordenar los materiales heredados del período precedente." [56] In accomplishing this, poets such as Quevedo relied upon their own genius, since the few Spanish literary theorists of the late sixteenth century had ignored the value of developing general rules for versification in the vernacular:

> Sería igualmente absurdo imaginar que un manual de arte métrica como el *Arte Poética Española* de Juan Díaz Rengrifo, publicado en 1592, y basado como autoridad máxima en el anacrónico comentario latino de Antonio da Tempo, pudo ejercer el menor influjo en la maestría técnica de los grandes poetas cultos del barroco, como Lope, Góngora o

---

[54] "Prevenciones al lector" reprinted in *Obras* II (1952), 1026.
[55] In making this distinction, I have followed T. Navarro Tomás, *Métrica española*. New York: Syracuse University Press, 1956.
[56] Ibid., p. 288.

Quevedo... Lo que sí es cierto es que la aparición de los primeros tratados de arte métrica en la España del siglo XVI, coincide con el período de máximo apogeo de la poesía del segundo Renacimiento y con la definitiva aceptación por parte de los eruditos y humanistas de la literatura en lengua vulgar. [57]

The literary theorist, Pinciano, admitted in the seventh "epístola" of his *Philosophia Antigua Poética* (1596) that there was a scarcity of studies of versification. [58] He lamented this because, "la fina [poesía] siempre siguió al metro y, aunque hay algunos poemas buenos sin él, no tienen aquella perfección que con él tuvieran." [59] Undisturbed by this lack of metrical precepts, Quevedo and his contemporaries followed their own poetic instincts, and through their efforts the borrowed Italian forms became thoroughly nationalized. [60]

Unlike the narrow traditionalism of Cristóbal de Castillejo (d. 1550) who fought the introduction of foreign verse forms into Spanish poetry, Quevedo adopted them and use them as freely as he did the traditional meters. In terms of quantity, the sonnet form is found most frequently in his poetry. [61] Quevedo employed the sonnet for serious as well as for burlesque purposes, and his mastery of this meter compares with that of his most renowned contemporaries: "Lope, Góngora y Quevedo, la gran 'trinidad lírica' de aquella magnífica época de la poesía, llevaron el romance y el soneto cerca de lo insuperable en cuanto a factura técnica se refiere." [62]

Along with the sonnet, Quevedo shows a preference for the traditional romance in octosyllabic meter. [63] This verse form, whose origin has been traced back to the fourteenth century, was exploited

---

[57] Antonio Vilanova, "Preceptistas españoles de los siglos XVI y XVII," in *Historia general de las literaturas hispánicas*, ed. Guillermo Díaz-Plaja, Vol. III. Barcelona: Editorial Barna, S. A., 1948, pp. 569-570.

[58] López Pinciano, *Philosophia Antigua Poética*, ed. A. Carballo Picazo, Vol. II. Madrid: Consejo Superior de Investigaciones Científicas, 1953, p. 218.

[59] Ibid., p. 220.

[60] See T. Navarro Tomás, *Métrica española*, p. 286.

[61] In Felicidad Buendía's edition (1964) of Quevedo's verse, there are approximately five hundred sonnets.

[62] E. Carilla, p. 152.

[63] F. Buendía's edition (1964) of Quevedo's poetry contains one hundred twenty-nine romances.

by many poets of the Golden Age. From its beginning as a fragmentary oral rendition of a longer epic poem, it evolved into a popular poetic medium for historical and imaginary themes of the most varied nature. The introduction of printing in Spain in the late fifteenth century made possible the publication of numerous "romanceros," or collections of popular romances, many of which were anonymous versions of traditional historical topics. In the second half of the sixteenth century, new types of "romances eruditos" and "romances artísticos" were written by poets who were inspired by a variety of pastoral, mythological, religious, historical, sentimental and burlesque themes,[64] During this period and in the seventeenth century, more "romanceros" were published, and the romance also became an integral part of the verse of the national theater.

Quevedo's extensive use of the romance meter might be ascribed to the preference which he so often expressed for clarity and simplicity in poetry. Unlike the sonnet which requires a more disciplined attention to form and rhyme scheme, the romance offers the poet more room for freedom and spontaneity. In contrast to the more serious tone of the majority of his sonnets, his romances are primarily light-hearted and burlesque in spirit and theme:

> En una época de inusitado brillo del romancero, en que el romance no sólo se canta entre el pueblo y circula profusamente en colecciones particulares, sino que se ha impuesto en el teatro y aun en la novela, el romance de Quevedo pone un sello propio, hecho juego, burla, ironía o sarcasmo, pero diferente del romance lírico que destaca a Góngora y Lope.[65]

Quevedo never lacked subjects for his playful romances. The following lines from a burlesque ode to a woman's nose demonstrate his facility with the romance form and the assonant rhyme which is traditional to this meter:

> A tus ojos y a tu boca
> acuden tantos requiebros,

---

[64] See García López, *Historia de la literatura española*, 5th ed. Barcelona: Editorial Teide, 1959, p. 102.
[65] E. Carilla, p. 153.

> que ya no caben de pies
> en labios y cobrecejos.
> Yo, que no requiebro en bulla,
> ando a buscar en tu gesto
> una parte reservada,
> alguna hermosura yermo.
> Yo soy tu ciego, zutana;
> como por el alma, rezo
> por la facción que más sola
> está de copla en tu cuerpo.
> A tus narices me voy,
> don fulano pañizuelo,
> y en figura de catarro
> a tus ventanas me acerco. [66]
> ... ...

The same characteristics may be pointed out in another famous romance by Quevedo entitled "La vida poltrona" (1630), one of the few autobiographical works in all of his writing. This romance is particularly significant as an example of the strong and dynamic rhythm which Quevedo often employed in his romance quatrains:

> Tardóse en parirme
> mi madre, pues vengo
> cuando ya está el mundo
> muy cascado y viejo.
> De hacer por los suyos
> hasta el diablo pienso
> que está ya cansado,
> perezoso y renco.
> Solían condenarse
> los del otro tiempo,
> con grande descanso
> por andar él suelto.
> Y agora los malos
> andan ellos mesmos,
> por falta de diablos,
> yéndose al infierno.
> Tristes de nosotros,
> dichosos de aquellos
> que el mundo alcanzaron
> en su nacimiento.

---

[66] *Obras* II (1964), 228.

De la edad del oro
gozaron sus cuerpos;
pasó la de plata,
pasó la de hierro,
y para nosotros
vino la de cuerno,
rica de ganados
y Diegos Morenos.
Yo, que he conocido
de este siglo el juego,
para mí me vivo,
para mí me bebo.
No se me da nada,
a ninguno temo,
porque a nadie agravio
ni a ninguno debo.
No pretendo cosa,
que todo lo tengo,
mientras con lo poco
vivo muy contento.
Ni desean mi muerte,
ni muertes deseo,
pues no hay que heredarme,
ni a ninguno heredo.
No vendrá a sobrarme
la vida, no puedo;
ni cuando me muera
sobrarán dineros.
No he de fatigarme
en buscar entierro,
que en nosotros vive
el sepulcro nuestro.
Dicen que me case,
digo que no quiero,
y que por lamerme
he de ser buey suelto.
... ...
Que a mí en esta celda,
donde alegre duermo,
hallo que me sobra
cuanto yo desprecio.
No ha de dar que hacer
a mi sufrimiento
ningún enfadoso,
ni ningún soberbio.
Pobre he de morir;
serviráme el serlo,

que si menos tuve,
que lo sienta menos.
Yo vivo picaño,
bien ancho y exento,
ni me pesa la honra,
ni frunce el respeto.
Hago yo mi olla
con sus pies de puerco,
y el llorón judío
haga sus pucheros.
... ...
Y sin pena alguna,
vergüenza ni miedo,
si Dios no me mata,
moriré de viejo.
Después de yo muerto,
ni viña ni huerto;
y para que viva,
el huerto y la viña. [67]

Behind the burlesque tone of this romance lies a serious appraisal of contemporary society which, in Quevedo's opinion, is a poor substitute for the glory of the past. He says that he would prefer to detach himself from his surroundings and lead a simple life which, in effect, he did shortly thereafter.

The spirit of Quevedo's letrillas is similar to that of his romances. Again, he uses a traditional verse form with regular rhyme scheme with a somewhat unconventional intent to satirize social types and customs. The "estribillos," or refrains, of his letrillas often satirize popular over-used expressions, as in the following excerpt:

Deseado he desde niño,
y antes, si puede ser antes,
ver un médico sin guantes
y un abogado lampiño;
un poeta con aliño,
un romance sin orillas,
un sayón con pantorrillas,
un criollo liberal.
Y no lo digo por mal.

---

[67] *Obras* II (1964), 340-342.

Ayer, sobre dos astillas,
andaba el señor Bicoca,
y hoy la barriga a la boca
lleva ya las pantorrillas;
eran todas espinillas
ayer las piernas de Antón,
y la una es hoy colchón,
y la otra es hoy costal.
Y no lo digo por mal. [68]
... ...

As a final note to Quevedo's versification, it should be pointed out that he respected traditional rhyme schemes in his sonnets, romances, letrillas, decimas and other diverse metric forms. However, on occasion, he would employ the rhyme of a poem as an additional burlesque feature, i.e.:

¿Qué te ríes, filósofo cornudo?
¿Qué sollozas, filósofo anegado?
Sólo cumples, con ser recién casado,
como el otro cabrón recién viudo.

¿Una propia miseria haceros pudo
cosquillas y pucheros? ¿Un pecado
es llanto y carcajada? He sospechado
que es la taberna más que lo sesudo.

Que no te agotes tú, que no te corras,
bufonazo de fábulas y chistes
tal, que ni con los pésames te ahorras.

Diréis, por disculpar lo que bebistes,
que son las opiniones como zorras,
que uno las toma alegres y otro tristes. [69]

The *udo-ado* variation in the above sonnet complies with the traditional rhyme scheme, while at the same time it injects another note of ridicule which complements the tone of the poem.

In his choice of poetic meter, Quevedo was as liberal as any poet of his time. Since the art of versification had gone virtually unnoticed in Spain until the latter part of the sixteenth century,

---

[68] *Obras* II (1964), 208.
[69] *Obras* II (1964), 387.

there were few precepts to be observed other than those dictated by custom. Like Lope and Góngora, Quevedo utilized both the traditional Spanish verse forms and the more modern Italianate meters which were rapidly becoming assimilated and nationalized in Spain. In view of this advanced state of assimilation, any objection to the originally Italian verse forms in Quevedo's time would have been pointless. The metrical variety of his poetry can therefore be regarded as natural and foreseeable, considering the historical circumstances of the art of versification and the diversity of his own talents.

"Gongorismos" in Quevedo's Poetry

In spite of Quevedo's avowed rejection of cultism, he himself is guilty of indulging in various traits of the cultist style on rare occasions. The number of "gongorismos" within the body of his complete works in verse is relatively small. However, I shall point out a few of them and try to analyze the reason for his deviation from the traditional style which he so ardently defended.

Gerardo Diego in his *Antología poética en honor de Góngora desde Lope de Vega a Rubén Darío* (1927) cites three of Quevedo's poems as examples of "gongorismos" in his style.[70] One of these is a sonnet to Lisi, Quevedo's secret love:

> En breve cárcel traigo aprisionado,
> con toda su familia de oro ardiente,
> el cerco de la luz resplandeciente
> y grande imperio del amor cerrado.
>
> Traigo el campo que pacen estrellado
> las fieras altas de la piel luciente,
> y a escondidas del cielo y del Oriente,
> día de luz y parto mejorado.
>
> Traigo todas las Indias en mi mano,
> perlas que en un diamante por rubíes
> pronuncian con desdén sonoro hielo,

---

[70] Diego, *Antología poética en honor de Góngora desde Lope de Vega a Rubén Darío.* Madrid: Revista de Occidente, 1927, pp. 20-21. Beside the two poems I shall discuss, Diego cites Quevedo's "A vosotras estrellas." See *Obras* II (1964), 500.

y razonan tal vez fuego tirano,
relámpagos de risa carmesíes,
aurora, gala y presunción del cielo. [71]

The subject of the poem, not mentioned with any clarity until the third stanza, is a ring the poet has on his finger which contains a portrait of his love; he refers to it figuratively in the first stanza as a "cárcel." The poem is essentially a metaphorical description of Lisi, and in these metaphors lies the principal influence of cultism. For example, in the third stanza, Quevedo compares Lisi's portrait to the riches of the Indies: by inference, her teeth are pearls, her lips, rubies, and her mouth, a diamond. In doing this, Quevedo becomes a target for his own satire in the afore-mentioned poem "¡Qué preciosos son los dientes" [72] in which he mocks the cultist fad of figurative description. Other "gongorismos" may be pointed out in the above sonnet: when Lisi speaks, her words are "relámpagos de risa carmesíes," and her tone of voice is described as "sonoro hielo." Because Quevedo relies upon the imagination and empathy of the reader to decipher his metaphors and images, he has obscured the meaning of his poem. However, the influence of Góngora here is only partial; the syntax and vocabulary are traditional, demonstrating that Quevedo has not surrendered himself completely to all the elements of cultism.

The second example which Gerardo Diego gives of "gongorismos" in Quevedo's poetry is the following letrilla:

(Estribillo)

Flor que cantas, flor que vuelas
y tienes por facistol
el laurel, ¿para qué al sol
con tan sonoras cautelas
le madrugas y desvelas?
Dígasme,
dulce hilgüero, ¿por qué?

Dime, cantor, ramillete,
lira de pluma volante,

---

[71] *Obras* II (1964), 122.
[72] *Obras* II (1964), 265. See the quote corresponding to footnote 20 in Chapter Four.

silbo alado y elegante
que en el rizado copete
luces flor, suenas falsete,
¿por qué cantas con porfía
invidias que llora el día
con lágrimas de la aurora,
si en la risa de Lidora
su amanecer desconsuelas?

(Estribillo)

¿En un átomo de pluma
cómo tal concento cabe?
¿Cómo se esconde en un ave
cuanto el contrapunto suma?
Qué dolor hay que presuma
tanto mal de su rigor
que no suspenda el dolor
al iris breve, que canta,
llena tan chica garganta
de orfeos y de vigüelas?

(Estribillo)

Voz pintada, canto alado,
poco al ver, mucho al oído,
¿dónde tienes escondido
tanto instrumento templado?
Recata de mi cuidado
tus músicas y alegrías
que las malas compañías
te volverán los cantares
en lágrimas y pesares
por más que a sirena anhelas. [73]

(Estribillo)

The influence of cultism in this poem, as in the one previously cited, is small and is primarily that of figurative description since the syntax, rhyme scheme and vocabulary remain traditional. Gerardo Diego points out the similarity between this letrilla and one by Góngora which begins "No son todos ruiseñores." [74] Not only is the

---

[73] *Obras* II (1964), 221-222.
[74] See Góngora, *Obras completas,* ed. J. Millé y Giménez and I. Millé y Giménez. Madrid: Aguilar, 1956, pp. 350-351.

subject of Quevedo's poem similar to that of Góngora's, but also some of the images are repeated, i.e., that of the "sirena" whose effect the bird wishes to imitate, and the musical instrument, a "lira," to which the bird is compared. One might be tempted to assume on the basis of this evidence that Quevedo was inspired by Góngora's poem. However, Luis Astrana Marín's 1952 edition of Quevedo's poetry gives the date of 1608 for this letrilla, [75] while Góngora's letrilla is dated 1609. [76] If these dates are correct, then it is possible that Góngora was actually inspired by Quevedo's poem to which he wrote a sequel in the following year. It must be noted that Góngora's letrilla shows an equally slight influence of cultism compared with other works he wrote in the same period. It is also possible that the similarities which we have pointed out in these two poems were merely coincidental.

A final example of "gongorismos" in Quevedo's work is the poem "Al jabalí a quien dió muerte con una bala la serenísima infanta Doña María" written by him in 1625. [77] As Emilio Carilla has noted, there are certain direct parallels between the images in this poem and those in the *Soledades* by Luis de Góngora. [78] Some of these are as follows:

        Escándalo de todas las riberas...
           (Quevedo, "Al jabalí")

        El girifalte, escándalo bizarro del aire...
           (Góngora, *Soledad segunda*)
              versos 753-754

...y el toro, que con piel y frente de oro rumia en el campo azul pasto luciente...
                        (Quevedo, "Al jabalí")

...en que el mentido robador de Europa ... en campos de zafiro pace estrellas.
                  (Góngora, *Soledad primera*) [79]
                    versos 2 y 6

---

[75] See *Obras* II (1952), 543.
[76] See Góngora, *Obras completas*, p. 350.
[77] See *Obras* II (1964), 502-503.
[78] See E. Carilla, pp. 173-175.
[79] Ibid., p. 174.

Certainly these parallels are apparent, and it seems that Quevedo may have consciously imitated Góngora's style in the *Soledades*. "Al jabalí," considered in its entirety, is far more "gongoristic" than the other poems we have discussed. However, Carilla, in pointing out these parallels, does not take into account the possibility that Quevedo's poem may have been a premeditated satire of Góngora's style. The very subject of the work, a eulogy to a boar, seems to strengthen the likelihood of it being a parody, as does the tone of the poem:

> Tú, blasón de los bosques,
> erizada amenaza de los cerros,
> temeroso escarmiento de los perros,
> que con las medias lunas espumosas
> de marfil belicoso y delincuente,
> más corto, sí, mas no menos valiente,
> su latir porfiado despreciabas,
> cuando las diligencias del olfato,
> que no pudiste desmentir, burlabas,
> pues nunca del venablo y del sabueso
> el hierro calentaste,
> el ladrido mojaste,
> ni fué al lebrel aplauso tu suceso,
> y en el cerco de telas
> al cáñamo burlaste las cautelas; [80]
> . . . .

If this is the case, then the "gongorismos" which Quevedo has parodied so successfully are not a serious and authentic manifestation of his own style.

Despite the fact that some of Quevedo's "gongorismos" may have been created with the intention of satirizing Góngora's style, it cannot be denied that other cultisms are found in his poetry which have no such excuse for being. They are the result of the pervasive influence of "gongorismo" in seventeenth century literature, an influence from which Quevedo could not escape:

> ¿Qué indican estos trazos cultistas en Quevedo? Pues nada más —ni nada menos— que el fuerte influjo del cultismo o, si se quiere, de Góngora sobre la poesía de su siglo. Quevedo, tenaz enemigo de Góngora en vida del cordobés,

---

[80] *Obras* II (1964), 502.

no pudo, por lo visto, evitar la "contaminatio", como tampoco la evitaron Lope, Jáuregui, Tirso de Molina y otros de menor categoría.[81]

The Problem of "Conceptismo" in Quevedo's Style

A discussion of Quevedo's poetry would be incomplete without an analysis of "conceptismo" and its relationship to Quevedo's traditionalism.

Quevedo has acquired particular renown as a "conceptista." Lope de Vega, in his *Rimas humanas y divinas del Licenciado Tomé de Burguillos* (1634), was one of many of his colleagues who admired Quevedo's dexterity in this capacity:

> Para cortar la pluma en un profundo
> ideal concepto y trasladarle en rima,
> hallé (peregrinando el patrio clima)
> que érades vos lo más sútil del mundo.
>
> Atento os miro, y tan valiento infundo
> alma al ingenio, al instrumento prima,
> que a escribir, a cantar, a ser me anima
> de vuestro claro sol Faetón segundo.
>
> Para alabaros hoy, pedíle al coro
> de Apolo (si es que tanto emprender puedo)
> permitiese mi pluma a su tesoro.
>
> Y respondióme con respeto y miedo:
> "Burguillos, si queréis teñirla en oro,
> bañadla en el ingenio de Quevedo."[82]

This literary phenomenon of "conceptismo" which developed alongside Góngora's "culteranismo" was concerned with the play of ideas, not with the refinement of words in themselves:

> Si las metáforas, ennoblecedoras de la realidad, son el recurso capital del culteranismo, la base del conceptismo se halla en las asociaciones ingeniosas de ideas o palabras ("conceptos"). A aquél le interesa ante todo la belleza de

---

[81] E. Carilla, p. 175.
[82] Reprinted in *Obras* II (1952), 1094-1095.

la imagen y la expresión refinada; a éste, la "sutileza del pensar" y la agudeza del decir. [83]

The distinction between these two styles is often blurred, and because of its obscure conceits, "conceptismo" is usually considered as reprehensible an affectation in Spanish literature as "culteranismo." For this reason, it is imperative that we try to understand why Quevedo was a "conceptista" in much of his poetry while in theory he condemned affectation and obscurity in writing.

The fact that these two styles are often dismissed by critics as synonymous maladies in Spanish poetry does not facilitate the solution of this problem. Although they both arose out of the same exaggerated tendency found throughout European art in the early seventeenth century to search for new and rare expressions of the creative instinct, [84] "culteranismo "and "conceptismo" are significantly different. In Góngora's style, the emphasis is upon new words, strange syntax and unusual metaphors, with scant attention paid to intricacies of thought. [85] Quevedo's "conceptismo," however, is not concerned with esthetic exoticism, but is rather an exercise in conceptual ingenuity. As Menéndez y Pelayo writes: "... el *conceptismo*, lejos de nacer de penuria intelectual, se fundaba en el refinamiento de la abstracción; era una especie de escolasticismo trasladado al arte." [86] Don Marcelino's analogy of "conceptismo" and scholasticism is, in my opinion, valid and useful in comprehending Quevedo's style. In the Middle Ages, the Scholastics appealed to

---

[83] García López, p. 223.

[84] See E. K. Kane, Chapters VIII through IX, *Gongorism and the Golden Age*, pp. 169-254.

[85] Kane has written: "one of the most noted qualities of gongorism is the barrenness of thought embedded at the same time in a wealth of exotic imagery," p. 257. Kane and Menéndez y Pelayo have followed Quevedo's lead by disdaining Góngora's style. Pedro Salinas and Dámaso Alonso represent the new school of critics who say that Góngora is "... a perfectly intelligible poet. Intelligible, even clear, when he is followed along his road, along the path he traced for his poetry. ... Every mysterious poet, if he is a true poet, gives us, with his poetry, a key with which to decipher its mystery. ... Góngora needed his difficulty. He could not have created his poetry without it. Difficulty was no mere whim or eccentricity of his. It corresponded with his poetical way of being." Salinas, *Reality and the Poet in Spanish Poetry*. Baltimore: The Johns Hopkins Press, 1940, pp. 136-137.

[86] M. Menéndez y Pelayo, *Historia de las ideas estéticas en España*, Vol. II, p. 326.

logic to solve problems, but the basis for their reasoning was always "the authority of the Church seconded by that of Aristotle." [87] In a similar manner applied to art, Quevedo sought through "conceptismo" new twists or associations of logical thought while relying constantly upon the bases of traditional language and traditional ideas. Alfonso Reyes, in agreement with this analogy, has said:

> El conceptismo, respetando la lengua tradicional, consiste en un esfuerzo interno, en una manera de conducir el pensamiento, en una mecánica de las ideas, que proceden mediante acertijos, antítesis, sutilezas y asociaciones inesperadas, y es ciertamente un producto de la educación escolástica. [88]

Quevedo's familiarity with Aristotle and the medieval Scholastics may thus have contributed to his facility in relating one concept to another.

The obscurity imputed to "conceptismo" is explained in part by the fact that the twists of thought and the language which Quevedo employed are now no longer in popular usage:

> No negamos que hay ocasiones en que es difícil entender a éste [a Quevedo]; pero no nace la dificultad de retorcimiento ideal, sino de otras causas; de la fineza del retruécano o del símil, para cuya cabal captación hoy nos falta conocer el matiz de una voz o de un giro, que se ha venido perdiendo con el curso de los años y que era patente en los tiempos de Quevedo. [89]

All too often, we forget the obvious fact that the lexicon and semantics of a given language change with the passage of time. It would be unfair to ask Quevedo to avoid the common expressions and popular puns of his time, just as it would be restricting for a contemporary Spanish author to omit similar modern locutions. Quevedo was, after all, writing for the people of seventeenth century

---

[87] Crane Brinton, *Ideas and Men: The Story of Western Thought*. New Jersey: Prentice-Hall, Inc., 1950, p. 193.

[88] Alfonso Reyes, *Cuatro Ingenios*. Buenos Aires: Espasa-Calpe Argentina, S. A., 1950, p. 96.

[89] Lucio Pabón Núñez, *Quevedo, Político de la oposición*. Bogotá: Editorial Agra, 1949, p. 31.

Spain, not for the reader of today. Moreover, it is interesting to note that Quevedo's contemporaries did not charge him with obscurity in his poetry as they did in Góngora's case. The lack of clarity in Góngora's poetry was the result of bizarre figures of speech and neologisms unknown to the Castilian vernacular.

In his own poetry, Quevedo maintained a respect for traditional language, although it cannot be stated that he was free of affectation. Quevedo, too, was susceptible to the artistic mood of his time which favored originality and ingenuity at any cost. One of the most representative of his "conceptista" poems is the following burlesque sonnet:

> Érase un hombre a una nariz pegado,
> érase una nariz superlativa,
> érase una nariz sayón y escriba,
> érase un peje espada muy barbado.
>
> Era un reloj de sol mal encarado
> érase una alquitara pensativa,
> érase un elefante boca arriba,
> era Ovidio Nasón más narizado,
>
> érase un espolón de una galera,
> érase una pirámide de Egipto,
> las doce tribus de narices era,
>
> érase un naricísimo infinito,
> muchísimo nariz, nariz tan fiera,
> que en la cara de Anás fuera delito. [90]

The appreciation of wittiness and ingenuity in Spanish literature was not limited to the Baroque era. According to Otis Green, "the Spanish taste for wit, for the 'conceit,' is observable earlier, especially in the poetry of the fifteenth century cancioneros." [91] Juan de Valdés, in his *Diálogo de la lengua* (1535), accentuates the Castilian tendency to use "vocablos equívocos":

> ... tenemos muy muchos vocablos equívocos, y más os digo que, aunque en otras lenguas sea defecto la equivocación de los vocablos, en la castellana es ornamento, porque con

---

[90] *Obras* II (1964), 380.
[91] Green, *Spain and the Western Tradition,* Vol. III, p. 445.

ellos se dizen muchas cosas ingeniosas muy sutiles y galanes. [92]

To prove his point, Valdés quotes the following poem which is a play upon the word "correr" (meaning "to run" and, in the reflexive, "to be annoyed"):

>   Vuestro rocín, bien mirado,
>   por compás y por nivel,
>   os es tan pintiparado
>   en lo flaco y descarnado,
>   que él es vos, y vos sois él;
>   mas una cosa os socorre
>   en que no le parecéis:
>   que él de flaco no corre
>   y vos de flaco os corréis. [93]

One might also recall the word-play in the verses devoted to "dueñas chicas" in Juan Ruiz's *Libro de Buen Amor*:

>   Quiero abreviarvos, señores, la mi predicación,
>   Ca siempre me pagé de pequeño sermón
>   E de dueña pequeña e de breve rrasón:
>   Ca lo poco e bien dicho finca en el coraçón.
>   Del que mucho fabla rríen, quien mucho rríe es loco,
>   Tyene la dueña chica amor grand e non de poco:
>   Dueñas dy grandes por chicas, por grandes chicas non troco;
>   Mas las chicas por las grandes non se rrepiente del troco. [94]

Although Spanish literature of the "concepto," or conceit, could be traced back to the works of the Latin satirist Martial, [95] the first Spaniard to write about it and describe it in detail was Baltasar Gracián in his *Agudeza y arte del ingenio* (1648, rev. ed.). In the prologue to this work, Gracián says that he has drawn upon examples of this art from several languages, but primarily from

---

[92] Juan de Valdés, *Diálogo de la lengua*, ed. J. P. Montesinos. Madrid: Ediciones de "La Lectura," 1928, p. 122.

[93] Ibid., p. 123. The poem is attributed to el Comendador de la Magdalena de Salamanca.

[94] Juan Ruiz, *Libro de Buen Amor*, ed. J. Cejador y Frauca, Vol. II. Madrid: Espasa-Calpe, 1963, p. 252.

[95] See Baltasar Gracián, *Agudeza y arte del ingenio* in *Obras completas*, ed. Arturo del Hoyo. Madrid: Aguilar, 1960, p. 458.

Castilian: "Si frecuento los españoles es porque la agudeza prevalece en ellos, así como la erudición en los franceses, la elocuencia en los italianos y la invención en los griegos." [96] In another part of this work, he writes:

> En España siempre hubo libertad de ingenio, o por gravedad, o por nativa cólera de la nación, que no por falta de inventiva. Sus dos primeros ingenios, Séneca en lo juicioso y Marcial en lo agudo, fundaron esta opinión, acreditaron este gusto. [97]

Agudeza y arte del ingenio is important for this study of Quevedo as it presents a definition of "conceptismo" from the viewpoint of one of his own contemporaries. One of Gracián's first considerations is to establish the separate identity of "agudeza" in the realm of the arts. He says that it is not a form of rhetoric nor of dialectics: "Atiende la dialéctica a la conexión de términos, para formar bien un argumento, un silogismo; y la retórica al ornato de palabras, para componer una flor elocuente, que lo es un tropo, una figura." [98] "Agudeza," according to Gracián, is superior to both of these "artificios" for the following reason: "No se contenta el ingenio con sola la verdad, como el juicio, sino que aspira a la hermosura." [99] The function of the "agudeza," or conceit, therefore, is not only to delight through its harmony of associations, but also to instruct, to impart truths.

The same dual purpose could not be attributed to the poets of "culteranismo" who were closer to believing in the idea of "art for art's sake." However, it would be misleading to imply that "conceptismo" was food for the common palate. Even though Quevedo's "agudezas" may be of instructive value, they are often too ingenious for the common reader to comprehend. Baltasar Gracián was correct in observing: "Si el percibir la agudeza acredita de águila, el producirla empeñará en ángel; empleo de querubines y elevación de hombres, que nos remonta a extravagante jerarquía." [100]

---

[96] Ibid., "Al lector," p. 234.
[97] Ibid., Discurso LI, p. 458.
[98] Ibid., Discurso II, p. 238.
[99] Ibid., Discurso II, p. 239.
[100] Ibid., Discurso II, p. 237.

If we now recall Fox Morcillo's words quoted at the beginning of this chapter, we find that an analysis of Quevedo's style has revealed a current of traditionalism which penetrates certain essential aspects of his style. However, this current does not preclude stylistic freedom. Although Quevedo vociferously defended the virtues of clarity and purity in writing, he is today often considered one of the most complex and demanding of all Spanish authors. With the passage of time, his poetry of conceits has become more difficult to appreciate because of the natural process of linguistic change. Moreover, his fame as a "conceptista" has drawn attention away from the traditional aspects of his style. In spite of this, the study of Quevedo's style shows that he was traditionalistic without being totally reactionary or revolutionary in his approach to writing. He maintained close contact with national literary traditions while, at the same time, experimenting with newer modes of artistic expression. That he gave free rein to his genius and wit in his style of writing is not unpredictable. It can only be considered a natural reaction on the part of a gifted writer who was eager to fulfill his creative abilities.

Chapter Six

THE LEGACY OF QUEVEDO'S TRADITIONALISM *

Quevedo: Forerunner of Traditionalism in Post-Renaissance Literature

We have seen in foregoing chapters how Quevedo supported traditional values in every area of Spanish life. Wherever he saw these traditions threatened by abuse or neglect, Quevedo led a crusade in their defense. The very fact that his traditionalism encompasses the total spectrum of national life is evidence of the reality of a general state of decadence in the first half of the seventeenth century. Quevedo's works viewed as a whole represent the most comprehensive analysis of Spain's situation of any writer of his time. Many other Spaniards were witnesses to this atmosphere of degeneration, but Quevedo alone protested not just one, but all of its manifestations, whether they were political, spiritual, social, cultural or literary in nature.

The uniqueness of Quevedo's position is enhanced by the historical immediacy of his writing. Since he lived precisely at the moment when Spain began to reveal the symptoms of decline, he found inspiration in specific events and attitudes which represented a visible departure from accepted traditions. Unlike many other writers of the Golden Age, Quevedo was not given to writing in the abstract:

---

* Although I have been concerned primarily with the study of Quevedo's traditionalism, I consider valuable the following rapid sketch of those writers who may be thought of as successors to Quevedo in their individual efforts to preserve the permanent values of Spanish culture.

"... siempre le guía una finalidad práctica."[1] In retrospect, the truth of this statement is substantiated by our analysis of Quevedo's attack against (1) the lack of monarchical authority evident in Felipe III and Felipe IV, (2) the excessive power of privados, such as the Duke of Lerma and the Conde-Duque de Olivares, (3) the weakening of the militant religious spirit in Spain, and the lack of support for Santiago, patron saint of Spain, (4) the moral relaxation of Spanish society, (5) the lack of pride in Spanish culture, and (6) the eccentric innovations of cultism in poetry. In each case, Quevedo combatted a specific weakness and defended the traditions endangered by these failings. His traditionalism, therefore, was unique in its motivation by practical problems, all of them relating to the ultimate course of Spain's future as a national entity. Without this historical immediacy, Quevedo's traditionalistic attitude would have been nothing more than a formality, a reaffirmation of existing values.

This unique factor in Quevedo's traditionalism is the basis for my contention that he initiated a literary attitude which is echoed in subsequent Spanish writers up to the present. Just as Quevedo reacted to the crisis of the seventeenth century, so other writers have adopted a similar defense of Spanish traditions during other moments of national concern. Until the reign of Felipe III, Spain had not truly experienced a need for a revitalization of her traditional heritage, since these traditions were still in the process of development and assimilation. The sixteenth century marked the culmination of incipient Spanish nationalism and the period of Spain's greatest influence in the Western Hemisphere. From the seventeenth century on, Spaniards were repeatedly tormented by the desire to understand why this greatness did not persist and how Spain could have avoided her fate. Quevedo, one of the first of his countrymen to perceive the widespread indications of national decline, may thus be considered the forerunner of a literary movement of traditionalism which sought the cure for Spain's crisis in the reawakening of traditional values.

There are certain aspects of Quevedo's traditionalism which faced greater difficulties in surviving the passage of time simply because historical circumstances proved them to be incongruous in modern European society. For example, his *Política de Dios* is based upon

---

[1] Pedro Pérez Clotet, "*La Política de Dios*" *de Quevedo*. Madrid: Editorial Reus, S. A., 1928, p. 15.

the belief that good government is achieved through the constant application of Christian ethics to the conduct of the ruler. In contrast to other seventeenth century political theorists such as Saavedra Fajardo (1584-1648), Baltasar Gracián (1601-1658) and Sánchez de Moncada (1586-1635), Quevedo was unwilling to compromise or make concessions to the concept of "razón de estado" which was evolving in Europe at the time. This concept, as mentioned earlier, sustains the Machiavellian principle that a ruler should be allowed to establish his own ethics by reason of what is required to promote the good of the state.[2] Quevedo's "ars gubernandi" was a science of absolutes in which there was no room for shades of good and evil.[3]

Above all, Quevedo maintained faith in the concept of the Spanish Empire and its messianic spirit of converting the world to Christianity even at the cost of war.[4] The weakening of monarchical authority under Felipe III and Felipe IV never led Quevedo to doubt the validity of the monarchical system in itself or the politico-religious goals with which it was identified. Over a period of nine centuries, Spain had identified her ideals as a nation with the universal aims of Christianity, and Quevedo knew that the essence of Spanish tradition was the inseparability of these two forces. His faith in this tradition remained secure and intact, but he had reason to fear that his fellow countrymen might be losing the aggressive spirit necessary to maintain this tradition. Even during Quevedo's lifetime, some of his literary contemporaries were beginning to compromise their faith in the Spanish Empire:

> Para Saavedra Fajardo ya no existe cristiandad, existe Europa. En esto es un hombre moderno. Le apremian las exigencias de los hechos consumados, y por ellos se encuentra dispuesto a abandonar el pensamiento tradicional español para adoptar, hasta cierto punto, el europeo que se abre paso. No porque Saavedra crea que éste sea mejor que el otro sino porque se trata del pensamiento que

---

[2] P. Frank de Andrea, "*El ars gubernandi de Quevedo*," *Cuadernos Americanos*, vol. IV, núm. 6, 1945, p. 170.

[3] Ibid., p. 172.

[4] See *Política* (Pt. II, Chapt. XXIII), *Obras* I (1964), 692-693.

triunfa en este tiempo y al cual hay que acomodarse para vivir en la realidad.[5]

Quevedo was not oblivious to this trend of thought caused by a gradual change in the European political atmosphere. He understood the danger which rationalism and secularization might hold for the future of Spain. He was, however, unwilling to admit its supremacy over the traditional goals of the Spanish Empire, and he thus redoubled his efforts to revitalize these goals.

As has been pointed out, Quevedo mistrusted "novedades": "Perdió el mundo el querer ser otro, y pierde a los hombres el querer ser diferentes de sí mismos."[6] His dislike of novelty extended to a general mistrust of science, since it was impossible, he thought, for man to arrive at the truth which is known only to God:

> ...por más que te fatigues en entender los secretos del cielo, no has de saber más de lo que tú inventares o soñares, disponiendo las cosas para entenderlas, y nunca las entenderás como están dispuestas, por más que estudies.[7]

Despite his own intellectual curiosity, Quevedo believed that there was a limit to what man could comprehend about the universe. Instead of wasting time with useless speculations, the good Christian should devote his energies to the exercise of virtue: "No me parece que el trabajo y el estudio del hombre se logrará en nada fuera de la consideración y ejercicio de las virtudes, que es sólo lo que a un hombre pertenece."[8]

This system of values was traditional in Spain during the Golden Age, but as the benefits of science made themselves known to the inquisitive men of the following centuries, the traditional reasoning was proved fallacious: "... Spain, owing to choices dictated by her own value system, remained in a very real sense caught on a sandbar while other European ships of state moved

---

[5] Vicente Palacio Atard, *Derrota, agotamiento, decadencia en la España del siglo XVII*. Madrid: Ediciones Rialp, S. A., 1949, p. 90.
[6] *Marco Bruto, Obras* I (1964), 827.
[7] *La cuna y la sepultura, Obras* I (1964), 1209.
[8] *La cuna y la sepultura, Obras* I (1964) 1208.

on to greatness."[9] Once this realization penetrated Spain in the eighteenth century, her men of letters understood that Spain could no longer lag behind Europe in this field of learning. Their feeling of cultural inadequacy heightened the attitude of disenchantment among Spanish intellectuals already concerned with their country's political and economic problems. The reaction on the part of many writers was to imitate Europe and repudiate traditional Spanish modes of thinking. To what extent this revolutionary spirit took root in different authors is the basis for determining the traditionalist vs. anti-traditionalist currents in post-Renaissance Spanish literature.

Eighteenth Century Traditionalism in Spain

Although he did not live to see it in its entirety, the decadence which Quevedo foresaw and tried to combat became a reality. The last years of the Hapsburg dynasty spelled doom for the traditional concept of the Spanish Empire as Spain saw her prestige diminish and her culture invaded by "extranjerismo." But did the spirit of traditionalism in literature which Quevedo had represented cease to exist? Francisco Puy, in a study entitled *El pensamiento tradicional en la España del siglo XVIII*, has shown that this spirit remained alive; as he writes:

> ...es ya hora de conocer de un modo crítico, apasionado y objetivo a un tiempo, la existencia, dimensiones y contenido del pensamiento tradicional español en uno de los momentos mas grises de su historia. Pues lo hay. A pesar de todos los esfuerzos de la revolución, España siguió distinguiendo la luz de las tinieblas, siguió siendo cristiana, y siguió pensando que valía la pena "perder" la vida buscando la Verdad y darla defendiéndola. El tradicionalismo jurídico-político de los siglos XIX y XX no es un ave fénix resucitando de sus cenizas. Existe un nexo con los clásicos, y es lo que hay que buscar.[10]

---

[9] Otis Green, *Spain and the Western Tradition*, Vol. III. Madison: University of Wisconsin Press, 1965, p. 236.

[10] Francisco Puy, *El pensamiento tradicional en la España del siglo XVIII* (1700-1760). Madrid: Instituto de Estudios Políticos, 1966, p. 233.

The traditionalistic spirit in the literature of the eighteenth century was expressed in different terms according to the individual interpretation of the writer. Alejandro Aguado, for example, wrote a work entitled *Política española para el más proporcionado remedio de nuestra Monarquía* (1746-1750) in which he defended the traditional ties between the Spanish monarchy and the Catholic religion as well as the universality of Spain's holy mission of achieving a Christian Empire.[11] Many writers, as Puy points out, expressed this politico-religious traditionalism along with a disdain for the foreign influences which were penetrating Spain.[12] There were, however, other writers who took an intermediate stand by sanctioning the importation of European innovations while realizing the importance of preserving the traditions of Spain. Among those who represent this moderate position is Fray Benito Jerónimo Feijóo (1676-1764), one of the most versatile and celebrated authors in eighteenth century Spain.

Although Feijóo is not usually thought of as a traditionalist, there exist several notable parallels between his thinking and that of Quevedo which demonstrate the fact that traditionalism was not forgotten in the literature of the "age of enlightenment" in Spain.[13] Despite being in favor of the European "nueva filosofía,"[14] Feijóo was sincerely dedicated to defending the glory of the Spanish heritage, as was Quevedo a century before. These words from an essay in his *Teatro crítico universal* recall the spirit of Quevedo's *España defendida*:

---

[11] See Ibid., pp. 124-125.
[12] See Ibid., pp. 125-129. The writers Puy mentions in this group are: José Antonio Butrón (*A la Francia*...) Joaquín Cases y Xaló (*Rasgo épico, verídica epifonema y aclamación cierta a favor de España*..., 1741), and Francisco Rábago (*Correspondencia* a Portocarrero, 1755).
[13] Francisco Puy believes that Feijóo, in accepting European innovations, unconsciously betrayed the traditional politico-religious aims of Spain: "La razón es simplemente que Feijóo juzgó de España y Europa con relación a bienes parciales, y sin darse cuenta de que sacrificaba el bien superior: la unidad religiosa, en cuya conservación se había empeñado España, hasta dar todos los demás bienes al lado. Sí, Feijóo amaba a España, pero "le dolía" de España el mal menor y sacrificó a su remedio el bien mayor. De modo que concedemos que hubiera patriotismo, pero sobre un concepto de España equivocado. ..." Ibid., p. 116.
[14] Feijóo, "Causas del atraso que se padece en España en orden a las ciencias naturales," in *Obras escogidas*, Vol. I. Madrid: Ediciones Atlas (BAE), 1952, p. 542.

> España, á quien hoy desprecia el vulgo de las naciones extranjeras, fué altamente celebrada en otro tiempo por las mismas naciones extranjeras en sus mejores plumas. Ninguna le ha disputado el esfuerzo, la grandeza de ánimo, la constancia, la gloria militar, con preferencia á los habitadores de todos los demás reinos. [15]

Spaniards of the present, adds Feijóo, are endowed with these same qualities:

> ...cuanto es parte de la naturaleza, la misma índole, igual habilidad, iguales fuerzas hay en nosotros que en ellos, y acaso superiores a las de otras naciones. Lástima será que cedamos a éstas en el uso, haciendo excesos en la facultad. [16]

The difficulty is that there is no national pride in the hearts of the Spanish people: "Busco en los hombres aquel amor de la patria que hallo tan celebrado en libros; quiero decir, aquel amor justo, debido, noble, virtuoso, y no lo encuentro." [17] Feijóo admits, as did Quevedo, that there has been a scarcity of indigenous works about Spanish history and culture; but this, he contends, is because Spaniards were more intent upon making history than writing it. His thoughts echo those of Quevedo:

> Todos tomaban la espada, y ninguno la pluma. De aquí viene la escasez de noticias que hoy lloramos. Y aún no es lo más lamentable que con muchos de nuestros ilustres progenitores se haya sepultado la memoria de ellos y de sus hazañas por faltar autores que la comunicasen, sino que haya hoy autores que quieren borrar la memoria de algunos pocos que por dicha especial se eximieron de aquel común olvido. [18]

Spain's glorious past must not be forgotten, nor is it profitable, says Fray Benito, to try to cast doubt upon the value of popular traditions which lack historical verification unless they are injurious to

---

[15] Feijóo, "Glorias de España" in *Obras escogidas*, p. 194.
[16] Idem.
[17] Feijóo, "Amor de la patria y pasión nacional" in *Obras escogidas*, p. 141.
[18] Feijóo, "Glorias de España" in *Obras escogidas*, p. 203.

the national spirit: "Si se hace juicio que la tradición presta algún fomento á la piedad, ya no sólo es empresa desesperada combatirla, mas sumamente peligrosa al que la intenta." [19] Feijóo's reasoning on this subject is the same as that which we have attributed to Quevedo, with the one difference being that Quevedo's approach was more subjective and less contrived.

Feijóo, although a devout Catholic monk, was not disdainful of the experimental sciences. He was aware of the Spanish tendency to be hermetic, to mistrust anything which might engender doubt concerning the truths upheld by Catholicism. Nonetheless, he did not hesitate to expose the error of this attitude in the hope of breaking down the barrier between Spain and the rest of Europe. Feijóo's evaluation of the human quest for knowledge is an eighteenth century answer to Quevedo's proposal that the wise man dedicate his life to the pursuit of virtue:

> No hay verdad alguna, cuya percepción no sea útil al entendimiento, porque todas concurren a saciar su natural apetito de saber. Este apetito le vino al entendimiento de el Autor de la naturaleza. ¿No es grave injuria de la Deidad, pensar que ésta infundiese al alma el apetito de una cosa inútil? [20]

Fray Benito's attitude was characteristic of other eighteenth century writers such as Gaspar Melchor de Jovellanos (1744-1810) and José Cadalso (1741-1782) who also sought reforms which would bring the benefits of progress to Spain while, at the same time, conserving traditional values: "Todos quieren que España adopte las corrientes innovadoras sin abandonar los cimientos de nuestro pensamiento tradicional y cristiano." [21]

QUEVEDIAN TRADITIONALISM IN THE NINETEENTH AND TWENTIETH CENTURIES

In the nineteenth century, due to the precarious position of the Spanish monarchy thwarted by civil war, the terms "traditionalist"

---

[19] Ibid., p. 206.
[20] Feijóo, "Causas del atraso que se padece en España en orden a las ciencias naturales," in *Obras escogidas*, p. 542.
[21] Palacio Atard, p. 154.

and "anti-traditionalist" acquire a modern political significance which does not apply to this study and to which I do not refer when using these terms.[22] The true spirit of traditionalism has no allegiance to political parties. It is an attitude which transcends temporary political programs because it is devoted to a broader perspective which comprehends the spiritual as well as the political and economic horizons of the national way of life.

The spirit of traditionalism is most evident in times of crisis, and the nineteenth century brought one upheaval after another to Spain. Monarchical instability, civil war, the independence of the territories in the New World, and a continuing sense of cultural inferiority precipitated a crisis among Spanish intellectuals who sought to understand the reasons for these occurences. For most of them, the answer lay in a reassessment of Spanish history and, in particular, in an analysis of the decadence of the seventeenth century: "El pensamiento de la decadencia se convierte desde Feijóo con resolución, con monotonía y volumen notorios, en pensamiento de las causas de la decadencia y de los congruentes remedios."[23] By reexamining the circumstances surrounding Spain's decline, nineteenth century writers hoped to find solutions to contemporary problems.

Several writers, such as Joaquín Costa in his *Poesía popular española y mitología y literatura celtohispana* (1881), Cánovas del Castillo in *Bosquejo histórico de la casa de Austria en España* (1869) and Macías Picavea in *El problema español* (1899), believed that Spain's decadence was caused by excessive religious intolerance, monarchical despotism and unasimilated foreign influences.[24] For them, the only recourse left to Spain was to "Europeanize" the Spanish mode of life, to promote religious tolerance, modern political and economic freedoms and scientific advancement:

> Desde finales de XIX estaba en pleno apogeo la fórmula lanzada por liberales, positivistas y krausistas: "Tenemos que

---

[22] At the present, one of the most common uses of the terms "tradicionalismo" and "tradicionalista" in Spain is in reference to the "carlista" movement.

[23] José Gaos, ed., "Introducción" to *Antología del pensamiento de la lengua española en la edad contemporánea*, México: Editorial Séneca, 1945, p. xx.

[24] See Palacio Atard, pp. 162-171.

europeizarnos". La "europeización", ese concepto tan en boga ya en el siglo XVIII, lo resucitaban ahora como panacea mágica los que culpaban de los desastres de España al aislamiento en que había vivido frente a Europa. [25]

This notion was favored by many writers of the generation of 1898. Three authors of this generation stand out from the rest because of their opposition to the trend toward "Europeanization": Ángel Ganivet (1852-1898), Marcelino Menéndez y Pelayo (1856-1912) and Ramiro de Maeztu (1875-1936). These writers had much in common with Francisco de Quevedo; their work was inspired, in varying degrees, by the same militant spirit of traditionalism. In 1965, in a lecture entitled "Panorámica y crítica del 98," Pedro Rocamora expressed this same relationship:

> Más que un movimiento literario —comenzó diciendo el conferenciante—, el 98 es una actitud intelectual. Su precursor más remoto fue Quevedo, porque en él también se daba aquella voluntad de superación de una realidad histórica, de la que era discrepante, a la vez que señalaba la esperanza de un futuro en que culminasen todas las cualidades del genio hispánico. [26]

Ángel Ganivet, both essayist and diplomat, was actually a precursor of the generation of 1898. Although he committed suicide at the age of thirty-three, his youthfulness and restless nature did not prevent him from understanding the importance of tradition in national life: "Cuanto en España se construye con carácter nacional debe estar sustentado sobre los sillares de la tradición." [27] In his most famous essay, *Idearium español* (1896), Ganivet evaluated the national heritage in terms of what it could contribute to the future. Tradition cannot be ignored, and yet, he writes, the spirit of traditionalism is more valuable than the exaltation of historical events:

> ... lo que nosotros debemos tomar de la tradición es lo que ella nos da o nos impone: el espíritu; en cuanto a los he-

---

[25] Palacio Atard, p. 172.
[26] "Pedro Rocamora habla en Lisboa sobre el 98," *ABC* (Madrid), miércoles, el 23 de julio de 1965, Edición de la mañana, p. 89.
[27] Ganivet, *Idearium español* in *Obras completas*, Tomo I. Madrid: Aguilar, 1943, p. 110.

chos, hay que examinarlos de cerca y ver el valor real que tienen, porque muchos no sirven para nada y otros son perjudiciales. [28]

From his experiences as a diplomat, Ganivet came to admire certain facets of European life. He saw no harm in foreign influences in Spain as long as they did not alter the national character:

> ... podremos recibir influencias extrañas, orientarnos estudiando lo que hacen y dicen otras naciones; pero mientras no españolicemos nuestra obra, mientras lo extraño no esté sometido a lo español y vivamos en la incertidumbre en que hoy vivimos, no levantaremos cabeza. [29]

Like Quevedo, Ganivet extolled the Spanish tradition of Stoicism as expounded by Seneca:

> Cuando se examina la constitución ideal de España, el elemento moral y en cierto modo religioso más profundo que en ella se descubre, como sirviéndole de cimiento, es el estoicismo; no el estoicismo brutal y heroico de Catón; ni el estoicismo sereno y majestuoso de Marco Aurelio; ni el estoicismo rígido y extremado de Epicteto, sino el estoicismo natural y humano de Séneca. [30]

The philosophy of Senequism is one of strength and fortitude:

> Toda la doctrina de Séneca se condensa en esta enseñanza: "No te dejes vencer por nada extraño a tu espíritu; piensa en medio de los accidentes de la vida, que tienes dentro de tí una fuerza madre, algo fuerte e indestructible, como un eje diamantino, alrededor del cual giran los hechos mezquinos que forman la trama del diario vivir; y sean cuales fueren los sucesos que sobre ti caigan,... mantente de tal modo firme y erguido, que al menos se puede decir siempre de ti que eres un hombre." [31]

This is the spirit which Spain must recreate, the traditional Stoic qualities of energy and determination which predominated in the

---

[28] Ibid., p. 213.
[29] Ibid., p. 207.
[30] Ibid., p. 89.
[31] Ibid., p. 90.

era of her greatest historical accomplishments. Spaniards are suffering from an affliction which Ganivet refers to as "abulia," "extinción o debilitación grave de la voluntad." [32] This "abulia," the same weakness which Quevedo saw in the seventeenth century, must be destroyed so that Spain can come to life again and follow the dictates of her traditional spirit:

> Nuestro espíritu parece tosco, porque está embastecido por luchas brutales; parece flaco, porque está solo nutrido de ideas ridículas, copiadas sin discernimiento; y parece poco original, porque ha perdido la audacia, la fe en sus propias ideas, porque busca fuera de sí lo que dentro de sí tiene. [33]

What does the future hold for Spain? How can she recreate an era of glory? The solution, says Ganivet, is to conserve her historical unity: "España tiene, acaso, caminos abiertos para emprender rumbos diferentes de los que le señala su historia; pero un rompimiento con el pasado sería una violación de las leyes naturales, un cobarde abandono de nuestros deberes, un sacrificio de lo real por lo imaginario." [34] The basis of that unity is a common faith in certain ideals and traditions; Spain's mission is that of establishing an intellectual and spiritual rapport among all Hispanic peoples:

> ...si por el solo esfuerzo de nuestra inteligencia lográsemos reconstituir la unión familiar de todos los pueblos hispánicos e infundir en ellos el culto de unos mismos ideales, de nuestros ideales, cumpliríamos una gran misión histórica y daríamos vida a una creación grande, original, nueva en los fastos políticos. [35]

Is this not a modern adaptation of the same goal which Quevedo sought in his support of the Spanish Empire?

Throughout the numerous tomes written by Marcelino Menéndez y Pelayo, there is a single unifying spirit which he has described as his one motivation in life. Receiving an award upon being elected director of the Spanish Real Academia de la Historia in 1910, he said:

---

[32] Ibid., 226.
[33] Ibid., p. 245.
[34] Ibid., pp. 221-222.
[35] Ibid., p. 222.

> Lo que honráis en mí no es mi persona, no es mi labor, cuya endeblez reconozco, sino el pensamiento capital que la informa y que desde las indecisiones y tanteos de la mocedad, me ha ido llevando a una comprensión cada vez menos incompleta del genio nacional y de los inmortales destinos de España.[36]

He knew that Spain was torn by doubts regarding her future: should she become "Europeanized" or assert her traditional Spanish qualities? His answer was decidedly in favor of traditionalism:

> Donde no se conserva piadosamente la herencia de lo pasado, pobre o rica, grande o pequeña, no esperemos que brote un pensamiento original ni una idea dominadora. Un pueblo nuevo puede improvisarlo todo menos una cultura intelectual. Un pueblo viejo no puede renunciar a la suya sin extinguir la parte más noble de su vida y caer en una segunda infancia, muy próxima a la imbecilidad senil.[37]

Menéndez y Pelayo's traditionalism was not only based upon patriotic zeal, but also upon a thorough knowledge of the cultural history of Spain and its relative value in contrast with other national cultures. Like Quevedo, Menéndez y Pelayo was one of the most respected writers of his generation, and his broad education rivaled that of any Renaissance humanist. Through his investigations of Spanish culture, he hoped to show his compatriots that there was no reason for them to feel inferior to Europe or to adopt a foreign culture:

> La ignorancia y el olvido en que estamos de nuestro pasado intelectual; las insensatas declamaciones que se enderezan a apartarnos de su estudio como de cosa baladí y de poco momento; el desacordado empeño de algunos en romper con toda tradición científica, persuadidos de que solo en su secta y escuela se halla la verdad completa; la facilidad que hoy existe para apropiarnos la erudición forastera, granjeando así la fama de sabios a poca costa, y las dificultades con que tropezamos para conocer, siquiera por enci-

---

[36] Menéndez y Pelayo, *Varia*, Vol. I (Discurso 7) in *Edición Nacional de las Obras Completas*. Madrid: Consejo Superior de Investigaciones Científicas, 1965, p. 356.

[37] Menéndez y Pelayo cited by Palacio Atard, p. 178.

ma, la nuestra; ...causas son que producen ese menosprecio de todo lo de casa, esas antipatrióticas afirmaciones que afligen y contristan el ánimo. [38]

To prove his point, he specified that there were several philosophical creations indigenous to Spain which "forman tradición y escuela e influyen en España y fuera de ella." [39] Among these, he said, are "senequismo," "averroismo," "maimonismo" (de Maimónides), "lulismo," "vivismo" and "suarismo." [40] Why is it that Spaniards do not realize the value of this heritage? Much of the cause resides in the "extranjerismo" of the national educational system, said Menéndez y Pelayo: "... nuestro actual sistema de estudios es un mosaico, en que hay de todo y para todos los gustos, menos para el gusto español puro y castizo." [41] Modern Spaniards are at fault because they lack confidence in themselves: "Fuerte cosa es que los españoles seamos tan despreciadores de lo propio." [42] Like Quevedo, Feijóo and Ganivet, Menéndez y Pelayo believed in a future for Spain which would be built upon traditional values:

> ...la tradición, maestra incansable, siempre vieja y siempre nueva, a la cual nunca se vuelve la espalda impunemente, porque es dura y tenaz en sus venganzas, y como paciente y eterna, nada respeta de los frágiles edificios que se labran sin la colaboración del tiempo. [43]

As a young journalist captivated by the revolutionary fever of the generation of 1898, Ramiro de Maeztu dreamed of a glorious future for Spain which would be made possible by breaking ties with "los misérrimos materiales que nos legó la España vieja." [44]

---

[38] Menéndez y Pelayo, "Indicaciones sobre la actividad intelectual en España en los tres últimos siglos," (1876) in *Ciencia Española*, Vol. I in *Edición Nacional de las Obras Completas*. Madrid: Consejo Superior de Investigaciones Científicas, 1953, pp. 53-54.
[39] Ibid., p. 212.
[40] Ibid., pp. 212-214.
[41] Ibid., p. 172.
[42] Ibid., p. 102.
[43] Menéndez y Pelayo, *Varia*, Vol. I (Discurso 3) in *Edición Nacional de las Obras Completas*. Madrid: Consejo Superior de Investigaciones Científicas, 1956, p. 328.
[44] Ramiro de Maeztu, "Dos palabras," in *Hacia otra España*. Bilbao: Biblioteca Vascongada, 1899, p. 5.

His youthful liberalism, however, was to change by the late 1920s after he made an extended visit to England. Maeztu came to realize that the answer to Spain's problems was not a rejection of tradition, but rather an acceptance of the past as an example for the future. Reflecting upon his earlier anti-traditionalism, he wrote in 1932:

> Era tan absurdo como querer borrar de mi existencia los cincuenta y ocho años que llevo encima. Esos cincuenta y ocho años son mi ser; suprimirlos es suprimirme. Así, en los pueblos, su ser moral se identifica con su historia... depósito de todos sus valores... Suprimidos esos valores, quedan los hombres reducidos a la animalidad.[45]

After his "conversion," Maeztu became an active exponent of traditionalism. This attitude culminated in his concept of "Hispanidad," a belief that all Hispanic nations share a common heritage of traditional spiritual values. Like Ganivet who had formed a similar concept, Maeztu believed that these values could become a source of unity to all Spanish-speaking peoples. What better source of unity than Catholicism whose creed proclaimed the equality of men before God and the possibility of salvation through faith:

> Estamos descubriendo la quintaesencia de nuestro Siglo de Oro. Podemos ya definirla como nuestra creencia en la posibilidad de salvación de todos los hombres de la tierra. De ello nacía el impetuoso anhelo de ir a comunicársela. En esta creencia vemos también ahora la piedra fundamental de progreso humano, porque los hombres no alzarán los pies del polvo si no empiezan por creerlo posible.[46]

Maeztu knew that this traditional ideal of spiritual unity could never become a reality unless those who believed in it were willing to fight for it. Like Quevedo, he understood that without a militant sense of patriotism, the regeneration of Spain would never occur:

> El espíritu no puede morir, pero la patria, sí, por abandonarlo o traicionarlo o cambiar sus valores por desvalores

---

[45] Maeztu, "Menéndez y Pelayo," *La Prensa* (Buenos Aires), 10 de julio de 1932, reprinted in *Autobiografía*, ed. Vicente Marrero. Madrid: Editora Nacional, 1962, p. 123.

[46] Maeztu, *Defensa de la Hispanidad*. Buenos Aires: Editorial Poblet, 1952, p. 77.

> que envenenan el alma. También en este plano del espíritu ser es defenderse. Ser es defender la Hispanidad de nuestas almas. La Hispanidad, como toda patria, es una permanente posibilidad... Puede morir, puede ser inmortal... todo depende de nosotros, que a nuestra vez no realizaremos nuestros destinos personales como abandonemos los que nos señala, como corriente histórica que apunta al porvenir, la tradición de nuestra patria.[47]

Maeztu was adamant in his defense of both the Spanish monarchy and the Catholic religion. In his opinion, the messianic ideal of the Spanish Empire was the most admirable attempt ever made in the course of history to achieve the moral unity of all men:

> ...no ha habido en el mundo propósito tan generoso como el que animó a la Hispanidad. No cabe ni comparación siquiera entre el sueño imperial de España y el de cualquier otro país. Por eso parece haberse escrito para nosotros el dilema que hoy nos obliga a escoger ente el valor o la nada absoluta. El hombre que haya llegado a compartir nuestro ideal no puede querer otro.[48]

Maeztu, in comparison with the other modern writers I have discussed, comes closest to echoing the philosophy of traditionalism as Quevedo understood it. Despite an interval of three hundred years, the spirit of tradition retains its force as one of the best possible solutions to contemporary problems and as a foundation upon which the future identity of Spain may be constructed.

In this final chapter, I have endeavored to prove that the attitude toward a recuperation of Spain's grandeur based on her great traditions, as sustained by Feijóo, Ganivet, Menéndez y Pelayo and Maeztu, represents a continuation of the same spirit which inspired the works of Francisco de Quevedo. In their respective approaches, each writer defends the values of Spanish history and culture against the revolutionary tendencies of those who wish to bury the past and open Spain's frontiers to European influences without reservations. These authors share a common desire to prove to their fellow countrymen and to the rest of the world the noble and unique

---

[47] Ibid., pp. 279-280.
[48] Ibid., pp. 290-291.

qualities of Spain's heritage. More than this, they felt, as did Quevedo, that to deny these traditions would be tantamount to denying Spain the possibility of future glory, for without an appreciation of her past, Spain would never again possess the feeling of identity and purpose which inspired the essential national unity of the Golden Age. It is my opinion that Quevedo initiated this literary attitude of traditionalism when Spain faced her first crisis as a nation in the seventeenth century. Since his time, this spirit has persisted through several eras of national upheaval and lives on in the works of modern writers who still seek the reaffirmation of the authentic Spanish character.

CONCLUSION

Menéndez Pidal once wrote these words in reference to what he termed "las dos Españas":

> Una lucha de tendencias opuestas, sobre todo entre tradición e innovación, constituye la vida normal de todos los pueblos; pero en España se da regularmente con una exacerbación grande que en otros pueblos aparece sólo en excepcionales momentos críticos. Aquí lo frecuente es que una y otra tendencia no hallen caminos de transacción, en especial respecto a los más vitales y apremiantes problemas derivados de hallarse la Península expuesta a las corrientes encontradas de dos continentes a que ella sirve de nudo, o recluída en el aislamiento a que la expone su finisterrismo. [1]

The normal balance between traditionalism and anti-traditionalism common to other cultures is not often found in Spain. Either one or the other of these two factions tends to dominate at different moments in history. From the eighth to the tenth century, for example, Spain remained isolated from the rest of Europe because of the force of Arab influence in the Peninsula. Later, during the eleventh and twelfth centuries, closer contact with France was achieved, and subsequently the enlightened reign of Alfonso X brought about unusual expansion and innovation in Spanish culture. According to Menéndez Pidal, these two forces reached a healthy balance in the sixteenth century: "... la España casticista no se encerraba en sí, rebasaba el aislamiento, y en cada español egregio se unían el espíritu tradicional y el innovador en concordia fecunda,

---

[1] Menéndez Pidal, *Los españoles en la historia* in *España en su historia*, Vol. I. Madrid: Ediciones Minotauro, 1957, p. 92.

de donde brotaron tantos frutos tardíos mezcla de la savia medieval con la moderna." [2] Once again, in the eighteenth century, Spain was forced to accept foreign rulers, and the influx of French philosophy and customs made any future hope of isolationism appear absurd. The modern world had penetrated the Peninsula, and the nineteenth century brought civil confusion and political conflict to Spain. Only recently, since the generation of 1898, has the voice of traditionalism been heard more clearly among Spanish writers. However, the controversy is far from being resolved, and the "two Spains" continue their dispute.

Another critic, Palacio Atard, has disagreed with Menéndez Pidal's theory of "las dos Españas," one "tradicionalista" and one "innovadora," on the grounds that this dualism does not truly exist. [3] He contends that such a separation cannot be made because even the writers of the eighteenth century who were essentially traditionalists were not opposed to intelligent reforms. They were not, as Menéndez Pidal implies, isolationists, or "misoneistas." And conversely, those who favored the influence of European ideas did not necessarily reject tradition. However, Palacio Atard accepts Menéndez Pidal's distinction between those modern writers who are traditionalists because they emphasize the glory of the sixteenth and seventeenth centuries in Spanish history in the belief that the decline came later in the eighteenth century, and those writers who insist that national decadence began much earlier. [4]

My motive in summarizing these theories of traditionalism vs. anti-traditionalism in Spanish culture has been to demonstrate that even today there is no unanimity as to how these concepts should be defined or even as to whether such a distinction is valid. The problem involved in any such controversy is that of agreeing upon an interpretation of traditionalism *per se*. It is my opinion that the distinction between traditionalism and anti-traditionalism is legitimate, but only within boundaries, such as a limited historical period or a well-defined ideological context.

---

[2] Ibid., p. 108.
[3] Vicente Palacio Atard, *Derrota, agotamiento, decadencia en la España del siglo XVII*. Madrid: Ediciones Rialp, S. A., 1949, p. 151.
[4] See Menéndez Pidal, pp. 119-120.

In discussing Quevedo as a traditionalist I have tried to isolate the differences between certain values actively sustained by him and the opinions or attitudes of his time which threatened to undermine these values. I have endeavored to point out, within the varied aspects of Quevedo's philosophy and style of writing, a unifying spirit of traditionalism. Although emphasizing this attitude in his work I have also indicated some areas, particularly in his style, where Quevedo did not adhere strictly to tradition. However, in those instances there existed no immediate threat to the integrity or well-being of the national culture.

The literary importance of Quevedo's traditionalism is best understood in terms of the evolution of Spanish history. It is my contention that Quevedo's perceptive nature, so quick to capture the essence of Spanish society, was also able to comprehend the greater significance of the decadence which he noticed. The persistent weakness of the Hapsburg monarchs presented a threat to the political traditions of the nation, and this Quevedo tried to remedy in his numerous essays on government. In addition, he observed the corruption in court society, the loss of support for Spain's patron saint, Santiago, the lack of pride in national cultural and historical traditions and the bizarre affectations of the cultist style in literature. All of these symptoms of moral enervation had come to the fore during his lifetime, and Quevedo understood the crisis which confronted Spain. His battle against these elements was actually a battle for the survival of Spain as a viable political and cultural power.

The significance of the traditionalism which Quevedo professed is better understood by us today than it was in his own generation, for history has shown that Quevedo's fears for Spain were justified. Not only on the Iberian Peninsula, but also throughout Europe, the first decades of the seventeenth century constituted a critical period of evolution. According to H. R. Trevor-Roper, it was around 1620 that the Renaissance in Europe came to an abrupt end: "... from the 1620s —here sooner, here later— the European courts are on the defensive. The voice of protest, even revolt, is rising; the courts' defenders know that they can only preserve them by admitting change."⁵ It was, however, too late to avoid the impending crisis. The bureaucracy of the sixteenth century courts had grown and multiplied to such an extent that the super-structure of a parasitic society was no longer tolerable: ⁶

> The court of Spain, once so simple, had been changed to a Burgundian pattern; the court of England, once so provincial, had become, under Queen Elizabeth, the most elaborate in Europe; and the princes of Italy and Gemany, with palaces and libraries, picture galleries and *Wunderkammer*, philosophers, fools, and astrologers strove to hold their own. As the [sixteenth] century wore on, social conscience dwindled, for social change seemed impossibly remote. ⁷

Around 1620, the turning point, and war in Europe and a general decay in trade changed the climate and brought the end of an age. ⁸

Quevedo, who lived precisely at the time when Spain was approaching this crisis, may thus be considered one of the last voices of Renaissance protest. Though his traditionalism may have proved futile in his own lifetime, it was a symbol of strength in an era of growing weakness.

---

⁵ H. R. Trevor-Roper, "The Sudden End of the Renaissance," *Horizon*, Vol. II,. No. 1, September 1959, p. 120.
⁶ Ibid., p. 121.
⁷ Ibid., pp. 29 and 120.
⁸ Ibid., p. 120.

BIBLIOGRAPHY

I. WORKS OF FRANCISCO DE QUEVEDO.

QUEVEDO Y VILLEGAS, FRANCISCO DE. *Obras completas,* ed. Luis Astrana Marín. 2 vols. Madrid: Aguilar, 1952 (3rd ed.).
———. *Obras completas,* ed. Felicidad Buendía. 2 vols. Madrid: Aguilar, 1964 (5th ed.).
———. *Obras,* ed. A. Fernández-Guerra. Tomo I. Madrid: M. Rivadeneyra (Biblioteca de Autores Españoles), 1876.
———. *Política de Dios: Gobierno de Cristo.* Madrid: Imprenta de Tejado, 1867.
———. *Política de Dios, Govierno de Christo,* ed. James O. Crosby. Madrid: Editorial Castalia, 1966.

II. OTHER SOURCES.

A. *Books:*

ALONSO, MARTÍN. *Ciencia del lenguaje y arte del estilo.* Madrid: Aguilar, 1949.
ASTRANA MARÍN, LUIS. *Ideario de don Francisco de Quevedo.* Madrid: Biblioteca Nueva, 1940.
ATKINSON, WILLIAM C. *A History of Spain and Portugal.* London: The Whitefriars Press Ltd., 1960.
BARJA, CÉSAR. *Libros y autores clásicos.* New York: G. E. Strechert and Co., 1941.
BATAILLON, MARCEL. *Erasmo y España, estudios sobre la historia espiritual del siglo XVI.* 2 vols. México: Fondo de Cultura Económica, 1950.
BLANCO-GONZÁLEZ, BERNARDO. *Del cortesano al discreto: Examen de una "decadencia".* 3 vols. Madrid: Editorial Gredos, 1962.
BLECUA, JOSÉ MANUEL, ed. *Floresta lírica española.* Madrid: Editorial Gredos, 1957.
BONET, JOAQUÍN A. *Grandeza y desventura de don Gaspar Melchor de Jovellanos.* Madrid: Afrodisio Aguado, S. A., 1944.
BOUVIER, RENÉ. *Quevedo, "Homme du diable, homme de Dieu."* Paris: Chez Honoré Champion. 1929.
BRINTON, CRANE. *Ideas and Men: The Story of Western Thought.* New Jersey: Prentice-Hall, Inc., 1950.
CÁNOVAS DEL CASTILLO, A. *Historia de la decadencia española.* Madrid: 1911 (2nd ed.).

CARILLA, EMILIO. *Estudios de literatura española*. Rosario: Imprenta de la Universidad Nacional del Litoral, 1958.

CARO BAROJA, JULIO. *Razas, gentes y linajes*. Madrid: Revista de Occidente, 1957.

CASCALES, FRANCISCO DE. *Cartas Filológicas*, ed. Justo García Soriano. Vol. I. Madrid: Espasa-Calpe, S. A., 1930.

CASTRO, AMÉRICO. *La realidad histórica de España*. México: Editorial Porrua, S. A., 1954.

———. *Santiago de España*. Buenos Aires: Emece Editores, S. A., 1958.

———. *Semblanzas y estudios españoles: Homenaje a Don Américo Castro por sus ex-alumnos*. Princeton: 1956.

CEJADOR Y FRAUCA, JULIO. *Historia de la lengua y literatura castellana*. Tomo IV. Madrid: Revista de Archivos, Bibliotecas y Museos, 1916.

CERVANTES SAAVEDRA, MIGUEL DE. *El ingenioso hidalgo Don Quijote de la Mancha*, ed. Justo García Soriano and Justo García Morales. Madrid: Aguilar, 1957 (6th ed.).

———. *Novelas ejemplares*, ed. F. Rodríguez Marín. 2 vols. Madrid: Espasa-Calpe, S. A., 1957.

CHAYTOR, HENRY JOHN. *Dramatic Theory in Spain*. Cambridge (England): University Press, 1925.

CROSBY, JAMES O. *The Sources of the Text of Quevedo's Política de Dios*. New York: Modern Language Association, 1959.

———. *The Text Tradition of the Memorial "Católica, Sacra, Real Majestad"*. Kansas: University of Kansas Press, 1959.

DANTE ALIGHIERI. *Monarchy and Three Political Letters*, trans. Donald Nicholl. London: Weidenfeld and Nicolson, 1954.

DAVIES, R. TREVOR. *Spain in Decline 1621-1700*. London: Macmillan and Co. Ltd., 1957.

DELEITO Y PINUELA, JOSÉ. *La mala vida en la España de Felipe IV*. Madrid: Espasa-Calpe, S. A., 1959.

DÍAZ-PLAJA, FERNANDO. *La historia de España en sus documentos: El siglo XVII*. Madrid: Instituto de Estudios Políticos, 1957.

DÍAZ-PLAJA, GUILLERMO. *Historia general de las literaturas hispánicas*. 3 vols. Barcelona: Editorial Barna, S. A., 1948.

DIEGO, GERARDO. *Antología poética en honor de Góngora desde Lope de Vega a Rubén Darío*. Madrid: Revista de Occidente, 1927.

DOLAN, JOHN P. *The Essential Erasmus*. New York: The New American Library, 1964.

FEIJÓO Y MONTENEGRO, FRAY BENITO JERÓNIMO. *Obras escogidas* Vol. I. Madrid: Ediciones Atlas (Biblioteca de Autores Españoles), 1952.

FERNÁNDEZ, SERGIO E. *Ensayos sobre la literatura española de los siglos XVI y XVII*. México: 1961.

FERNÁNDEZ CLÉRIGO, LUIS. *Aspectos de Quevedo*. México: Universidad Nacional, 1947.

FONT RIUS, JOSÉ MARÍA. *Instituciones medievales españolas*. Madrid: Consejo Superior de Investigaciones Científicas, 1949.

GANIVET, ÁNGEL. *Obras completas*. Tomo I. Madrid: Aguilar, 1943.

GAOS, JOSÉ, ed. *Antología del pensamiento de la lengua española en la edad contemporánea*. México: Editorial Séneca, 1945.

GARCÍA GALLO, ALFONSO, and ROMÁN RIAZA. *Manual de historia del derecho español*. Madrid: Librería General de Victoriano Suárez, 1935.

GARCÍA LÓPEZ, J. *Literatura española*. Barcelona: Editorial Teide, 1959 (5th ed.).
GARCÍA MERCADAL, JOSÉ. *España vista por los extranjeros*. Vol. III. Madrid: Biblioteca Nueva, 1917.
GARCÍA MORENTE, MANUEL. *Idea de la hispanidad*. Madrid: Espasa-Calpe, S. A., 1961.
GATES, EUNICE JOINER. *The Metaphors of Don Luis de Góngora*. Philadelphia: Pennsylvania University Publications, 1933.
GÓMEZ DE MERCADO Y DE MIGUEL, FRANCISCO. *Dogmas nacionales del Rey Católico*. Madrid: Ediciones Cultura Hispánica, 1953.
GÓNGORA Y ARGOTE, LUIS DE. *Obras completas*, ed. J. Millé y Giménez and I. Millé y Giménez, Madrid: Aguilar, 1956.
GONZÁLEZ DE AMEZÚA Y MAYO, AGUSTÍN. *Cervantes, Creador de la novela corta española*. 2 vols. Madrid: Consejo Superior de Investigaciones Científicas, 1956.
GRACIÁN, BALTASAR. *Obras completas*, ed. Arturo del Hoyo. Madrid: Aguilar, 1960 (2nd ed.).
GREEN, OTIS H. *Courtly Love in Quevedo*. Boulder (Colorado): University of Colorado, 1952.
—. *Spain and the Western Tradition*. 4 vols. Madison: University of Wisconsin Press, 1963-1966.
GUEVARA, ANTONIO DE, *The Dial of Princes*, trans. Sir Thomas North. London: Philip Allan and Co., 1919.
HAMILTON, BERNICE. *Political Thought in Sixteenth Century Spain*. Oxford: Clarendon Press, 1963.
HATZFELD, HELMUT. *Estudios sobre el Barroco*. Madrid: Editorial Gredos, S. A., 1966 (2nd ed.).
HENRÍQUEZ UREÑA, PEDRO. *La versificación irregular en la poesía castellana*. Madrid: Centro de Estudios Históricos, 1933.
HERRERO GARCÍA, M. *Ideas de los españoles del siglo XVII*. Madrid: Editorial Voluntad, S. A., 1928.
HUME, MARTIN. *The Court of Philip IV: Spain in Decadence*. New York: Brentano's, [1927].
JOVELLANOS, GASPAR MELCHOR DE. *Obras*. Tomo I. Madrid: Ediciones Atlas (Biblioteca de Autores Españoles), 1963.
JUDERÍAS Y LOYOT, JULIÁN. *Don Francisco de Quevedo y Villegas: La época, el hombre, las doctrinas*. Madrid: Estab. tip. de J. Ratés, 1922.
KANE, ELISHA KENT. *Gongorism and the Golden Age*. Chapel Hill: University of North Carolina Press, 1928.
À KEMPIS, THOMAS. *The Imitation of Christ*, trans. Rev. William Benham. London: George Routledge & Sons, Ltd., 1905.
Las Siete Partidas del Sabio Rey Don Alonso, ed. Gregorio López. Vol. I. Madrid: 1611.
LEMAN, A. *Richelieu et Olivares: leurs négociations secrètes de 1636 pour le rétablissement de la paix*. Lille: Facultés catholiques, 1938.
L'ESTRANGE, SIR ROGER. *Seneca's Morals*. New York: National Book Co., 1890.
LLORENTE, JUAN ANTONIO. *The History of the Inquisition of Spain*. London: Geo. B. Wittaker, 1827.
LÓPEZ PINCIANO, ALONSO. *Philosophia Antigua Poética*, ed. A. Carballo Picazo. 3 vols. Madrid: Consejo Superior de Investigaciones Científicas, 1953.

MACHIAVELLI, NICCOLÒ. *The Prince*, trans. Thomas G. Bergin. New York: Appleton-Century-Crofts, Inc., 1947.

MAEZTU, RAMIRO DE. *Autobiografía*, ed. Vicente Marrero. Madrid: Editora Nacional, 1962.

———. *Defensa de la Hispanidad*. Buenos Aires: Editorial Poblet, 1952.

———. *Hacia otra España*. Bilbao: Biblioteca Vascongada, 1899.

MARAÑÓN, GREGORIO. *El Conde-Duque de Olivares: La pasión de mandar*. Madrid: Espasa-Calpe, S. A., 1959 (4th ed.).

MARAVALL, JOSÉ ANTONIO. *Carlos V y el pensamiento político del Renacimiento*. Madrid: Instituto de Estudios Políticos, 1960.

———. *La Philosophie Politique Espagnole au XVIIe Siècle*. Paris: Librairie Philosophique J. Vrin, 1955.

MARIANA, PADRE JUAN DE. *Obras*. Madrid: Ediciones Atlas (Biblioteca de Autores Españoles), 1950.

MARTÍNEZ NACARINO, RAFAEL. *Don Francisco de Quevedo, Ensayo de biografía jurídica*. Madrid: Imprenta Ibérica, 1910.

MARTÍNEZ RUIZ, JOSÉ (Azorín). *Obras completas*, ed. Rafael Caro Maggio. Madrid: 1919.

MAURA Y GAMAZO, GABRIEL. *Conferencias sobre Quevedo*. Madrid: Editorial "Saturnino Calleja," 1946.

MENÉNDEZ PIDAL, RAMÓN. *El Padre Las Casas: Su doble personalidad*. Madrid: Espasa-Calpe, S. A., 1963.

———. *España y su historia*. Tomo I. Madrid: Ediciones Minotauro, 1957.

———. *Idea Imperial de Carlos V*. Madrid: Espasa-Calpe, S. A., 1955 (4th ed.).

———. *Poesía juglaresca y orígenes de las literaturas románicas*. Madrid: Instituto de Estudios Políticos, 1957 (6th ed.).

MENÉNDEZ Y PELAYO, MARCELINO. *Edición Nacional de las Obras Completas*. 65 vols. Madrid: Consejo Superior de Investigaciones Científicas, 1941-1965.

MÉRIMÉE, ERNEST. *Essai sur la vie et les œuvres de Francisco de Quevedo 1580-1645*. Paris: 1886.

MONTAIGNE, MICHEL DE. *Trois essais*, ed. Georges Gougenheim and Pierre-Maxime Schuhl. Paris: Librairie Philosophique J. Vrin, 1951.

MONTOLIU, MANUEL DE. *El alma de España y sus reflejos en la literatura del Siglo de Oro*. Barcelona: Editorial Cervantes, 1942.

MOREL-FATIO, ALFRED PAUL VICTOR. *L'Espagne au XVIe et au XVIIe siècle*. Paris: Librería española de E. Denne, 1878.

NAVARRO TOMÁS, TOMÁS. *Arte del verso*. México: Cía. General de Ediciones, S. A., 1959.

———. *Métrica española*. New York: Syracuse University Press, 1956.

OLIVER BELMÁS, ANTONIO. *Don Luis de Góngora y Argote: Genio y figura*. Madrid: Nuevas Editoriales Unidas, n. d.

PABÓN NÚÑEZ, LUCIO. *Quevedo, Político de la oposición*. Bogotá: Editorial Agra, 1949.

PALACIO ATARD, VICENTE. *Derrota, agotamiento, decadencia en la España del siglo XVII*. Madrid: Ediciones Rialp, S. A., 1949.

PAPELL, ANTONIO. *Quevedo, su tiempo, su vida, su obra*. Barcelona: Editorial Barna, S. A., 1947.

PÉREZ CLOTET, PEDRO. *"La Política de Dios" de Quevedo*. Madrid: Editorial Reus, S. A., 1928.

PFANDL, LUDWIG. *Introducción al estudio del Siglo de Oro*. Barcelona: Casa Editorial Araluce, 1929.
Poema de Mío Cid, ed. Ramón Menéndez Pidal. Madrid: Espasa-Calpe, S. A., 1963 (10th ed.).
PUY, FRANCISCO. *El pensamiento tradicional en la España del siglo XVIII (1700-1760)*. Madrid: Instituto de Estudios Políticos, 1966.
REYES, ALFONSO. *Cuatro Ingenios*. Buenos Aires: Espasa-Calpe Argentina, S. A., 1950.
RODRÍGUEZ-CASADO, VICENTE. *De la monarquía española del barroco*. Sevilla: Escuela de Estudios Hispanoamericanos de Sevilla, 1955.
RUIZ, JUAN (Arcipreste de Hita). *El Libro de Buen Amor*, ed. J. Cejador y Frauca. 2 vols. Madrid: Espasa-Calpe, S. A., 1963 (8th ed.).
SAAVEDRA FAJARDO, DIEGO DE. *Obras*. Madrid: M. Rivadeneyra (Biblioteca de Autores Españoles), 1866.
SAINT AUGUSTINE. *The City of God*, trans. Marcus Dods, D. D. New York: Random House, Inc., 1950.
SALINAS, PEDRO. *Reality and the Poet in Spanish Poetry*. Baltimore: The Johns Hopkins Press, 1940.
SÁNCHEZ-ALBORNOZ, CLAUDIO. *Españoles ante la historia*. Buenos Aires: Editorial Losada, S. A., 1958.
SANTA TERESA DE JESÚS. *Obras completas*, ed. Padre Isidoro de San José. Madrid: Editorial de Espiritualidad, 1963.
SCHACK, ADOLFO F. *Historia de la literatura y del arte dramático en España*. Tomo II. Madrid: Imprenta y fundición de M. Tello, 1886.
SERRANO PONCELA, SEGUNDO. *Formas de vida hispánica*. Madrid: Editorial Gredos, 1963.
SEVENSTER, J. N. *Paul and Seneca*. Leiden: E. J. Brill, 1961.
SHEPARD, SANFORD. *El Pinciano y las teorías literarias del Siglo de Oro*. Madrid: Editorial Gredos, 1962.
SUÁREZ, FRANCISCO. *Selections from Three Works*, ed. G. L. Williams, A. Brown and J. Waldron. Vol. II. Oxford: Clarendon Press, 1944.
UNAMUNO, MIGUEL DE. *Ensayos*. Madrid: Aguilar, 1945.
VALDEAVELLANO, LUIS GARCÍA DE. *Historia de España de los orígenes a la baja Edad Media*. Madrid: Revista de Occidente, 1952.
VALDÉS, JUAN DE. *Diálogo de la lengua*, ed. José F. Montesinos. Madrid: Ediciones de "La Lectura," 1928.
VEGA Y CARPIO, LOPE DE. *Colección escogida de obras no dramáticas*. Madrid: Ediciones Atlas (Biblioteca de Autores Españoles), 1950.
VON RANKE, LEOPOLD. *La monarquía española de los siglos XVI y XVII*, trans. Manuel Pedroso. México: Editorial Leyenda, S. A., 1946.
VOSSLER, KARL. *Introducción a la literatura española del Siglo de Oro*, trans. José F. Montesinos. Madrid: Cruz y Raya, 1934.
WERKMEISTER, WILLIAM H., ed. *Facets of the Renaissance*. New York: Harper Torchbooks, 1963.
ZAMBRANO, MARÍA. *Pensamiento y poesía en la vida española*. México: Fondo de Cultura Económica, 1939.

B. *Articles*:

ALATORRE, ANTONIO. "Quevedo, Erasmo y el Doctor Constantino," *Nueva Revista de Filología Hispánica* (México, D. F.), vol. 7, núm. 3-4, julio-dic. de 1953, pp. 673-685.

BENICHOU-ROUBAUD, SYLVIA. "Quevedo helenista," *Nueva Revista de Filología Hispánica* (México, D. F.), vol. 14, núm. 1-2, enero-junio de 1960, pp. 51-72.
BENÍTEZ CLAROS, RAFAEL. "Influencias de Quevedo en Larra," *Cuadernos de Literatura* (Madrid), I, enero-feb. de 1947, pp. 117-123.
BLEZNICK, D. W. "La *Política de Dios* de Quevedo y el pensamiento político en el Siglo de Oro," *Nueva Revista de Filología Hispánica* (México, D. F.), vol. IX, 1955, pp. 385-394.
BONILLA Y SAN MARTÍN, ADOLFO. "Erasmo en España," *Revue Hispanique* (Paris), Tome XVII, 1907, pp. 379-548.
BORGES, JORGE LUIS. "Menoscabo y grandeza de Quevedo," *Revista de Occidente*, vol. VI, 1924, pp. 249-255.
CALVO SERER, RAFAEL. "Del 98 a nuestro tiempo," *Arbor* (Madrid,) núm. 37, enero de 1949, pp. 1-34.
CROSBY, JAMES O. "Nuevos manuscritos de la obra de Quevedo," *Revista de Archivos, Bibliotecas y Museos* (Madrid), Tomo LXIII, núm. I, 1959, pp. 165-174.
———. "Quevedo and the Court of Philip III: Neglected Satirical Letters and New Biographical Data," *Publications of the Modern Language Association of America*, Vol. LXXI, 1956, pp. 1117-1126.
———. "A Little-Noticed *Parecer* by Francisco de Quevedo," *Modern Language Notes*, Vol. LXX, No. 7, 1955, pp. 518-521.
———. "Un *Sueño* desconocido," *Nueva Revista de Filología Hispánica* (México, D. F.), vol. XIV, núm. 3-4, julio-dic. de 1960, pp. 295-306.
DELACROIX, PIERRE. "Quevedo et Sénèque," *Bulletin Hispanique* (Bordeaux), Tome LVI, Num. 3, 1954, pp. 305-307.
DEL PIERO, RAUL A. "Algunas fuentes de Quevedo," *Nueva Revista de Filología Hispánica* (México, D. F.), vol. XII, núm. 1, enero-marzo de 1958, pp. 36-52.
DURÁN, MANUEL. "Algunos neologismos en Quevedo," *Modern Language Notes*, Vol. LXX, No. 2, February 1955, pp. 117-119.
FERNÁNDEZ-GUERRA, A. "Quevedo como escritor político," *Revista de Madrid*, vol. V, 1883, pp. 513-522.
FRANK DE ANDREA, P. "El ars gubernandi de Quevedo," *Cuadernos Americanos* (México), vol. IV, núm. 6, 1945, pp. 161-185.
FRIEDERICK, W. P. "The Unsolved Problem of Dante's Influence in Spain (1515-1865)," *Hispanic Review*, Vol. XIV, 1946, pp. 160-164.
GREEN, OTIS H. "A Hispanist's Thoughts on *The Anatomy of Satire*," *Romance Philology* (Berkeley, Calif.), Vol. XVII, 1963, pp. 123-133.
GREGORES, EMMA. "El humanismo de Quevedo," *Anales de Filología Clásica*, 6, 1953-1954, pp. 91-105.
HAFTER, MONROE Z. "Sobre la singularidad de la *Política de Dios*," *Nueva Revista de Filología Hispánica* (México, D. F.), vol. XIII, 1959, pp. 101-104.
HENDRIX, W. S. "Quevedo, Guevara, Le Sage and the Tatler," *Modern Philology*, Vol. XIX, 1921-1922, pp. 177-186.
JOVER, JOSÉ MARÍA. "Sobre la conciencia histórica del Barroco Español," *Arbor* (Madrid), núm. 39, marzo de 1949, pp. 355-374.
LAÍN ENTRALGO, PEDRO. "Quevedo y Heidegger," *Jerarquía*, pp. 197-215.
LANZA ESTEBAN, JUAN. "Quevedo y la tradición literaria de la muerte," *Revista de Literatura* (Madrid), vol. IV, núm. 7, 1953, pp. 367-380.

LÁSCARIS COMNENO, CONSTANTINO. "Senequismo y agustinismo en Quevedo," *Revista de Filosofía* (Madrid), núm. 34, julio-sept. de 1950, pp. 461-485.
LIDA, RAIMUNDO. "Estilística: Un estudio sobre Quevedo," *Sur* (Buenos Aires), núm. 4, 1931, pp. 163-172.
―――. "La España defendida y la síntesis pagano-cristiana," *Imago Mundi* (R. Argentina), vol. II, núm. 9, pp. 3-8.
―――. "Quevedo y la *Introducción a la vida devota*," *Nueva Revista de Filología Hispánica* (México, D. F.), núms. 3-4, julio-dic. de 1953, pp. 638-656.
―――. "Quevedo y su España antigua," *Romance Philology* (Berkeley, Calif.), Vol. XVII, No. 2, November 1963, pp. 253-271.
LIDA DE MALKIEL, MARÍA ROSA. "La tradición clásica en España," *Nueva Revista de Filología Hispánica* (México, D. F.), Tomo V, 1951, pp. 183-224.
―――. "Para las fuentes de Quevedo," *Revista de Filología Hispánica* (Buenos Aires), 1939, pp. 369-375.
LIRA SS. CC., OSVALDO. "La monarquía de Quevedo," *Revista de Estudios Políticos* (Madrid), vol. XV, núm. 27-28, 1946, pp. 1-46.
MARAVALL, JOSÉ ANTONIO. "Quevedo y la teoría de las cortes," *Revista de Estudios Políticos* (Madrid), vol. XV, núm. 27-28, 1946, pp. 145-149.
MARICHAL, JUAN. "Feijóo y su papel de desengañador de las Españas," *Nueva Revista de Filología Hispánica* (México, D. F.), núm. 3, julio-sept. de 1951, pp. 313-323.
―――. "Montaigne en España," *Nueva Revista de Filología Hispánica* (México, D. F.), núm. 1-2, enero-junio de 1953, pp. 259-278.
MORREALE, MARGARITA. "Luciano y Quevedo: La humanidad condenada," *Revista de Literatura*, Tomo VIII, núm. 16, oct.-dic. de 1955, pp. 213-227.
"Pedro Rocamora habla en Lisboa sobre el 98," *ABC* (Madrid), miércoles, el 23 de julio de 1965, Edición de la mañana, p. 89.
PÉREZ DE GUZMÁN, J. "Academias literarias de ingenios y señores, bajo los Austrias," *La España Moderna*, vol. LXXI, 1894, pp. 68-107.
PRICE, R. M. "A Note on the Sources and Structure of 'Miré los muros de la patria mía'," *Modern Language Notes*, Vol. LXXVIII, 1963, pp. 194-199.
REGLÁ, JUAN. "Un dato para la biografía de Quevedo," *Revista de Filología Española*, vol. XL, 1956, pp. 234-236.
RODRÍGUEZ-MARÍN, FRANCISCO. "Doce cartas de Quevedo," *Boletín de la Real Academia Española*, Tomo I, Cuaderno V, diciembre de 1914, pp. 586-607.
RODRÍGUEZ-MOÑINO, ANTONIO. "Los manuscritos del *Buscón* de Quevedo," *Nueva Revista de Filología Hispánica* (México, D. F.), núms. 3-4, julio-dic. de 1953, pp. 657-672.
ROMERA-NAVARRO, M. "Querellas y rivalidades en las academias del siglo XVII," *Hispanic Review*, Vol. IX, 1941, pp. 494-499.
SÁNCHEZ-ALBORNOZ, CLAUDIO. "El culto de Santiago no deriva del mito dioscórido," *Cuadernos de Historia de España* (Buenos Aires), vol. XXVIII, 1958.
SÁNCHEZ ALONSO, B. "Los satíricos latinos y la sátira de Quevedo," *Revista de Filología Española* (Madrid), Tomo XI, Cuaderno 1, 1924, pp. 33-62 and Cuaderno 2, 1924, pp. 113-153.
SOMERS, MELVINA. "Quevedo's Ideology in *Como ha de ser el privado*," *Hispania*, Vol. XXXIX, No. 3, September 1956, pp. 261-268.

TREND, J. B. "Musical settings of famous poets," *Revue Hispanique* (Paris), Tome LXXI, 1927, pp. 547-554.

TREVOR-ROPER, H. R. "The Sudden End of the Renaissance," *Horizon*, Vol. II, No. 1, September 1959, pp. 28-29, 120-121.

VALLE, RAFAEL HELIODORO. "Santiago en la imaginación de América," *Cuadernos Americanos* (México), vol. XX, 1945, pp. 150-167.

VIVES COLL, A. "Algunos contactos entre Luciano de Samosata y Quevedo," *Helmántica*, 1954, pp. 193-208.

WERNER, ERNST. "Caída del Conde-Duque de Olivares," (Nach verschiedenen Handschriften in Müenchen, Dresden und Stuttgart.), *Revue Hispanique* (Paris), Tome LXVI, 1927, pp. 1-156.

The Department of Romance Studies Digital Arts and Collaboration Lab at the University of North Carolina at Chapel Hill is proud to support the digitization of the North Carolina Studies in the Romance Languages and Literatures series.

www.ingramcontent.com/pod-product-compliance
Lightning Source LLC
Chambersburg PA
CBHW030236240426
43663CB00037B/1153